Plains Histories

John R. Wunder,
Series Editor

ROUTE 66

ROUTE 66

A Road to America's Landscape, History, and Culture

MARKKU HENRIKSSON

Plainsword by Susan A. Miller

Texas Tech University Press

This book is typeset in Minion Pro. The paper used in this book meets the minimum requirements of ANSI/NISO Z39.48-1992 (R1997). ∞

Designed by Kasey McBeath
Cover design by Ashley Beck

Library of Congress Cataloging-in-Publication Data

Henriksson, Markku.
Route 66 : a road to America's landscape, history, and culture / Markku Henriksson ; foreword by Susan A. Miller.
pages cm. — (Plains histories)
Includes bibliographical references and index.
Summary: "Offers insight into America as revealed through the author's perspective on the peoples, histories, cultures, literature, and music of US Route 66"
— Provided by publisher.
ISBN 978-0-89672-677-2 (hardcover : alk. paper) — ISBN 978-0-89672-825-7 (pbk. : alk. paper) — ISBN 978-0-89672-826-4 (e-book) 1. United States Highway 66—History. 2. West (U.S.)—Description and travel. 3. West (U.S.)—History, Local. 4. Henriksson, Markku. Travel. I. Title.
F595.3.H46 2014
917.804—dc23

2013028355

14 15 16 17 18 19 20 21 22 / 9 8 7 6 5 4 3 2 1

Texas Tech University Press
Box 41037 | Lubbock, Texas 79409-1037 USA
800.832.4042 | ttup@ttu.edu | www.ttupress.org

Dedicated to the memory
of Barbara and Willard Rollings,
amigos en route

Do not resent growing old;
many are denied the privilege.

Writing on the wall of the Cozy Dog Café

Contents

Illustrations

Plainsword:
A Finn Gets His Kicks
on Route 66

We learn from the following narrative that you do not have to be an American to buy into our grand myth of The Road. Woody Guthrie, *The Grapes of Wrath*, On the Road, and the rest of American road lore invite anyone so inclined into the suite of fantasies (freedom, adventure, self-creation, landscape, history, local color) that we project onto a stretch of highway snaking out across the landscape toward the western horizon. Growing up in Finland, the author of this book heard Bobby Troup's anthem to our famous highway, "(Get Your Kicks On) Route 66," in both its original form and the Finnish language. He watched the American dramatic series "Route 66" on Finnish TV. He tells us that Europeans name restaurants after Route 66 and create works of art around icons of the Road. So Americans are not alone in our road fantasies. When that lonesome road starts to callin' us, likeminded Europeans (and even South Africans) also hear the call.

Markku Henriksson, who wrote this book, is a professor at the University of Helsinki in Finland. His specialty is North American Studies. That means he views the United States (and Canada) through the multiple lenses of history, anthropology, ethnic studies, sociology, economics, literature, art, architecture, music, communications, film, religion, folklore, and any other discipline that strikes his fancy. So this is a thoughtful multifaceted look at the Mother Road. It describes Route 66 at two moments: the author's drives from Chicago to Los Angeles in 1996 and in the reverse direction in 2002. In part, his narrative reads as a reflection on the "literary 66," the road found in the pages of classic works by Jack D. Rittenhouse, Michael Wallis, Jerry McClanahan, Tom Snyder, and a few others. To that canon, Henriksson brings a Finnish sensibility and an American Studies perspective that highlight and expand on Road lore in unique ways.

Much has changed along the Road since its literary canon took shape. Beloved characters have passed on, iconic businesses have folded, and the Road itself has lost its federal status and has partly disappeared. Conventionally, we bemoan all that change as the loss of a good way of life. Henriksson deals lovingly with old symbology, but—a historian at heart—he indulges his fascination with how things change through time. What American historical currents destroyed parts of our storied Road? Who are the new characters along the way? What kinds of markets flourish there now? This is a view of the Road in deep, deep historical perspective.

Before there was a highway, before there was an America, people built their communities here; farmed and harvested; mined and manufactured; married and raised families; shared knowledge, technologies, philosophies, games, arts, and institutions; and traded along a network of roads. Their languages provided the names of the states along the route: Illinois, Missouri, Kansas, Texas, New Mexico, Arizona, and probably California. "From an American Indian point of view, the area has never been empty," Henriksson reminds us. He is talking about the Llano Estacado of West Texas, but the same is true for the rest of the Route. No other book on Route 66 gives so much attention to the communities and histories of these original peoples. Henriksson highlights the Indian foundations of the state of Oklahoma, Custer's massacre of Cheyenne families on the Washita River, the Comanchería of the Southern Plains, the Pueblos and tourism, the Navajo and Hopi land dispute, and the historic roles of Jesse Chisholm, Will Rogers, and Chief Manuelito. "Indians have influenced many aspects of Route 66, and the Road has revolutionized their lives," he tells us.

Of course, this book is also full of cafes, motels, tourist traps, museums, natural wonders, unique buildings, side trips, alternate routes, anecdotes, and cowboys on horseback—the complete iconography to be found in any guide to Route 66. It is a love letter to America's Main Street. For all its historical and cultural context, this is, ultimately, a Finn's celebration of that fantasy of the American Road.

Susan A. Miller

Prologue: Before the Trip

Hit the road, man!
Hit the road at early dawn
—no, no, no, no!
hit the road before
the sun lights the asphalt canyons of the Windy City,
get going before
the sun glitters the high-rise of Chicago.
get on the road,
travel west,
take the road that's the best, go south
Through the fertile valleys of Illinois,
across the Old Man River in St. Louis, Missouri,
and on along the softy meadows
and Joplin
to the Southwest,
where the wind comes sweeping down the plains,
and where the corn is as high as the elephant's eye,
and you're OK
Yes, indeed, Oklahoma City still looks pretty,
and you'll see Amarillo
Leave right the roaming plains,
leave left the endless of Llano Estacado
and enter into the land of the Zia sun:
Albuquerque, Gallup, New Mexico,
the Indian country of the Old Southwest,
where legends are still created,
where Apaches and Navajos once rode, now drink.
Flagstaff, Arizona—and don't forget Winona,

Kingman, Barstow, San Bernardino
Travel through the Purgatory of the Mojave Desert
in order to enter the paradise of California
Hear the ocean call
Santa Monica
And it's the end of the road
It's the end of the journey
It's the end of the world
Make the trip,
Take the trip;
Get your kicks on Route 66!

My Connection with the Road

I must have first heard about Route 66 through the song "(Get Your Kicks on) Route 66." The song is older than I am, so it has always been there for me. I have always been able to recognize the song but have no recollection of when I first heard it. My younger brother claims that I can recognize only two songs: one is "Route 66," and the other isn't. For many years that American recording and a Finnish version by Eero & Jussi that appeared in 1964 remained but a song to me. I remember watching the TV series in the early 1960s in which two young men traveled around the United States on Route 66, but it was but another TV series among many from America. In 1989, on a trip with Navajo artist David Johns to Meteor Crater in Arizona, he pointed out a grass-covered short piece of former road and called it "the Old 66." Four years later, at the second annual international Route 66 festival in Flagstaff, I remembered his reference and realized that Route 66 was making a major comeback. No longer was the song just another song; no longer was the TV series just another series.

I had been looking for a topic to teach as a multidisciplinary American Studies course at the university level. Having already taught courses on American history, American Indians, and even the American West, I wanted something that was not tied so closely to geography or a distinct group of people. What I was looking for was truly to be a topic of American Studies. Route 66 was a perfect match. Much of American culture was tied to the Old Road or could easily be attached to it. This topic allowed me to explore many disciplines and many ways of teaching, creating a holistic and a complex picture of the United States: its past and present, its landscape and culture. I could also throw in some of my own experience, as I had traveled widely on the Road and its vicinity without really knowing that I was on Route 66. Since 1994 my courses on Route 66 both in Helsinki and Tampere have been successful, and I have learned much from my students. I have even given a few lectures on 66 at the University of Tartu in Estonia and discussed the topic widely with my colleagues in Sweden and elsewhere in Europe, not to mention Canada and the United States. Clearly, Route 66 had made a comeback with many of them as well.

For a long time I thought I was the first and only professor teaching Route 66 at any university. In spring 2002, however, I learned that Ned O'Malia had been teaching a course on the Old Road for the honors program at the University of New Mexico. I envy him, as he has the advantage of having his university right on Route 66 and can take his students to tour the Old Road. So far I have not had a chance to do that. Professor O'Malia has given me several good hints, for which I am very grateful.

My wife and I first came to the United States in 1974 as young graduate students to study at the University of Wisconsin-Madison. During the Christmas break, we took a long bus trip west, visiting many Route 66 sights, particularly in the American Southwest. Later, our work, studies, and conferences took us to places like Chicago, St. Louis, Albuquerque, Santa Fe, Oklahoma City, and Los Angeles. Finally, in 1996 I drove the whole length of the Old Road from Chicago to Los Angeles with my brother. Shorter trips followed, and in the spring of 2002, I again practically did the whole length of Route 66, this time from west to east just to get a fresh and different perspective. I drove with my wife, and we rendezvoused with my brother in Flagstaff at the Museum Club right on Route 66.

This book draws from my experiences of those two full-length trips, some short visits, and my readings and research on the historic highway, the places it went through, and the people who traveled and lived on it. Parts of this book are based on my *Amerikan tiellä—Route 66*, published in Finnish in 1998 by Alfamer, Helsinki, Finland. Hannu Tervaharju translated most of the Finnish book into English to help me write this book.

This is a trip into the cultural history and presence of Route 66, a journey through American landscape and culture. Many of the stories here are old, some are new, and a few are mine. Some of the stories have been told before, but I have included them, as I think that they are important in understanding the big story of the Old Highway. You cannot write about Route 66 without writing about the Cozy Dog, Shea's top, the TV series, Bobby Troup, Will Rogers, and Woody Guthrie. In the same way, it is impossible to write about US history without the Revolution, the Indian Wars, the Great Depression, and the tragic events of 9/11, or George Washington, Abraham Lincoln, and Theodore Roosevelt, even if you only repeat what others have already said. I have tried, however, to avoid repeating too much of the stories already well known. Instead, I have added material on American Indians, for example, and on the locations Route 66 runs through. Place names, particularly, have provided me with interesting side trips to American history.

No book is written alone by the author and certainly not a book on Route 66. I owe many thanks to numerous people who have helped me create and shape the manuscript. My foremost thanks, as always, are due to my wife Ritva Levo-Henriksson, my companion on the road of life, my map-reader and photographer; and, secondly, to my younger brother Jyrki Henriksson as my driver, map-reader, and research assistant.

I am grateful to the actual people of and on Route 66 and in its vicinity, to my colleagues in North America and in Europe, and to my students at the Universities of Helsinki and Tampere. Among the people I need to mention are Dag Blanck of the University of Uppsala; Marian Clarck of the *Route 66* magazine; the late Robert Crunden of the University of Texas at Austin; Vilma Delgadillo of Delgadillo's; the late Ernie Edwards of the Pig-Hip; Elyse Engelman of Boston University; Catherine Feher-Elston of the University of Texas at Austin; Benjamin Franklin V of the University of South Carolina; Glaida Funks of Funk's Maple Sirup; Clifford Haby of the University of Texas at Austin; Melvin Holli of the University of Illinois at Chicago; Harold Hously of Arizona State University; Peter Iverson of Arizona State University; David and Gloria Johns of the Navajo Nation; Ted Julien of the Roadrunner; the late Dina Rampelotto Matus of Delgadillo's; Jerry McCLanahan of Texas; Jeff Meikle of the University of Texas at Austin; N. Scott Momaday of the Kiowas; John Moore of California State Polytechnic University in Pomona; Tina Parke-Sutherland of Stephens College; Laura Pellinen of the University of Helsinki; Pauliina Raento of the University of Helsinki; Jussi Raittinen of Helsinki; the late Barbara and Willard Rollings of the University of Nevada-Las Vegas; Michael and Sue Saffle of Virginia Polytechnic and State University; Margaret Connell Szasz and the late Ferenc Szasz of the University of New Mexico; Kelli Shapiro of Los Angeles Conservancy; Bill Shea of Shea's Top; Loris Taylor of KUYI Hopi Radio; Paul Taylor of the *Route 66* magazine; Wayne Taylor of the Hopi Tribe; Sam Truett of the University of New Mexico; Dave Warren of the Indian Art Institute; John Wunder of the University of Nebraska-Lincoln; Erik Åsard of the University of Uppsala; and Steve Österlund of the University of Helsinki.

My sincerest thanks are due to Susan Miller who made the book readable for American and other English speaking audiences.

Route 66 has, indeed, made a comeback. It has become big business and also a big tourist attraction. As more and more entrepreneurs use the magic shield shape sign, the sign also appears more and more on the roadside to stop travelers to wonder at an old bridge or a cracky piece of asphalt that once was the mighty highway. The old and the new, the relic and the life, side by side, as always in human history, the past and the future. It is only we who are tied to the present.

Most of this book was written in the summer and fall of 2002. By the time you read this book, many details herein may be obsolete. The people mentioned may already be dead; businesses may have turned unprofitable, gone bankrupt, or moved elsewhere. But that is the way Route 66 has been changing all along, and it is still out there and will stay there. As it is also a road of the imagination, I believe everybody will find on it whatever they long for.

As a reader, your views are also important and your presence of utmost importance. Thank you for joining me on this travel on the Prairie Road and across the enchantment of the American Southwest—this trip on Route 66, a road to American landscape, history, and culture.

Helsinki, 2014

ROUTE 66

The Mother Road

Main Street of America

It is the most famous highway in the world. The American road. Route 66.

Traveling on it, the Okies tried to leave behind the Depression and the Dust Bowl. With its name on his lips, Woody Guthrie sang people through the Southwest to California. Bobby Troup's song gave it a place in musical history. And on it, Carl Bark's Donald Duck is speeding. John Steinbeck called it "the Mother Road."

In Steinbeck's *The Grapes of Wrath* Highway 66 was "the main migrant road." It was "the long concrete path across the country, waving gently up and down on the map, from Mississippi to Bakersfield—over the red lands and the gray lands. Twisting up into the mountains, crossing the Divide and down into the bright and terrible desert, and across the desert to the mountains again, and into the rich California valleys." Still, a very apt description.

Route 66 runs, indeed, through green, red, gray, and yellow lands. It crosses the Mississippi, the Rio Grande, and the Colorado Rivers. It's the mother of all roads, running through the imaginations of John Steinbeck and Jack Kerouac. It's the road where movies come to life; the highway *Easy Rider* travels in the wrong direction. It leads to the core of the United States and cuts right through the heart of the country. It's the old Federal Highway 66. In this book we will follow it from the Windy City of Chicago to Santa Monica by the gentle waves of the Pacific. We will follow the Road looking for landscapes, for people, for

America—and for ourselves. On it we follow the sun west. This book is a tourist trip on the American artery, a trip into American landscape, history, and culture.

This book is similar to all other Route 66 books as it also tells the basic history of the Old Road, travels it from state to state, meets and interviews some of the people along the road, visits some of the legendary places, and introduces some of the 66 icons, although I have tried to avoid repeating the well known facts already told in every other Route 66 book except what is necessary to understand the 66 story.

Unlike most Route 66 books, this one pays more attention to the natural and historical environment along the road. This book not only sees Route 66 going through places but also uses the road to interweave many historical events into United States history and culture—Americana, if you will. Canadian historian Phil Jenkins examines in *An Acre of Time* the history of a tiny piece of land in the center of present day Ottawa, the capital of Canada. He traces historical events that have affected the acre. Applying the same techniques to a road gives a wider perspective. Much history has affected Route 66 but much has also taken place in its vicinity. Route 66 touches surprisingly many interesting and meaningful events of United States history.

Route 66 is a road with difference. It does not merely link various localities in the American Midwest and West. It is a part of their attraction and of the history, culture, and mythology so important in and for the United States. It has a place in the American mind and heart. No wonder it has become officially by an act of Congress the National Historic Highway.

This book also remembers Native Americans, forgotten by other Route 66 books that overlook the Indian presence and importance to the Road and the area it traverses. And this book is rich in references to movies and music.

The mythologizing of Route 66 began in the 1920s through the marketing activities of its builders. Road societies in certain states promoted Route 66 until the 1960s, and some of their leaders became local, even national, celebrities. With the recently renewed interest, some of them have been elevated as legends along the legendary Route.

Even in decline, Route 66 has remained the most famous road in the United States throughout the post-World War II era. When cartoonists, artists, or advertisers require a road with a number, they almost always choose 66. Seeing the number, even with no frame of reference, reminds people of the Old Road—or Bobby Troup's song—regardless of what they know of the Route itself. By no coincidence, Carl Barks, the most famous of Donald Duck cartoonists, drew "66" on the road sign as poor Donald speeds away from town. In his short animated film *Wild and Woolfy*, Tex Avery sets a nineteenth century stagecoach on a road marked with the same sign. In the TV series, Route 66 was the setting for tales of young people on the road. Route 66 has long been an essential part of American motoring in the free and expansive landscape of the West.

Even today, marketers shoot car commercials against the dramatic backdrop of the Southwest, often in Monument Valley, where Route 66 signposts often mark the roads these cars drive, although Route 66 does not pass through there. An amusing United Airlines billboard uses both Illinois and California Route 66 signs to make the point that a flight from Los Angeles International to O'Hare provides a quick connection—quicker than the Old 66.

Route 66 is a familiar name everywhere in the United States. A brand of that name exists for men's clothing. I own a magnet from Sault Ste. Marie in Michigan that bears the magic number along with the town's name, although the Old Road lies some five hundred miles to the south. Route 66 wallpaper covers the walls of Rick's Family Restaurant in Greencastle, Indiana. I asked if there was a story behind this. "No story," the waitress replied. "It was here when we moved in." Too bad. I bet there is a story, but she just doesn't know it. Was the previous owner a Route 66 nut, or did he get the wallpaper cheap, or was he or she a child of the Mother Road?

The Route has come to fascinate not only America but Europe and the rest of the world as well. Japan, Belgium, France, and Germany now have Route 66 societies. The German airline Lufthansa arranges two-week package holidays to Route 66 from Europe. Oulu in northern Finland has a restaurant called Route 66. In Tampere the local American Diner has good food, large portions, and Route 66 memorabilia all over its walls. Neighboring Sweden boasts a full chain of restaurants called Route 66. The chain used to advertise: "US food for Swedish roads." The menu was in fact straight from the map of the Old Road: "Arizona Whiskey Chicken, Classic Chicago Burger, St. Louis Hot Dog, Amarillo Pasta, Oklahoma Baked Potato, Tulsa Pancake or

Dixie Trucker Sandwich." Diners who didn't go for the exotic US cuisine could order "today's special," usually Swedish meatballs. As the twenty-first century began, however, the restaurant chain reduced its menu to "normal" Scandinavian cuisine but retained the name Route 66.

A European internet service named Route 66 provides you with driving directions from any major European city to another with maps, distances, and estimated times of travel. And "Route 66" was the title of the winning work of art in a contest titled "America!" in Heinola in the spring of 2007. The young American-Finnish artist Timo Berry and his wife glued eight hundred miniature model toy cars in spirals around the trunks of birch trees to produce the winner. In Europe you can buy Route 66 rulers, folders, erasers, and pencils, many of them manufactured in Holland. Bob Groeneveld, a Dutch businessman, has registered the sign of the Route for the private use of his company. This license is not acknowledged in the United States, and lawsuits in other parts of the world dispute Groeneveld's claim to exclusive rights. And why not? How can anybody take the sign of Route 66 as a private trademark? It is not a commercial brand. As a sign of a US highway, it belongs to all American citizens; as an American icon, it belongs to all the people in the world. Quite rightly, Paul Taylor, the editor-in-chief of *Route 66* magazine, spelled out this opinion on the matter in the spring 1998 issue.

Yes, a magazine of that name does exist, and every 66 fan should subscribe to it. It was founded in Nevada in 1994 and publishes four issues a year. Later it moved to Williams, Arizona, to be right on the Road itself. Nowadays, however, it seems to operate from Port Richey in Florida. Many of the Route 66 societies also publish their own magazines and regional news.

Thus, the Old Federal Highway has acquired its own magazines and conquered the worlds of commerce, advertising, cartoons, movies, and even cyberspace. Today several 66 societies, as well as practically every business on the Route, have their own home pages on the worldwide web. The web provides pictures, maps, and stories related to the Road, not to mention advertisements for all the paraphernalia for sale. The last time I checked, my Google-search resulted in more than thirty-seven million links to websites having "Route 66" in their headings. Even on the new information highway, the Old Route is alive and kicking.

Other countries have national highways, but Route 66 is the best in the world. South Africa boasts Route 62 and marks it with a shield-shaped sign similar to the US highway system's. The African scenery is great and the traffic terrible, but it is no match for the original American highway. The Trans-Canada Highway (TCH) runs from coast to coast and is the longest highway in the world, but do you know anyone who is dreaming of driving it from one end to another? I have done it,

and others must have, too, but TCH is really more of a political concept than a highway of dreams. Other roads have local fame, but none has the worldwide reputation of United States Federal Highway Number 66. None has the mythology and the nostalgia associated with it. It is the most famous highway in the world. As Susan Croce Kelly described it, "Route 66 . . . was a real highway

that grew to be a symbol for the American people's heritage of travel and their national legacy of bettering themselves by moving west."

Roads, Canals, and Railways

The United States is the most motorized nation in the world, and good roads are an essential part of its history and culture and the lifestyle of its citizens. Road travel has grown with the nation from its colonial origin. All the original thirteen colonies were on the Atlantic coast and connected mostly by sea routes. By the Revolutionary War, when the British navy controlled the coastal waters, messages and goods from one rebel colony to the next had to be carried by land.

After the colonies gained independence, increasing traffic among them caused a rapid growth of road networks on the East Coast. White settlement and the political power of the United States expanded simultaneously westward into territories that could only be reached by land. Westward expansion therefore necessitated the construction of roads, including the turnpike system in the early nineteenth century. The turnpikes were federally maintained toll roads leading from centers on the Atlantic coast, like Boston, New York, Philadelphia, and Baltimore, to the newly settled areas in the West, Ohio, and Kentucky. The name "turnpike" is still in use today.

Because horse-drawn transportation was inefficient and costly, canals were initially as important as roads, if not more so. The building of canals retarded the construction of roads, especially during the first half of the nineteenth century. On the Great Plains, however, waterways were often useless. In the winter they froze, in the summer they dried up; and waterways could not traverse the mountains. Wagon trains and stagecoaches were slow and their cargo space limited. The Pony Express was faster but unable to deliver heavy shipments. All these problems were solved as railroads penetrated further and further into the West during the latter half of the nineteenth century.

Railroads and telegraph lines revolutionized transportation and communications. Both replaced life with technology. Living horses gave way to inanimate machines. Invented by man to satisfy his needs, the machines had sneaked in like the snake into paradise. Oil fields were now more important than fields of hay. Corn, carrots, and other specialties of the garden were not suitable food for locomotives. Animals had been replaced as providers of transport, and nature moved aside by cold iron, puffing steam, haste, and capitalism.

The West Coast and the Great Plains were joined to the rest of the United States by railroads built after the Civil War. In 1884 the Atchison, Topeka and Santa Fe (ATSF), one of the most legendary companies of the West, finally finished a connection to Los Angeles through the Southwest. In American mythology, the Santa Fe is the railroad of railroads. Whenever trains are discussed, the red and yellow locomotives of the Santa Fe come up. In innumerable Western movies, these trains carry both outlaws and heroes to one place or another. The company's main railroad even boasts a movie of its very own.

The Santa Fe Railroad Company was founded by Cyrus K. Holliday in 1859. Four years later the name was changed when the railroad's point of departure became Atchison, Kansas; it also ran through Holliday's hometown of Topeka. The idea was to build the railroad all the way to legendary Santa Fe in New Mexico, a town whose mere name was believed to attract investors. The tall mountains surrounding Santa Fe stopped the disappointed Holliday and his companions from building the main railroad to the town proper. Despite the name of the company, it never entered this historic town; instead, in February 1880 the company ran its rails to Lamy, fifteen miles south of Santa Fe. The name of the station commemorated Santa Fe's Catholic bishop.

During the building of the early railroads, Arizona and New Mexico were still largely uncharted areas. Under the lead of William Barstow Strong, Albert Alonzo Robinson, Ray Morley, Henry Holbrook, and Lewis Kingman, ATSF charted a suitable route for its rails. Stations of the railway were properly christened Barstow, Holbrook, and Kingman. In New Mexico the railroad naturally followed the Rio Grande south to Albuquerque. The northern route was chosen in Arizona, not because it was an easy one but because the Southern Pacific Company had a good head start on the southern route and was not about to capitulate to a new and smaller competitor.

In 1883 the Santa Fe railroad crossed the Colorado River to Needles, California. At that time, the building of a railroad inland from the West had already begun, following the old California-Santa Fe route to San Bernardino and through Cajon Pass over the San Gabriel Mountains to Barstow. The track through Cajon Pass was ready in 1885, and a couple of years later the ATSF got a permit to build directly to Los Angeles. Strong founded the Chicago, Santa Fe & California Company, and in the late 1880s the company ran a railroad from Chicago to Los Angeles via Kansas City and Albuquerque.

Later, Route 66 provided a highway connection through the same area. It did not go through Kansas City, however, but through St. Louis, running southeast of the ATSF railroad as a rule near its southeastern end. From Las Vegas, New Mexico, it followed the old railroad quite closely, in many places practically paralleling it. As late as in the 1950s billboards by the roadside of Route 66 urged people to take the train the next time. Many drivers on the highway watched ruefully as the Santa Fe's red and yellow engines puffed past them in the middle of the Arizona desert.

Later, Amtrak replaced the ATSF as a carrier for passengers, but the Santa Fe Railroad still hauls a lot of cargo. A typical and recurring sight is a column of freight cars hundreds of yards long drawn by four red and yellow engines. These locomotives have now been joined by silver, blue, and green engines since the ATSF and the Burlington Northern joined forces in 1996. Atchison and Topeka were dropped from the name of the company, and the letters BNSF now adorn the sides of the locomotives. In the southwestern United States, railroads still compete successfully with highways. The railroad that runs through Flagstaff in northern Arizona still transports about one-half of all goods between California and the Midwest.

With the construction of Route 66, stories about the railroad as the conqueror of the West or Southwest were revised to include the highway as the agent of change. In this way, Route 66 absorbed US heritage as the main route to the West and evolved into a legend still alive today. Route 66 also assumed many of the ATSF's early side activities such as advertising the Grand Canyon and other tourist attractions.

Civilizers of the West

The long westward journey could be tiring and dull for railroad passengers. The train had to stop every hundred miles or so, as the steam

engines required more water. Soon passengers started to demand some nourishment for themselves during the stops; they were no longer satisfied with the dry biscuits or poor coffee the conductor might offer them.

Fred Harvey diners filled the passengers' needs beside the railroad and sometimes even on it. Harvey had come to New York as a fifteen-year-old English immigrant in 1850. He made his first dollars mainly as a dishwasher in local diners. Later, he established his own restaurant in St. Louis but had to close it during the tumult of the Civil War. After the war, Harvey traveled west on the Atchison, Topeka, and Santa Fe. He built the first Fred Harvey diner in Topeka, the capital of Kansas, in 1876. By 1889 Harvey had a diner at each important ATSF station from Topeka to Santa Monica, California. The young women waitresses were nicknamed Harvey Girls. Eventually, they became such a legend of the West that Metro-Goldwyn-Mayer made a movie musical about them starring Judy Garland.

Harvey's first help-wanted advertisement was published in midwestern and eastern newspapers in 1883. It called for single women between the ages of eighteen and thirty who were intelligent, charming, and good-natured. The promised salary was $17.50 a month, free board and lodging, and possible tips. The story has it that there were plenty of applicants, and the posts were generally filled reasonably quickly.

Many still see the Harvey Girls as civilizers of the West. The *Tope-*

ka Capitol wrote in 1951, first quoting the old saying that went, "No ladies west of Dodge City; no women west of Albuquerque," but then continued to claim that "Harvey tamed the West with good food and pretty girls."

At the time of Fred Harvey's death in 1901, his company operated sixteen restaurant hotels, twenty-six other restaurants, and twenty dining cars on the Santa Fe railroad and by the roadside. The company was taken over by Harvey's sons and son-in-law John Frederick Huckel. Huckel's right hand man was Herman Schweizer; together Huckel and Schweizer extended the company's operation. Harvey hotels were *crème de la crème* as hotels go and frequently incorporated southwestern architectural elements in their design. Magnificent interiors were created either in Pueblo or mission styles and decorated with Navajo blankets, Apache baskets, and Pueblo pots, creating the image of the Southwest that still exists in our minds today. Some hotels operated separate Indian departments, where they sold Indian and local Spanish handiwork and jewelry of high quality. The Hopi House in the Grand Canyon consisted of nothing but the Indian department. Hopi Indians often also made their jewelry and pots there and danced to please the tourists and make money for the Harvey companies. With such performances, Navajo weavers and Hopi dancers created the foundation for Southwest tourism.

The first of Harvey's Indian rooms was established in the Alvarado Hotel in Albuquerque in 1902. Much of it was designed by Mary Elisabeth Jane Colter, who later became the chief designer and architect for the company. Her sensitivity to local materials and styles and her views of Southwest Indian cultures may be largely blamed for our concept of Southwestern style. It may be a mixture of colonial Spanish influences and Colter's misunderstandings of Native American art but; nevertheless, it delighted the visitors of Harvey hotels, and, I admit, it also pleases my eye.

In order to find enough high-quality Indian "products," the Harvey company started early on to cooperate with trading stations in New Mexico and Arizona. John Lorenzo Hubbell's extensive trading post network in Navajo country was particularly useful to Harvey. Hubbell had learned the Navajo language and created close relations with the Indians. As the saying goes, "Whenever the Navajo needed a friend, Hubbell was there." The Navajo traveled long distances to the posts and wanted new ones to be established deeper in the Navajo country; Hubbell heard them and began creating a trading post empire of his own. At the peak of the operations, Hubbell owned thirty-six enterprises on Navajo and Hopi Reservations. In addition to the trading posts, his conglomerate included farms and a cattle ranch. When Hubbell died in 1930, the family enterprise gradually shut down. Most of the old trading posts are now in ruins.

The last of Lorenzo Hubbell's offspring died in 1963. Subsequently, a couple of female relatives tried to take care of the diminished business but, unfortunately, in vain. In 1967 Hubbell's last remaining, and also oldest, trading post was sold to the federal government; today, it is a national monument. With improved roads and increased motorization, Indians also gradually began driving to Flagstaff and Gallup. Better roads also brought new entrepreneurs to the area. A few old trading posts function today as cooperative retail shops or village shops operated by Indians.

Enticing Indians to work at Hubbell's or Harvey's trading posts and Indian houses was not always easy. Women at the beginning of the century earned approximately twenty dollars or less a month, about as much as the Harvey Girls. On the other hand, the girls often got higher tips. Both businesses paid male weavers ten to twenty dollars more a month than they did women. The Harvey people managed to find a Navajo couple, Ellen and Tom from Ganado, who worked for the company some twenty years. Herman Schweizer had a particularly close relationship with the couple. Ellen became famous after she wove a rug for President Theodore Roosevelt in 1903.

The most important Indian department was the Hopi House at the Grand Canyon. It was built in 1903 simultaneously with El Tovar Hotel on the southern rim of the Canyon, where the Santa Fe ran from Williams. The house, planned by Mary Jane Colter, copied the dwellings of the Oraibi Hopi village. Outside, the Hopi performed their dances, while, inside, Nampeyo and other Hopi artists made ceramics. After World War II, the Hopi no longer wished to be tourist attractions, and the Native American performances were stopped. The house itself, however, still stands.

The Depression and World War II brought significant changes to the activities of the Harvey companies. During the war, the companies employed women whose only job was serving the soldiers traveling by train. These girls were usually hired locally, and they did not receive the traditional and even severe education the Harvey Girls did. There was no time for it. Instead, they lived where they worked and were on call twenty-four hours a day whenever a train full of soldiers happened to arrive. As a result of the war, Harvey also employed Spanish-speaking and Native American girls. The waitresses at the Gallup Navajo Hotel were all Navajo, with the exception of two head waitresses. In 1943 most of the staff at the Alvarado Hotel in Albuquerque was of Spanish descent.

Because of the war, service at the luxury hotels had to be compromised. The same happened at restaurants when foodstuffs were rationed. The quality of equipment and food was lowered, and perhaps the service was not as good as before. After the war there was no return to the way things used to be. Huckel had died before the war in 1938 and Schweizer during it in 1943. The last members of the Harvey family sold their shares, and the original family operation was turned to a normal enterprise. Since 2002, it has been part of the Xanterra Parks & Resorts that operates in several national parks.

Motorization also affected the decline of the Harvey companies. When passenger traffic on the railroads diminished, both customers and incomes decreased accordingly. When automobiles replaced trains and roads replaced railroad tracks, the Harvey companies often attempted to transfer their operations to Route 66 and other roads. Sometimes this worked, sometimes not. In any case, Harvey restaurants, hotels, and girls became an important part of the history of Highway 66 and its diners. Some of these restaurants are of course still open along the roads and in the major tourist centers of the West. At El Tovar and Bright Angel Lodge on the south rim of the Grand Canyon, and at Grand Canyon Lodge on the north rim, Harvey hotels, restaurants, and shops are still in business. The same is true with two trading stations in the Petrified Forest National Park, right next to the Old Highway 66 or the new I-40.

Thus, Harvey Girls still work even in the new West although their position and importance pale beside those of their legendary predecessors. In many parts of the Old West, they were the only "marriageable" (white) women for hundreds of miles around. Thanks to them, even the wild Southwestern territory did not completely lack "the touch of a woman's hand"—a Euro-American notion totally lacking respect for Native women.

The operations of Harvey and Hubbell also had a great impact on Indian trade, especially in the Southwest. American Indians were allowed a place to sell their jewelry, ceramics, and roasted piñon nuts. When Route 66 was constructed, white Americans were persuaded to travel the road to see Indians. The American Indians who used to sell their goods to train travelers on stations moved to peddle their goods by the roads. They are still there. As a result of this process, American Indians entered the circle of cash and became a part of America's economy. Indian artifacts became national (ethnic) art. The smiles of the Harvey Girls sometimes helped make this possible.

The Birth and Death of Route 66

In the beginning of the twentieth century, Henry Ford and other automobile manufacturers loosed a large number of these modern vehicles on poor cart roads. The increase in the number of cars soon resulted in demands to improve the road conditions. Many states reorganized their road administrations. For example, the state of Oklahoma founded a new and larger road commission in 1915 and gave it new tasks. Federal officials responded to calls for a national road network. In 1916 the US Congress passed the Federal Aid Road Act that brought federal money to road construction and emphasized cooperation between states regarding choice of routes.

The army also needed good roads; World War I had proved that. In July 1919, then-Captain Dwight D. Eisenhower led a cavalry detachment ordered to assist a column of motorized vehicles traveling from coast to coast. The column included forty-two trucks, "mobile kitchens," ambulances, and a number of motorcycles. The intention was to emphasize the necessity of good roads, and in this task the expedition succeeded. It only progressed four or five miles per hour even on the best roads of the time. On the worst roads, the cars broke the surface and sank into holes. Tractors and horses were often needed to pull the cars back onto the road. In September the troops finally reached San Francisco after many hardships. Eisenhower often recalled the trip and stated that it really had made him think about the need for good two-lane roads.

In 1920 only horses and carts could use most of the nearly three million miles of US highways. Only about thirty-six thousand miles had some type of all-weather surfacing able to endure motor traffic. The nation needed good roads in a hurry because in the 1920s the car and motorization became the popular symbol of the United States. In

1920 there were 6.5 million cars, more than twice the number of five years before. By 1930 the number was rapidly approaching 50 million. Today more than 200 million vehicles drive around the fifty states.

The car has made many things possible. Many considered it a blessing for the environment, because the cities could get rid of the many horses and the droppings they left on the streets. A car made possible a longer commute to work in a shorter time. It alleviated the isolation of country life and made tourism, and family touring in particular, available to many more people.

Congress responded quickly to the new situation with the Federal Aid Highway Act of 1921. The act called for the creation of a unified national road network covering the whole United States. Each state was to give a minimum of 7 percent of its roads to the national road network to be eligible for federal subsidy for its future road construction projects. The act naturally resulted in hectic competition, both within the states and between them, for the national highway routes, road maintenance expenditures, and even naming or numbering of the roads. For Route 66, the central figure in this scramble was Cyrus Stevens Avery from Oklahoma. He is generally considered the father of the Double-Six.

Cy Avery was a real estate agent in Tulsa. He brokered oil lands and was involved in the operation of local coal quarries. He wanted to develop the roads especially to facilitate oil and coal transportation. In 1921 he became the chairman of the Associated Highways Association of America, an umbrella group for associations from forty-two states. Two years later Avery became the chairman of Oklahoma's three-member road commission. Soon he was the chairman of the American Association of State Highway Officials. This association, meeting in San Francisco in 1924, presented an appeal to the Secretary of Agriculture to nominate a national highway board. The appeal led to action and a twenty-one-member board was established. Avery was appointed as the board's special consultant. In 1925 the planning of a national highway network began.

Even before the work of the board began, highway clubs or societies planned and maintained more than 250 mapped US highway routes. Most of these routes combined and improved old Indian paths and wagon trails. The highway clubs, not wanting their own work to go to waste, pressed and lobbied the federal highway board through means fair and foul. Avery, however, opposed all attempts at manipulation and kept strictly to his own policy regarding the choice of highway routes.

The highway from Chicago to Los Angeles traditionally ran through St. Louis, Missouri, and then either west through Kansas and then along the old Santa Fe trail or southwest into Arkansas and Oklahoma via the more southern Butterfield overland mail road. Avery chose a third route between these two: it roughly followed an old gold mine trail from Fort Smith, Arkansas, to Oklahoma City and, as if by coincidence, ran through Avery's hometown Tulsa. As one of the early Route 66 revitalization writers, Susan Croce Kelly wrote, "Unlike other national highways, Route 66 did not follow a single trade route established by generations of travel. It traversed sections of several old trails at its eastern and western ends, but it cut out on its own through the young state of Oklahoma and covered a lot of empty space before it finally reached California."

Traditionally, all routes linking important places had names. The 1920s road clubs had usually given names to their own bit of road, too. In order to avoid confusion, the federal highway board decided to give the new highways numbers instead of names. This system of identifying roads by numbers and letters had started in Wisconsin a few years earlier. The board decided to give odd numbers to north-south roads and even numbers to east-west routes. Signs shaped like shields designated highways crossing state borders, and round signs the roads inside states. The main highways received numbers smaller than one hundred, and the most important became so-called 0-roads or decade roads (their numbers reading 10, 20, 30, and so on).

The highway between Chicago and Los Angeles ran roughly east to west. It was also an important highway, and so Avery and his friends chose 60 as the suitable number for it. Representatives of Georgia and Virginia, however, opposed this plan; in their opinion, the number 60 belonged to the highway running west from Newport News, Virginia, on the Atlantic Coast, through Kentucky to St. Louis, Missouri. Neither party would give in. Avery and his partners even started making Highway 60 road signs. No fewer than six hundred thousand maps on which Highway 60 crossed the state from northeast to southwest were printed in Missouri. Finally, the argument threatened to collapse the entire highway planning system, and the two sides began to fear intervention by Congress.

Early in 1926 the road officials of Oklahoma, Illinois, and Missouri met to consider alternatives among the available numbers. Eventually, 66 was chosen from among them. In Avery's opinion "double six" was easy to remember. He announced to the Federal Highway Office that Route 66 is a road running through Oklahoma that the US government will be proud of. The federal and state road officials met in Pinehurst, North Carolina, on November 11, 1926 and signed the road plan concerning forty-eight states. Route 66 was born.

The highway system did not correspond exactly to the requirements of the constantly increasing motorization. During World War II, General Dwight D. Eisenhower had been impressed by the Autobahn highways in Germany and, as president during the 1950s, wanted to reform the US highway network into a system of freeways after the German fashion. As a result, the Federal Aid Highway Act of 1956 created the present interstate system. In Congress the act was forced through as a part of national defense policy. In case the Cold War  turned hot, troops and equipment could be moved quickly from one place to another, and, in case of a Soviet nuclear strike or a landing of Communist soldiers, the population could be evacuated swiftly.

The old principle of numbering was retained on the new freeways. Odd numbers run north and south and even numbers east and west. On April 1, 1966, the number 66 was proposed as the number of the new highway from Chicago to Los Angeles, but it was considered an April Fool's joke and was not approved by Congress. A part of the Old Highway 66 actually ran from north to south, and it would have been confusing to keep the even number as the number of the highway between Chicago and St. Louis. Officially, the Old US Federal Highway 66 ceased to exist in 1977.

On a freezing Chicago day in January, the signs marking Highway 66 were unceremoniously removed. A new one replaced the last section of the Old Highway in October 1984, when the section of road near Williams, Arizona, was officially moved to I-40. This funeral of the 66 did at least include appropriate ceremonies. Eric Eikenberry, chairman of Williams's Chamber of Commerce, delivered a speech, and Bobby Troup was flown to Williams on a helicopter. He sang his song and many burst into tears. According to unofficial information, the day's lowest temperature was 40 degrees on the Fahrenheit scale, the highest 66.

Route 66 itself was by then physically too narrow to manage the increasing traffic, and it was completely abandoned in many locations. Today, the corresponding route runs from Chicago to St. Louis as I-55; from St. Louis to Oklahoma City as I-44; through the Texas Panhandle, New Mexico and Arizona as I-40; from Barstow, California, to San Bernardino as I-15 and I-215; and from San Bernardino to Santa Monica mainly as I-10. Despite the many road numbers, it is still easy to discern the "direct" connection from Chicago to Los Angeles on a map.

Rebirth of the Old Road

Route 66's premier status—and traveling in general—was changed dramatically by the new interstate highway system. Highways became necessary evils leading from one place to another; they were no longer an integral part of the journey, let alone the adventure. The bends of the old highway were straightened, and it was broadened to a minimum of four lanes throughout. Centers of small towns were bypassed, and many of them and their businesses ceased to be.

Route 66, however, refused to die. Perhaps it disappeared officially, but many of its original tracks remained to be used and traveled by people. It was a road of loving memories to some, bitter memories to many. These memories found new expressions when some young researchers and writers took an interest in the road in the late 1980s and began collecting stories related to it before the tales passed into oblivion along with their tellers.

Jack D. Rittenhouse's *A Guide Book to Highway 66* from 1946 got a new printing by the University of New Mexico Press in 1989, but the first real literary breakthrough was *Route 66: The Mother Road*, carefully researched and warmly written in 1991 by Michael Wallis. He has since practically become the new father of the Mother Road. A couple of years earlier, Quinta Scott published her *Route 66: The Road and Its People* with plenty of dramatic black-and-white photographs. Scott could not have predicted that a wave of nostalgia would soon lift the Old Road to new splendor and that a plethora of new books, some with pictures and some without, plus videotapes, maps and guidebooks would follow. Scott herself has published many since 1989.

Even the fictional literature related to Route 66 has enjoyed a revival. Tony Hillerman sets his Navajo detective stories in the neighborhood of the Route and even mentions it at times. Other books and movies have also used Route 66 as their backgrounds. In 1994 the Native American writer William Sanders situated *A Death on 66* on the Route itself, proving not only his skills as a writer of detective stories but also his knowledge of the remaining parts of the Old Route and the surrounding culture in eastern Oklahoma.

The rebirth infused new energy into the withered 66 societies. Their activities have become lively, and various signs reminding passersby about the historical road have been erected along the Route. Since the Route became a national historic highway in the year 2000, the National Park Service has become involved with its protection.

New tourist interest has, of course, helped the economy on the Road. Elysa Engelman's studies show that Route 66 has become a "pilgrim path and economic icon." Except, perhaps, for Disneyland, there is no Mecca at the end of the Road; instead, the whole Road has become the Mecca. Many shrines, equally important, dot the roadside, but of course only certain things are eligible for shrineage. Some gas stations, but not all. Some motels, but not all. Who decides this has, unfortunately, also become a contest.

Various events and festivals now take place along different parts of the Route throughout the year. Especially in towns and villages in Arizona, the competition to stage events is fierce and at times overlapping festivals compete for the audience. Beautiful cars and beautiful women go together in advertising, especially on Route 66. Annually, a Miss Historic Route 66 is chosen, and local beauty pageants are held along at least on the Arizona stretch of the Historic Route.

Beauty pageants, Route 66 festivals, and car shows are also great opportunities to see the commercial side of the Old Road. Route 66 T-shirts, caps, belt buckles, sleeve badges, pot holders, and other paraphernalia abound, most of it manufactured far from the Route in Taiwan, Singapore, or Guatemala. In Thailand a T-shirt manufacturer received a photographic negative by mistake and printed T-shirts to commemorate Route 99 still showing the states of the original 66.

The present retro-tourism, the quest for the last good decade of the

United States via the 1950s Route 66, is not entirely positive. Elysa Engelman admits that often the sacred has also become profane. There are many businessmen and businesswomen on the Road with no other idea than to take your money. Dr. Engelman wonders if there are really enough pilgrims in the whole wide world to buy all the trinkets and rubbish that are marked with the 66 sign.

After the revitalization, the first travelers on Route 66 were not typical tourists but a different kind of traveler. Naturally, they bought stuff and services along the way, but they were more interested in the history and nature, perhaps the philosophy, of the Road, than in rushing through it because doing so was a trend. The masses are more likely to fall into cheap imitations and useless paraphernalia. Why buy a Hopi Indian *katsina* doll for 180 dollars, when you can get a factory-made knock-off for 18 dollars? They look the same to the uninformed eye, and even the latter can serve as a souvenir of the trip. What difference does it make that it's made in Mexico or Taiwan?

Kelly Shapiro has worked with the Los Angeles Conservancy to preserve shrines along Route 66, such as the Edward Azusa Foothill Drive-In Theatre, which was designated a California historical resource in 2002. Increasing tourism on the Old Road helped the preservation, but tourism also has negative features. According to Shapiro, many tourists have paternalistic attitudes toward the local people. In many cases, they know better how things should be. If a 1950s gas station has a modern pump, it is no longer eligible to be called a Route 66 legend. By the same reasoning, if an American Indian is not dressed in feathers, he is no longer truly an American Indian.

As long as businesses remain local family affairs, they help the little towns survive. Increasing traffic, however, may bring in big chains that will kill the local enterprises. Tourism brings other unpleasant side effects. Pollution is worse, and it's no longer safe to let your children play by the road. Route 66 may be an interesting nostalgic drive to the 1950s, but it has also remained in that decade with its attitudes about the environment and Native Americans, says Shapiro. As much as I love Route 66, I am afraid that she is right.

The rapid growth of renewed interest has also caused disputes. Some people participate in the activities solely for economic reasons. Some feel that cherishing the culture and memories—the spirit of the Old Road—is more important than the actual location of the Route. Fundamentalists argue about the Route's original location, and disputes about where along the road to erect commemorative signs have often resulted in no signs at all.

A one and only genuine official Route 66 never really existed. The location of the road varied almost annually. Even though road maintenance kept making Route 66 straighter, local interests and politics often changed the pathway of the Route. For example, in St. Louis the Route has crossed the Mississippi on no less than five different bridges at different times.

The Old Federal Route 66 is by no means the only US road crossing the country with memories. Actually, Route 66 does not even cross the whole continent. Nor is it the only road in the United States historically joined to patterns of increased motoring. It isn't and wasn't culturally different from several other roads built around the same time under similar legislation and as parts of the same federal highway network. Route 66 is only one representative of its culture among a multitude of similar highways. Other roads attracted travelers. Bars, diners, cafés, and motels lined other roads. Tourist attractions on other roads tempted travelers and tried to empty their wallets. These other roads met exactly the same fate as Route 66: the new interstate system with four-lane freeways replaced them, their gas stations were abandoned, and their motels dilapidated. Scattered throughout the United States are ruins of old buildings and remains of the Old Road culture from early years of motoring, from times when the traveling itself was as important as reaching the destination. 1950s gas stations can still be found on Routes 50 and 34 as well as on Route 66. Some of them are still open; some have been gnawed by the ravages of time.

In many midwestern and western towns blocks of buildings from the 1920s or the 1950s are crumbling just as they do on Route 66 in Joliet, Gallup, and Williams. Art deco houses can still be seen elsewhere than along Route 66; movie theaters, cafés, hardware stores—all remnants of America's Golden Age, nostalgic memories from the times when ice-cream sodas tasted sweet on young lips, chewing gum was frowned upon, youth culture took its first toddling steps, and rock 'n roll had not yet corrupted everybody's musical taste. That age we now imagine as completely different from its historical reality. The memories are gilded with romance. So are the roads we travel in our memories. Although Route 66 was only one among many, it has become the symbol of all those roads and all those memories—a symbol of a time that never really was but nevertheless still is and of our habits that we can remember, although we never behaved like that at all.

But then, Route 66 is America at its best: not how the US has been, but how it should have been.

Historic Highway

Route 66 was and is the road to and of the West. Asphalt or concrete, its surface streams like a river on the map, down from Illinois to Southern California and ultimately to the Pacific Ocean. It does not run through the north and the large cities on the East Coast. It steers clear of the old plantations and cotton fields of Dixie. Instead, it winds from Chicago, the center of the Old West, to Los Angeles, the center of the new West. It wanders through both the most fertile and the driest soils in the United States, the richest and the poorest areas. It cuts right through the heart of America.

For more than three decades, Route 66 was THE ROAD west. It combined minor roads into a coherent Main Street of the United States, crossing the nation, the backbone of the country. Although it was miserable and in poor condition for most of its life, it guaranteed economic survival for previously isolated communities. Especially in the Southwest, the Route took on universal status. Professor Dave Warren of Santa Fe explains that in his youth in the 1930s and 1940s people always "took Route 66"—regardless of where they were going or whether they ever drove the actual Double-Six.

Route 66 connected the West and the Southwest in particular to the rest of the country. After World War II, it became the most popular tourist route in the nation. Hopis and Navajos beckoned in advertisements, and families responded by going to see the Grand Canyon and other sights of the Southwest. Moms and dads drove whimpering kids to Disneyland along Route 66; people hitchhiked the road in search of happiness at the dream factory of Hollywood. When you traveled to Los Angeles, you had no other roads to choose from.

The heyday of Route 66 came in the 1950s; until the late 1960s, it provided almost the only direct link connecting Chicago to Los Angeles and New York and the other eastern centers to California. It became the symbol of American mobility. Bobby Troup wrote a song for it, and John Steinbeck memorialized it in *The Grapes of Wrath*. These classics have given the Road eternal life.

At its birth in 1926, however, Highway 66 was far from a passable link between Chicago and Los Angeles. Only a good 800 miles of the road had some kind of paved surface and the rest, 1,600 miles, were either gravel road, bricks covered with asphalt, hard clay, or simple wooden planks. A long time passed before the existing sections of the Highway were in good shape and new sections had been built to link them. Local politics frequently confused things. Highway 66 was not truly in a drivable condition until 1937. Even then, it was far from being completely hard-surfaced.

In mythology and song Highway 66 enjoys mainly a positive image, but the Highway has also had its somber features. It was the road on which thousands of poor sharecroppers, pickers, and other victims of the Depression from Oklahoma and farther east made their way towards California. Some of them, like Grandma Joad in Steinbeck's *Grapes of Wrath*, never made it.

During Prohibition, bootleggers thrived on Route 66; the road was lined with speakeasies, gambling joints, and brothels. It served as an escape route for John Dillinger, Al Capone, and Bugsy Malone. At times, newspapers and news agencies warned of criminals who might infiltrate tourist groups.

Some of the gasoline sellers were dishonest, and various tourist attractions tried to relieve unfortunate travelers of their money. The same kind of attractions, with the same purpose, still exists in abundance along Route 66 and other US highways, as, no doubt, elsewhere in the world.

In certain localities good road conditions tempted travelers to step on the gas. Some papers called Route 66 the worst speed trap in America. The American Automobile Association urged its membership at times to steer clear of certain stretches of the Highway unless they were willing to contribute to local policemen's funds.

Traffic safety often left much to be desired, and the Highway was sometimes known as "Bloody 66." Local nicknames tell somber stories of their own. According to roadside entrepreneur Lyman Riley, the section of the Highway from Waynesville to Conway in the Missouri Ozarks was a "two-lane killer." In this area lies the town of Devil's Elbow at a bend in the road known as "death's corner of the world." In the Texas Panhandle the nickname of Route 66 still is "Death Alley" or "Blood Alley." On the eastern border of New Mexico the story goes that on Route 66 only a couple of inches and a cigarette paper stood between the driver and death. In Arizona, Route 66 was given the Spanish name *El Camino de la Muerte*—the Road of Death. In 1956 one out of six car accidents in Arizona took place on Highway 66.

Speeding was not the only problem. In many places for many years the Road had no paving, and rain would turn the surface into impassable mud and sludge. This happened frequently in Jericho east of Groom in the Texas Panhandle. This sector of the Road, called Jericho Gap, would become impassible, so that travelers had to stop and wait in Groom for the road to dry. The reputation of Jericho Gap was such that even when it was properly grounded and covered in the 1930s, worried travelers coming to Groom on beautiful days years later would ask where the gap was located.

Many highway accidents were linked to booze. Drinking and driving was a problem from the very beginning. The song "Wreck on the Highway," written by Dorsey Dixon and recorded in 1942 by Roy Acuff and His Smokey Mountain Boys, is an apt warning against the rising number of road fatalities caused by alcohol.

Hitchhikers have also been both a danger and in danger on Route 66, as everywhere. Signs warn drivers not to take in hitchhikers, as they may be escaping inmates from nearby prisons. You hear stories of hitchhikers who robbed their driver, but you also hear of drivers who molested hitchhikers. In 1964 West Virginian Paul Hluska and his friend Jerry were hitchhiking on 66 inspired by Jack Kerouac and bound for the Olympic Games in Los Angles. Paul had relatives in the LA area, and as he was a good runner, he was hoping to make the Olympic team. Somewhere in Missouri a traveling salesman gave Paul and Jerry a ride. The discussion turned to safety, and the salesman pulled a gun, pointed it at Paul's head, and said that this is how he secures himself. The boys were happy to get off at the next town. In Amarillo, Texas, a local rodeo hero took them into his truck. He was distraught, having been arguing with his lady. Abruptly, he drove off toward the south and did not stop until they reached Mexico.

Sometimes rumors alone caused accidents. Once a local story developed around a hitchhiking ghost, who was said to vanish into thin air in the middle of the ride. A midwestern salesman (these things seem always to happen to traveling salesmen) picked up a middle-age hitchhiker somewhere in the Missouri countryside on a rainy night. The hitchhiker sat in the back, and on they went southwest on Route 66. A few minutes later the driver looked at his inside rear mirror to see how his passenger was doing but saw no one on the backseat. "This must be the ghost," he  thought and got so scared that he pulled off the road and ended in the ditch. When he got out of his car so did his passenger. He had only bent down to tie his shoelaces.

Travelers on the Road

Cy Avery of Oklahoma and John Woodruff of Missouri founded the National US 66 Highway Association as soon as the Federal Highway 66 officially came into existence. The principal task of the association was to make the general public aware of the Highway and encourage people to use it. Another goal was to press for hard surfacing for the entire Highway. Members from each of the eight states crossed by US 66 were elected as vice-chairmen. Lon Scott was hired as the association's PR man.

At the first meeting of the National US 66 Highway Association on February 2, 1927, Chairman Avery stated that the Double-Six was the Main Street of America. The charter of the association stressed specifically that Route 66 was the shortest route from the Great Lakes to the Pacific and described the trail of the Route through Illinois prairies, past the vistas of the Ozarks in Missouri, the lead and zinc production areas in Joplin-Miami, the oil fields of Oklahoma and the Texas Panhandle, the southern Rockies in New Mexico, the Grand Canyon area in Arizona, and Southern California. In other words, Route 66 ran through the center of the United States and covered the essential—according to some, the absolutely most essential—part of the United States.

Lon Scott came up with the idea of a footrace across the United States on Highway 66. In order to gain more publicity the track was extended from coast to coast, first to Chicago on 66 and from there to New York. Already famous for arranging mass events, C. C. Pyle—whose initials stood for "Cash and Carry" or "Cold Cash," depending on whom you talked to—organized the race. The Highway Association promised to pay Pyle sixty thousand dollars. The money was supposed to come from various side events, from the localities chosen as over-night stops for the competitors, and of course from the competitors themselves, who had to pay one hundred dollars each as an entry fee.

The race started from Los Angeles on March 4, 1928, at 3:46 p.m. Pacific time. Some half a million spectators witnessed the event. As many as 275 competitors began the race but many soon quit. Seventy-seven competitors dropped out the first day, twelve more gave up on the second, and eighteen on the third. The Mojave Desert wore the runners down fast. Most of them suffered from blisters and chafes on their heels and toes. Soon the race took on its nickname, "The Bunion Derby."

Seventy competitors reached Chicago, and fifty-five made it all the way to New York. A couple of Finns were among the competitors who reached the goal. Ville Kolehmainen even led the race for a long time, and, initially, Olli Wantinen also kept up with the pack. The winner of the race, however, was Andrew Payne, a twenty-year-old Oklahoma Cherokee, with a running time of 573 hours, 4 minutes, 34 seconds. With night stops, the race took 87 days in all. Payne used his prize of twenty-five thousand dollars to pay off the debts on his parents' farm. In 1934 he became Secretary of Oklahoma's Supreme Court and was re-elected to this post no less than seven times.

Cold Cash Pyle suffered an economic loss, however, and he never got the money he was promised. Several towns did not pay the participation fee Pyle demanded, nor did the side events produce as much money as he had anticipated. Besides, others apart from Pyle's organization also arranged side events and cashed in on them. Several economic scandals marked the race. Often competitors ran down empty stretches of road while spectators waited in the wrong place at the wrong time. Pyle probably had to pay compensations for some of his empty promises. Representatives of the media enjoyed Pyle's hospitality to the full at times, but the cook hired to prepare food for the competitors was fired—not because the food was bad but because he embezzled the profits.

Despite the economic losses, the race did publicize Highway 66. Through press coverage of the race, the American public learned quickly and thoroughly about the Route and its location. Cy Avery's dream of Route 66 as America's Main Street began to come true.

After 1928 people kept walking and running on the Double-Six. Many longer and shorter races were arranged near or on the old highway. Even C. C. Pyle organized another coast-to-coast race in 1929. In that same summer "Happy" Lou Phillips and "Lucky" Jimmy Parker roller-skated from Washington, DC, to San Francisco on old-fashioned roller-skates with two parallel rows of four wheels. They skated Route 66 from Missouri through Arizona to California. Phillips and Parker financed their trip by selling photos of themselves, participating in all kinds of events, and selling newspapers along the way. On the paved sections of the highway, the skaters could roll up to seventy-five miles a day.

In the late 1950s, Pete McDonald walked from New York City to Los Angeles on stilts and earned 1,500 dollars for his stunt. From Chicago on he walked Route 66. Hobo Dick Zimmerman traveled on Route 66 routinely from California to Michigan to visit his mother. She lived to be 101 years old, the boy 78. "Pushcart" Dogherty, with his white beard and turban-covered head, pushed his earthly possessions along the Route for years, walking nine to sixteen miles a day.

In 1972 John Ball, a forty-seven-year-old South African, jogged Route 66 from California to Chicago, then on from Chicago to the East Coast. The jog lasted only 54 days; many less than in 1928, because the road had been improved. Bob Wieland, who had lost his legs in Vietnam, traveled along the Route on a rack in 1979. Five years later, in 1984 and again in 1996, the Olympic torch was carried on the Route through New Mexico, Arizona, and California. Also in 1996 sixty-six-year-old Margie McCauley walked all of Route 66.

In summer 2001, to celebrate the seventy-fifth anniversary of Route 66, a website company called Route66.com organized a "Bunion Run." David Williams led it and anyone could join for whatever distance they wanted to run. This was not a race but a publicity and fundraising event. New walkers and runners are certain to come forth in the future. And we should all join with Alan Rhody and Kevin Welsh when they in their song titled "The Mother Road" ask the Lord to "let them get where they are going, those children of the mother road."

Despite this surprising amount of foot traffic, most people have always traveled 66 by car. So did the job-seeking Okies, so did the many looking for their fortune in Hollywood, and so did the parents taking their kids to Disneyland. The Old 66 was designed, after all, for wheels, not for feet, and for peaceful travel, not for competition. It should be traveled so that the journey itself is as important as the destination.

Highway of Music

The memory of Highway 66 lives on best in the song "Route 66," written by Robert (Bobby) William Troup, Jr., in 1946. Spencer Crump I think is right when he, in his book *Route 66: America's First Main Street*, claims that "The Man responsible, more than any other person, for elevating Route 66 to cult status is Bobby Troup."

Troup, born in Harrisburg, Pennsylvania, in 1918, was already a successful songwriter before World War II; a song of his called "Daddy," performed by Sammy Kaye, topped the charts. In the war, Troup served in the Pacific theater from 1942 to 1946 and achieved the rank of captain. After the war, he did not want to continue a career in the family's music store but decided to try his luck writing more songs.

In the postwar world of American entertainment, a songwriter in principle could succeed in only two places: New York or Los Angeles. Troup decided to make a name for himself in Hollywood and took to the road with his 1941 Buick. Somewhere in the western parts of Pennsylvania, Troup's wife suggested that he write a song about the road they were on, Highway 40. Troup thought it was a silly idea, particularly as they were about to move to Route 66 for most of the trip. However, the idea of a road song wouldn't leave Cynthia Troup alone, and after St. Louis she turned to her husband and whispered: "Get your kicks on Route 66, then." That got Troup's attention: what a great name for a song! Soon he was measuring distances on his ruler and building his song into a musical map of the Route.

In Los Angeles, Bobby Troup got the chance to perform some of his songs for Nat King Cole, who liked the unfinished 66 song and wanted to record it at once. Troup finished his song, and Cole went on to record it. It became a big hit and soon reached number three on US charts. Cole re-recorded the song at least twice. All of his versions are relatively slow and include a lengthy piano solo. Even his daughter Natalie Cole sang a version of "(Get Your Kicks on) Route 66." The arrangement proved that she was daddy's girl.

Bobby Troup made enough money with the song to be able to stay in California and buy a house. Later, he took up acting and appeared in minor roles in several Hollywood films. He eventually divorced Cynthia and married actress Julie London. He also continued to write songs. Some of them succeeded, but none has become as popular as "(Get Your Kicks on) Route 66." Even Troup himself has recorded the song; his live performance is slow and smooth.

Nat King Cole's pronunciation has had an effect on the pronunciation of *route*. Most Americans would normally pronounce the name of the highway something like *rowt*, rhyming with *out*. In Bobby Troup's own version, the songwriter uses this pronunciation when he sings it the first time, but later he also adopts the more British-like pronunciation Cole used throughout the song: *root*. Outside the United States, this pronunciation is the most common.

"Route 66" has subsequently been recorded by a number of artists, and it is still frequently performed live and recorded everywhere in the world. The song's European break-through took place first in 1956 when Chuck Berry recorded it and again after he toured England in the early 1960s. Berry's version was faster than Cole's, with the piano solo taken over by a guitar and shades of rock 'n roll added. Other famous performers of "Route 66" include Perry Como, Manhattan Transfer, Paul Anka, Sammy Davis, Jr., the  Andrews Sisters, Bing Crosby, and the Rolling Stones. It can also be heard in the soundtrack of the 1993 movie *Kalifornia*.

The song was recorded in Finland in 1964 as a single by Eero, Jussi & The Boys. Later that same year they re-recorded it for their first album. Some ten years later Jussi Raittinen wrote the lyrics in Finnish locating the song on the Finnish Highway 66, which runs northwest from central Finland toward the western coast. Jussi complained in his words that the Finnish 66 was in poor condition and managed to irritate the Finnish Department of Transportation into making improvements. Then Jussi had to rewrite the Finnish version praising the new 66.

There also exist other editions of the song in Finnish. One refers to the Finnish road with that number and one to a pub in eastern Helsinki. A Helsinki-based rock group, Mailroad, has made the original "(Get Your Kicks on) Route 66" their favorite number so much so that their vocalist is sometimes referred to as Mr. 66 of Finland. Even their record *Left Chicago* shows the beginnings of Route 66 on its cover. The license plate of their vocalist's pick-up is RTE-66. This is as close as you can get in Finland with license plates.

Before his death, Bobby Troup said he was glad his 66 song is a blues, as blues numbers attract even the most avant-garde rock groups. And hundreds of recordings of Bobby Troup's song must have been made outside the United States and in virtually any language you can imagine.

While writing the song, Troup paid careful attention to the map. Not all of the performers have been equally accurate. Many of the singers do not travel through Joplin; they just drive "down to Missouri," as does, for instance, Depeche Mode. Great confusion also concerns the towns near the end of the Highway in Arizona and California. Even with the best of intentions and ears, one cannot possibly hear the towns of Kingman, Barstow, and San Bernardino mentioned in the Rolling Stones version. In the Charles Brown and Manhattan Transfer versions, "Kingman" becomes "Kingsman," and that extra "s" can even be heard in Chuck Berry's recording when he mentions the town for the first time.

Some have even located the Route in a totally wrong place. The Four Freshmen urge the listeners to remember not only Winona but Disneyland as well. Disneyland has indeed been one of the attractions of Route 66 ever since its founding, but the park is not on the highway. The Brian Setzer Orchestra has the highway make a detour through Nevada, as the "three town list" changes from "Kingman, Barstow, San Bernardino" to "Barstow, Reno, San Bernardino." Reno is in northern Nevada, far from Route 66. The black street duo Juliette Cartwright and Bruce Brooks, a.k.a. the Chicago Brother and Sister Blues Band, are equally lost, as their up-tempo rhythm and blues arrangement misses the "three town list" altogether but includes San Francisco and New York.

Rather special versions of the song include Cal Collins's instrumental where acoustic guitar and bass steal the attention, and Mel Tormé's live performance. Tormé's ragtime arrangement does not mention Joplin and mixes some other songs into the soup. Tormé adds a long section of Ella Fitzgerald-type scat singing, and in fact he mentions Fitzgerald in the middle of the song, suspecting that the lady could scat much better than he could.

People other than Bobby Troup have also made music about the Old Highway. The most famous of them is probably Woody Guthrie, a folk singer from Oklahoma, who composed songs of the Road in the 1930s. You can fairly claim that his songs made 66 known throughout the country. His songs often eased the pain of economic depression and were quite popular. Too bad that many of them are not often played anymore and never really became hits outside the United States. Guthrie is a Route 66 person and an Oklahoma person, and we will meet him again in this book when we take 66 through the Sooner State.

When a TV series was made of Route 66, Bobby Troup thought his song would be included as the theme music, but the producers chose Nelson Riddle's music instead. Understandably, Troup was infuriated. From then on his song would advertise the TV series of the same name, and he would gain nothing from it. According to David Sanger, a musician from Austin—the capital of Texas and, many say, "the live music capital of the world"—Nelson Riddle's theme song captures the laid-back feeling of the Old Route. Hearing it now, fifty years later, the song seems like such a standard US entertainment tune that I'm not surprised I had forgotten it completely, although I can recall the TV series vividly.

Most songs dealing with Route 66 have been influenced by Troup's melody and follow in its footsteps. It would seem difficult to compose music or write songs about the Road without reference to Troup. David Sanger has collected 66 tunes on a record called *Music from the All-American Highway*. The compilation also contains Troup's and Charles Brown's versions of the original song.

All 66 songs reminisce about the golden age of the Highway, now replaced by the new highway system. Alan Rhody sings about the people on the Road, "Children of the Mother Road." Jason Eklund's nostalgic lyric, "What's Left of 66," explains that the Road was named Will Rogers Highway, that Jesse James hid out in Missouri, that Indians were removed by force—and that you don't have to pay sales tax for cigarettes if you buy them from a shop on Indian land. Finally, the song urges listeners to experience some of what is still left of Route 66.

The lament continues in "The Long Red Line," mourning the replacement of the Old Highway with Interstate 40. The following tune, "Used to Be," is set in Oklahoma between the towns of Kelly and Bristow, but the same concerns are true everywhere along the Route. It expresses the fear that the Old Highway will vanish along with its roadside inns, crumbling sandstone cottages now marked with holes and surrounded by weeds. Once cotton grew in this tired soil and wagons rolled by, but now there's nobody picking cotton anymore. "There used to be dancing in this town . . ."

In the song "2200 Miles," Cindy Cashdollar and the Mad Cat Trio (with Finnish Erik Hokkanen on the acoustic guitar, violin, and vocals) lay before us the entire length of Route 66. This is traditional country music to commemorate the Old Road. Jimmy LaFave's return to the Highway in "Route 66 Revisited" is more up-tempo. Playing this song and the one by Bobby Troup in succession shows clearly how time passes and things change, but the tradition lives on.

Aside from the Road itself, many of the localities it runs through have also made it into songs. This will become clear when we hit the road to meet these towns in music. A number of songs have also been written about roads and traveling. They are not directly related to Route 66, but they express a mood that people committed to the memory of 66 wish to maintain. Chuck Berry has excelled here as well. He drives his Ford Mustang. In his classic "No Particular Place to Go," Berry and his girlfriend drive about aimlessly, and Berry is unable to unbuckle the safety belt at a critical moment in their relationship. The song is a favorite of Al Bundy's in the TV series *Married with Children*. On the other hand, the song also illustrates American youths' favorite pastime—or the only one available in small midwestern and southwestern towns.

"CC Rider" by Elvis Presley and Jerry Lee Lewis is, of course, the song of all travelers, but motorcyclists have attempted to adopt Steppenwolf's "Born to be Wild" as their own. After all, the song opens the road movie of all time, *Easy Rider*. The term "heavy metal" comes from this song and has subsequently become the name of an entire music genre.

Several collections on Highway 66 have been published during the past few years. A package of no less than five CDs with over one hundred songs is titled *Get Your Kicks on Route 66: 100 Songs for the Road*. Steppenwolf, Canned Heat, and the Lovin' Spoonful are all there, along with Chuck Berry. Berry's version of the title song opens the fourth record. The front cover has a picture of the Southwest desert and a truck; a smaller picture shows a Route 66 sign from California. The back cover has a big picture of a US 66 sign from New Mexico.

The *American FM* collection presents songs from the 1970s as if played by US radio stations. This record includes Canned Heat's "Let's Work Together." Lynyrd Skynyrd's "Sweet Home Alabama" has nothing to do with Route 66, and in fact it has hardly any reference to cars or travel; neither do most songs in this collection. However, Americans still listen to the radio a lot while driving. This is probably the reason why the record collection's front cover has a picture of a straight stretch of road somewhere in the Southwest. The Route 66 sign is impossible to miss. The same photograph appears in the cover of the 1996 edition of the *Rough Guide* traveler's guide to the United States.

Unbridled nostalgia for the 1950s and 1960s can be found in the four-record compilation by Penny recording company with performers like Chuck Berry, Jerry Lee Lewis, Elvis Presley, the Platters, and Fats Domino. One of the records is titled *Rebel Rouser*, another *Blue Suede Shoes*, and the third claims, with the help of a car parked outside a bar, that *There's Good Rockin' Tonight*. The title of the fourth record is *American Diner*. The cover has a picture of—what else—the 66 diner in Albuquerque, New Mexico.

Advice for the Road

An old-timer told his daughter when she was about to embark on a trip: "Beware of unknown men and public lavatories." This advice should be kept in mind on Route 66. Although most people in the United States—like most people everywhere—are very friendly, you will need to be careful about whom you keep company with. Do not pick up hitchhikers, particularly on the eastern edge of the Mojave Desert. These guys have their ways to detect rented cars. Too many a tourist has had to pay dearly for an act of kindness, although Route 66 has never had the kind of systematic robbing of travelers that has taken place occasionally in Florida.

To follow the old-timer's advice literally, you may want to construct a "Texas T-shirt" on the toilet seat as a sound protective method. In places with more quality this device is usually on the house. The model used by American Airlines at Chicago airport is probably the most modern: push a button, and you'll automatically get a fresh plastic sheet between your butt and the toilet seat.

The best advice for any trip is to use your wits and keep an open mind. In order to achieve something you usually have to sacrifice something else; you gain some, you lose some. In the case of Route 66 there is no reason to lose anything but time and money—and gain an experience of a lifetime, maybe even of two lifetimes.

Route 66 is free and full of adventure. Adventure need not spell danger—or wallowing in dirt or sleeping on train station floors. After all, Route 66 is a road of civilization, a road of dignified people and their dignified businesses, a road of beautiful scenes and genuine travelers. Therefore, Route 66 should be the road taken. It is the road that will take you to the West. It's the trip that the sun makes every day. It can give you "your kicks."

Route 66 is no place for mass tourism, but if you want to see a whole different America in addition to the most important United States natural wonders, it may be for you. The road is free, but it is best to plan the trip with care. It is of course possible to travel by train or bus, and that may even be the best alternative if you plan to travel alone. The trains do not travel on 66, however, nor do the bus lines visit the smaller places. A bus will take you to the largest towns and the most important tourist attractions, though. You can enjoy the local atmosphere and charm at least in some places.

But you can only catch the atmosphere of the Old Road itself through traveling on it. Therefore, you will need a car or a motorcycle—well, a bicycle will do, if you want to be sporty. For safety reasons, I will not recommend walking, although, as we have seen above, many have tried that, too.

In principal you can follow Route 66 from Chicago to Santa Monica by just following the signs, but new traffic arrangements change roads all the time. Due to the disputes of local Route 66 associations, even the "Historic 66" signs may change places. Different traveler's guides give different instructions about the Road and its location. Sometimes Route 66 fanatics even steal the signs.

It is reassuring to see brown Historic Route 66 signs by the road, but they never are where you really need them. At least I would like to see them just before the next intersection to help me decide which way to go. The signs are less useful on a long straight of road with no options ahead.

Jack D. Rittenhouse wrote the first Route 66 traveler's guide in 1946. Rittenhouse was born in Kalamazoo, Michigan, but moved later to Los Angeles. He made a living writing about events in the oil fields and as an advertising man. His work often took him to Albuquerque on Highway 66. Eventually, he decided to write a guidebook. Rittenhouse started to take careful notes every time he traveled on 66, and, finally, he took a couple of journeys to both directions almost from one end of the Road to the other only with his guide in mind. *A Guide Book to Highway 66* presents practically everything on Route 66 at the time, mile by mile. Rittenhouse was so excited about New Mexico when he was writing the book that he even made the Gulf of Mexico the Gulf of New Mexico.

Critics either missed or neglected the guidebook, and Rittenhouse's hopes for a second edition seemed doomed forever, although the first three thousand copies were sold very quickly. His traveler's guide, however, was published again in 1989 as a facsimile for which the author still had time to write a new preface. This second edition is available to all, thanks to the University of New Mexico Press. It remains the primary reference book of Route 66 travelers, today almost as useful as it was sixty-five years ago. The real first edition is immeasurably valuable—even in terms of money.

A more modern guidebook is Tom Snyder's *Route 66 Traveler's Guide and Roadside Companion* published originally in 1990. The even more useful and up-to-date version includes a preface by Bobby Troup, which he wrote just before passing away. Nick Freeth's *Route 66: 2,297 Miles from Chicago to LA* is nothing but an extended travel guide with great pictures and a magnificent layout. Freeth has had obvious difficulty measuring his miles, as four months earlier he published *Traveling Route 66: 2,250 Miles of Motoring History from Chicago to LA* with another publisher. Both books are interesting reading, but, surprisingly for a former music reporter and writer of guitar books, Freeth's prose does not flow, and the book lacks the personal touch. One wonders whether he really traveled the whole length of Route 66 regardless of what the mileage is.

Practically every Route 66 guidebook, and other 66 books, too, takes the reader on the road from Chicago to Los Angeles, as does this book that you are reading. Jamie Jensen's *Road Trip USA: Cross-Country Adventures on America's Two-Lane Highways*, however, introduces Route 66 refreshingly from west to northeast. Swa Franzen provides a full route description on the World Wide Web from Belgium.

Local guides for various sections of the Route are also many. All the Route 66 state associations and some of their local branches have excellent introductions to their neighborhoods. Often they are but Xerox copies of one or two pages, but they are useful and filled with interesting stories.

The best of the book-form regional guides is probably John Weiss's *Travelling the . . . New, Historic Route 66 of Illinois*, already in its seventh printing. Excellent and very useful for the whole trip is a collection of maps put together by Pro-Map publishing company into a single poster/map of the Mother Road. It is also the easiest to follow and keep handy while you're driving.

Also postcards, old and new, can serve as guides to interesting places along the Road—or, at least, they can arouse your curiosity on where to stop and what to see. As important as the travelling itself has been sending messages along the way to those who were left behind. With postcards, the traveler cannot only send greetings or tell about the weather but also show the homefolks what the scenery is like. Even before World War II, many towns along the Route were selling postcards featuring their major sights. Later, this habit spread even to the smallest villages. Many entrepreneurs on the Road began making their own cards to advertise their businesses. Hotel and motel owners often gave away their postcards free of charge and thus induced their guests to advertise their accommodations literally throughout the world.

With Route 66 nostalgia, old postcards have come to be valued again, even while new cards are produced each year. Several collections of Old Route 66 postcards have appeared. Many of them are the kind that can be detached from a booklet. Even the author Michael Wallis is involved with this kind of business.

Two recent Route 66 artists perhaps have risen above the others. Both Jerry McClanahan and the late Bob Waldmire have created whole series of cards depicting present and bygone scenes of the Old Road. Many drawings by Bob Waldmire have found their way onto postcards amounting to a collection of already more than sixty different cards. Every self-respecting Route 66 tourist shop will have at least some of them on sale. Very popular is the series that maps the Road through each of the eight Route 66 states. These cards are so full of text and details that you can amuse yourself with them for a while and really use them as your guide to the Old Road.

The Texan Jerry McClanahan is an accomplished writer, photographer, and painter of the Route 66 tradition. He has produced several series of postcards depicting some of the most important Route 66 sights like the Jack Rabbit Trading Post in Joseph City, Arizona; the Blue Swallow Motel in Tucumcari, New Mexico; or the Club Café in Santa Rosa, New Mexico. Most often the cards also show parts of 1950s cars.

Several museums, photographers, and other entrepreneurs are involved with the postcard business. Probably the busiest of these is the Smith-Southwestern Company of Mesa, Arizona. Among their great variety of Route 66 cards is a thematic series showing sections of the Old Road together with a map, a photograph of one of the local sights, a picture of an old car, and a picture of a 1950s postcard from the Curt Teich postcard collection in the Lake County Discovery Museum, Wauconda, Illinois. And, of course, each postcard also carries the magic shield symbol of Route 66.

2

Land of Pigs and Corn

The Windy City

After all this introduction, finally, let's put the pedal to the metal and hit the road itself, and be, as John Steinbeck wrote, "on 66—the great western road," and, like the Joad family in his *The Grapes of Wrath*, "we stay on this road right straight through."

Route 66 starts right here by the art museum. The sign says so. Just on the corner, the fine Irish-type Bennigan's provides food before the long drive. Then a couple of blocks and under the tracks of the elevated electric train. Soon, we'll cross the river and drive west through Chicago.

Chicago is the beginning and the end of Highway 66. The highway began here for people heading west and ended here for people coming from Los Angeles. If Route 66 is the mother of all roads, Chicago is an excellent point of departure for it. After all, it is in many ways the archetypal American city. The local residents are right to comment that, if you haven't visited Chicago, you haven't seen the United States. The French actress Sarah Bernhardt called it the Artery of America.

Chicago lies in the Midwest of the United States, pretty much in the center of North America, on the southern shore of Lake Michigan. In the winter the weather can be extremely cold, and some twenty degrees below is not exceptional. Chicago is the most freezing place I've ever been (and I come from Finland, close to the Arctic Circle, where cold winters are not rare). In January 1981 the meters read close to -40°, regardless of whether the scale was Fahrenheit or Celsius. Because of the wind, the cold felt to the skin like -72° Fahrenheit (about -57°C). And that, I'll tell you, is COLD. (Can you see the frost biting the letters?) And yet, it had been colder still a day before.

The weather is often windy in Chicago, summer or winter. The gusts come from Lake Michigan so frequently that Chicago has been nicknamed the Windy City. (Although the name originally referred to the windy politics of Chicago.) On March 9, 2002, the wind blew the scaffold of the John Hancock Center down from more than forty floors and killed three women in their cars below. Several similar wind-related events mark the town's past.

Nevertheless, the summers in the city are warm, often quite humid and hot. During a heat wave in the summer of 1995, a couple of hundred city dwellers died of heat, some of them because they lacked either the sense or the courage to open their windows. The television news gave instructions on how to survive the heat. Of course, the heat wave eventually ended in violent thunderstorms, rains, and flooding. In the summer of 2012, all of the Midwest suffered from draught, and Chicago constantly reached temperatures of a hundred.

Both air conditioning and heating equipment are needed in this city that has preserved its original Indian name in a distorted English version. According to several interpretations, "chicagu," or something like that, in the Potawatomi language means bad smelling or swamp-smelling. Others interpret the word to refer to an onion-smelling place or river. The mouth of the Chicago River was a familiar trading place for American Indians a long time before Europeans strayed to America. When Europeans arrived, they soon became part of the trading activities. The French had a small trading post there probably by the end of the eighteenth century. As an American center of any meaning, Chicago began in 1804 with the building of Fort Dearborn, just south of the river. Indians destroyed it in 1812. A new Fort Dearborn was built four years later on the north side, still right at the very center of the present town. A bridge still crosses the river pretty much on this spot.

After the occupation of the Ohio Valley between 1812 and 1815, Chicago quickly became the northern center of westward expansion. In 1820 the white town population was about one hundred, and most of the people were involved with the fur trade. Particularly in the 1830s and 1840s Chicago grew thanks also to the Erie Canal, and soon the

French were a minority. By 1850 the city already had fifty thousand inhabitants. Fifty years later, the population had grown past 1.7 million, and Chicago was already bigger than any of the old East Coast cities except New York. These two cities then held their respective positions for a long time. New York City still has the largest population in the United States, but in the latter half of the 1970s Chicago yielded second place to Los Angeles on the West Coast. The population shift from east to west mirrors the tradition of Route 66, as in the mythology, the tales, and Bobby Troup's song, the Route was always traveled from Chicago to Los Angeles, never vice versa. Frank Lloyd Wright, the famous architect from the Chicago area, has indeed commented that Highway 66 is a slide across the tilted continent, on which everything loose seemed to roll down to Southern California.

In the pale blue and white-striped flag of Chicago, four stars symbolize the important events of the city. One star is dedicated to Fort Dearborn, two to the Chicago World Fairs. The second of the stars is a reminder of the fire that destroyed Chicago in 1871, when Mrs. O'Leary's cow kicked over an oil lamp and it fell on dry straw, or so the story goes. Only the water tower and its pumping station, built in 1867, were spared from the fire and are still standing. The pumping station still pumps water to 400,000 Chicago residents north of the city center.

A couple of decades after the fire, architect David Burnham created an extensive reconstruction program that, almost by accident, transformed some twenty-five miles of Lake Michigan shoreline into public parks, swimming beaches, and harbors. The work was completed by Louis Sullivan, a pioneer of modern architecture, and later by Mies Van der Rohe, Frank Lloyd Wright, and others. They created the foundation of the city's skyscraper silhouette so eminent from Lake Michigan. In the late nineteenth and early twentieth centuries Chicago was a "model for the future," a "dream city." It seemed to many, and probably still does, a result of man's natural progress. According to an American Studies professor from Texas, Jeffrey Meikle, Chicago naturalized mechanics. The hurry of the Chicago residents and the swiftness of all changes especially amaze European visitors.

Elevators, electrification, and new construction techniques made it possible to build tall buildings. Previously, houses with more than six stories required a strong wall of stone or brick to support them. The Chicago people developed beams made of Bessemer steel and changed stone buildings into steel buildings. The tradition of constructing tall buildings with steel frameworks still continues in Chicago. The four-square plan of the city center with its tall buildings has served as a model for the rest of the United States and for other countries. The sixth or seventh tallest building in the world, the Willis Tower with its 108 stories, is in Chicago by Route 66, between Adams going west and Jackson going east. A wonderful view over the city awaits those who take the tour to the observation level. If you dare, you can actually step outside the building over a glass floor to look straight down on the street. It almost feels as you are in the air. Higher still, the tower's top is used to monitor the ozone level of the atmosphere. The Windy City also has improved on ozone: with new equipment and energy-saving methods, the town is producing less pollution than before.

I first learned to know and visited Willis Tower as Sears Tower. At the time of its completion in 1973, this 1,451-foot tall tower was the tallest building in the world. Around that time, its owner and builder, the Sears, Roebuck & Co was also the world's largest retailer. Later on the tower was sold to other companies and the Sears' naming rights expired in 2003. Six years later its name was changed to Willis Tower by Willis Group Holdings that now owns the naming rights. Most Chicagoans think that changing the name was one of the most unfortunate things that ever happened to their city and still continue to refer to the building as Sears Tower.

Famous Chicago buildings apart from the Sears Tower—sorry, Willis Tower—include Marina City with its two round towers by the Chicago River. One can enter this building on a boat straight from the river, just as cars can enter their own parking lots a couple of stories up. The John Hancock Center, the Time-Life Building, and the NBC Tower are skyscrapers on the northern side of the river. Helmut Jalm's State of Illinois Building, built in 1985 but renamed James R. Thompson Center in 1993 to honor former Illinois governor, creates a hyper-modern or postmodern version of the city square with its round floors, atriums, and open or glass-covered elevators and escalators exposing their users for others to gawk at.

Chicago is the third largest metropolis in the United States, although it is still often referred to as the "Second City." There are some 7.5 million inhabitants of all colors and races and speaking almost all languages. Only Warsaw has more Polish-speaking city-dwellers than Chicago. The Windy City is inhabited by United States citizens of German, Nigerian, Burundian, Russian, Mexican, Jewish, Italian, Swedish,

Chinese, and Irish origin, to choose but a few examples. It is a city of neighborhoods, suburbs, barrios, ghettoes, and "silk stocking districts." American Indians of the Great Lakes region gather in Chicago annually for a powwow in the fall. Chicago really is a mix of ethnic groups and languages like the old tower of Babel in the Bible. Outside the city center, the city is still like a jungle, as Upton Sinclair aptly described it in his 1906 novel *The Jungle*. Around that time, Jane Addams started Hull House as a refuge for the poor. A Chicago writer, the late Studs Terkel, has attempted to give the jungle a more human face in his interview studies. In *American Dreams* many of the dreamers come from Chicago.

Like many old city centers, Chicago's boasts a subway, even if originally it never went underground. An elevated electric train, the EL, runs on rails above the streets. Its first route made a loop on the southern side of the Chicago River in the old downtown area, as it still does, and, therefore, the center of Chicago is still known as the Loop. Most of the tall buildings, however, have moved to the northern side of the river right next to the Lake Michigan shoreline. Public transport is organized almost in good European fashion by the CTA, the Chicago Transit Authority.

Chicago was born to equip the migration movement westward and grew largely through transportation, regardless of whether the goods transported were furs, cattle, or grain, or whether they came by canoes, ships, horses, or trains. During the nineteenth century, live cattle were brought by train to Chicago slaughterhouses from Abilene, Cheyenne, and other cattle towns where the livestock had often been herded by cowboys on horseback all the way from Texas. As the technology of transportation and packaging developed, refrigerated railroad cars replaced cars carrying live cattle, but the destination was still Chicago.

At the beginning of the twentieth century, the city became a new center of trade and also culture. It was the locus of both water traffic and railroad traffic. It was the center for processing Midwest farm goods and for meatpacking also. Upton Sinclair's book on Chicago's meat packing industry described how workers stuffed the meat quickly into packages and how the packagers themselves were spat out of the factory once the workday was done. Chicago's slaughterhouse, meat processing, and meat packing industries are still important in the city's economic life. The Chicago Stock Exchange still trades "livestock," or cattle. As Tom Snyder said, Chicago is a "hub—importing and exporting anything movable, anything thinkable." You can change everything in Chicago and everything can change in the Windy City. "Chicago, Chicago, that wonderful town," goes the song; "on State Street, that great street you see things you never see on Broadway."

The machine-shop industry that supports the transport services provides many jobs, and Chicago continues to be a busy traffic junction. Even if railroads have diminished in importance, the rails from east and west, north and south still cross in Chicago. And then there are the highways. Interstate 90 runs through the city from east to west, from Boston  to Seattle, and so does the more northern route I-94 through Minneapolis. The central transcontinental highway I-80 from New York to San Francisco also runs through Chicago. Could it be that the Chicago Sister and Brother Blues Band confused this highway with the Old 66 in their song? Highways I-57 and I-55 run south from Chicago, the latter following in the footsteps—excuse me, in the wheel tracks—of Highway 66.

London-Heathrow and Hartsfield Atlanta may have surpassed Chicago's international O'Hare Airport, but for many years it was the busiest airfield in the world, based on the amount of goods transported and number of passengers served. In the number of airplane takeoffs and landings, it was surpassed in the United States only by Anchorage, Alaska, and even that only in the summer, but in Anchorage almost all of the planes are hydroplanes or other small aircraft.

City of Big Shoulders, Big Boys, and Big Scenes

Chicago is a city known around the world. It has set the time for the rest of the world, literally. In Chicago's Grand Pacific Hotel, a building that no longer stands, an agreement was made in October 1883 to divide the world into time zones. A month later "standard time" began.

Famous American poet Carl Sandburg said about Chicago that it was "Hog Butcher for the world, Tool Maker, Stacker of Wheat, Player with Railroads and the Nation's Freight Handler." Chicago was "stormy, husky, brawling, City of the Big Shoulders."

During Prohibition in the 1920s, Chicago became a center of smuggling and bootlegging. The TV series *The Untouchables* and many movies on the subject, including one with Kevin Costner, have brought stories of gangsters Al Capone and Frank Nitti and federal agent Eliot Ness to a worldwide audience. The movie *Bad Boys*, set in a juvenile prison, begins with night shots of downtown Chicago. Much of *Ferris Bueller's Day Off* is located in the Windy City; the St. Patrick's Day parade hints, of course, at the city's Irish inhabitants. This film also mentions the Chicago Cubs, the lovable losers of the baseball circuit; they haven't won a World Series for some ninety years. But maybe next year.

Another film showing the St. Patrick's Day parade, and even the coloring of the river green, is *The Fugitive*. Chased by Tommy Lee Jones, Harrison Ford is looking for a one-armed man in the streets, hospitals, and elevated electric trains of Chicago. A TV series of the same title preceded it with David Jansen playing Richard Kimble, the fugitive, but nothing like that really happened in Chicago. In Brian de Palma's *The Fury*, Kirk Douglas is also chased in the Windy City and saved, at least temporarily, by the elevated electric train and its tracks.

Betrayed, starring Tom Berenger and Debra Winger, depicts the right wing violence of America and shows a lot of Chicago. A showdown in gangster circles is the point of departure for *Some Like it Hot*, a play whose film version has become a classic. In the movie, directed by Billy Wilder, Tony Curtis and Jack Lemmon play musicians who dress up as women, and Marilyn Monroe adds her feminine charm. Although most of the movie takes place in Florida (although filmed in San Diego, California), it begins in Chicago with a series of events involving the St. Valentine's Day Massacre of 1929.

The Front Page, a play about the world of the press by Ben Hecht and Charles MacArthur, also involves Chicago gangsters and the corruption of the city. Of a plethora of movie versions, the most famous is probably the 1970s film starring Walter Matthau and Jack Lemmon. The first film version, made in 1931 by director Lewis Milestone, features Adolphe Menjou as the managing editor and Pat O'Brien as the journalist who wants to quit the paper and go on his honeymoon. In 1940 Howard Hawks cast Rosalind Russell as the journalist and divorced wife of the managing editor played by Cary Grant in *His Girl*

Friday. As late as 1988 the same theme was modernized for the world of television in *Switching Channels*, starring Kathleen Turner and Burt Reynolds.

The first controlled nuclear chain reaction took place in Chicago in 1942, so it is more than fitting that Chicago be seen as a city of science in *Chain Reaction*. In this movie, a group of university scientists invent a cheap way of making energy. The film has a few wonderful overviews of Chicago, although it intersperses them with scenes from New York and other places. Even Chicago's Field Museum of Natural History changes right in the middle of the scene into the Washington Science Museum. The main character, however, runs to meet his partner at Chicago's Union Station, which lies right on Route 66.

Unfortunately for Chicago, its gangster past has become a concept in the outside world. When the city of Lahti in southern Finland suffered from violence, it was soon nicknamed the Chicago of Finland. The present upheaval and lawlessness in Russia has drawn for that nation the sobriquets "the Wild West" and "Old Chicago." In Austria, the city council of Vienna justified increased regulation by affirming that they did not want their town turned into "a Chicago." Richard M. Daley, the second-generation mayor of Chicago, expressed irritation with such labeling of his city. How can you judge Chicago on the basis of only one of its inhabitants, Al Capone? he demanded. Should we also damn Vienna because of one of her citizens, Adolf Hitler?

Although Chicago's gangster past may have been exaggerated, it cannot be completely denied. Violent showdowns between police and gangsters happened in the city during Prohibition. Sometimes even competing gangster groups shot each other, as in the Valentine's Day bloodbath. According to the calculations of Melvin Holli, a Professor of History in Chicago, some 150 criminals were killed in skirmishes between gangsters from 1923 through 1929. The police killed an additional 150 gangsters and about a hundred innocent bystanders died in the heat of the fight.

Even violent clouds have a silver lining, though. Gangster bosses usually paid in cash, and musicians liked that. After World War I, many black musicians moved from New Orleans to Chicago, where racial boundaries were not as strict as in the South. Whereas only white musicians were admitted to the musicians' trade union in Louisiana, color did not mean so much in Illinois. The union insisted that members be able to read music, however. Some pioneers of jazz learned a couple of songs by heart and sat down to play them in front of a music rack as if reading the notes. Thus, they passed the entrance test of the musicians' union and continued to play in Chicago saloons. Chicago can be considered the home of the blues just as much as New Orleans and St. Louis.

Throughout the 1920s, 30s, and 40s, Central Station in Chicago was an important meeting place particularly for blacks. They came there from the south side and even farther away to meet people arriving by train, maybe to make a few bucks at their expense or to instruct their country cousins where it was safe for blacks to go in Chicago. So many people passed through the station that some have compared it to Ellis Island. In addition to blacks arriving from the agricultural south, many immigrants from Eastern Europe also found their way to the Windy City.

Benny Goodman, a son of a poor Jewish family, was there, the clarinetist who became the master of swing. Al Capone fancied the pianist Earl Heinz and put him on his payroll for twelve years. Chicago became the great city of jazz. Louis Armstrong and King Oliver played there with many others. The reality of the big city combined with memories of the sharecropper South created new music that lured musicians to the town. Chicago jazz, a new hard driving electric blues, was born. It was and is clearly urban, but its roots are still in the country and its lyrics often long for the homeland in the South.

Americans of Italian descent were often responsible for the bootlegging and corruption during Prohibition. Unlike the Irish and Anglo-Saxons, Italians and Jews were relatively friendly toward blacks and supported jazz music. The golden age of jazz in Chicago ended abruptly, however, when Irish and Anglo-Saxon Democrats joined forces to clean the city of bars and cabarets. The courts supported Chicago's Irish police force and its strict enforcement of Prohibition, so by around 1928 musicians, particularly black musicians, could find few places to make a living. Many of them had already packed up and headed to New York. Jazz did not return to Chicago until after World War II, and even then Chicago never became the kind of jazz center it had been during the early years of Route 66.

As an industrial city, Chicago has often been a theater of worker unrest. In 1886 during the struggle for the eight-hour workday, at least eleven people were killed in a melee that disrupted a peaceful demonstration of workers at Haymarket Square. Four leaders of the demonstration were hanged and a fifth committed suicide in jail. The five are buried at Waldheim Cemetery in Forest Park, Illinois, near the Old Route 66. In 1997 the cemetery, now part of Forest Home Cemetery, was designated a National Historic Landmark. Workers around the world observe May Day to commemorate their lost comrades of Haymarket massacre.

Chicago has also known political upheaval. In 1968, during the era of resistance to the Vietnam War and youth culture in search of alternatives in general, many young people demanding change made their way to the Windy City and the Democratic Party's National Convention. Mayor Richard Daley, the elder, who ruled his city with an iron grip, refused them entrance to the convention arena. Conflict between demonstrators and the police escalated into a colossal fight that was televised inside the party's convention facilities. The police quickly lost both their nerve and their sense of judgment and began indiscriminately beating people nearly at random with their billy clubs. Many of the party convention participants were appalled. Others demanded even stronger measures against the "young trash." Still others realized that something had gone badly wrong. Why does the United States beat up its children at the beginning of Route 66, the highway on which it should send its children to the world?

In addition to *The Untouchables*, many TV series are set in Chicago. "The mother of all police series," *Hill Street Blues*, never named the city it happened in, but initially the episodes clearly took place in New York. Later the scenes became more Chicago-like, even to the extent that the Chicago River was clearly identifiable in some of the opening shots. All the filming took place at the other end of Highway 66, however, in Los Angeles.

In *Hill Street Blues*, the cops were not all necessarily good guys, nor were city administrators. Corruption is indeed Chicago's other vice, besides the unequal treatment of its inhabitants. A popular story illustrates that theme: The Pope was visiting Chicago. Returning to his lodgings after midnight mass, he persuaded his chauffeur to let him drive the brand new limo that his hosts had provided. The Pope was an inexperienced driver, however, and he soon crashed the limo into a lamppost. The two policemen who arrived to investigate were Catholic, one Irish and the other Italian. After a brief conference, they decided not to write a ticket. If the chauffeur was the Pope, who was the big shot in the back seat?

The television series *ER* and *Chicago Hope* are both set in the Windy City. In one episode of *ER* young Doctor Carter (Noah Wyle) drives along Route 66 toward Chicago with nurse Abby (Maura Tierney) after picking up her drug-abusing mother (Sally Field) in Oklahoma. *Married with Children* also takes place in Chicago; the opening scene features Buckingham Fountain in Grant Park. Abruptly, the fountain's water stops, perhaps in symbolic honor of shoe salesman Al Bundy's flagging masculinity.

Al Bundy played American football in high school, and Chicago is indeed a sports Mecca. The city has hockey teams, baseball teams, and football teams. The professional hockey team, the Chicago Black Hawks, is named after the Indian chief of the Sauk tribe who fought the white invaders in the Chicago area during the 1830s. The Chicago Bears is another famous team. Wrigley Field, named for William Wrigley, Jr., the chewing gum magnate, is home to the Chicago Cubs baseball team. The basketball team Chicago Bulls has often won the North American championship, or world championship, as the Americans like to put it. Michael Jordan and Dennis Rodman, whose hair keeps changing color, are Bulls figures familiar to every sports enthusiast in the world. Scottie Pippin of the Chicago Bulls played on the US Olympic team in 1996 and also paid a short visit to *ER* on television.

Chicago sports have also made it to the movies, but not always in a positive limelight. Sports history and baseball are mixed with corruption in John Sayles's motion picture of *Eight Men Out*, in which the 1919 Chicago White Sox take money to "throw" the world series—lose it deliberately. Chicago is a city of big things: big gangsters, tall basketball players, big corruption, big games, big business, and big vistas from the tops of its skyscrapers.

Besides skyscrapers, Chicago has other important buildings: museums, hotels, commercial buildings, you name it. The city boasts at least three state universities and twice as many private universities or their campuses. The Newberry Library on the north side of the river holds famous historical collections. At the southern corner of Grant Park lies the famous Field Museum of Natural History dating to the time of the 1892/1893 Chicago World's Fair. The Fair opened during the four hundredth anniversary of Christopher Columbus's "discovery" of America and, aside from European marvels, it exhibited the achievements of the New World and the United States as well as relics from its past. Even the streets of the fair site were named after European explorers or, more accurately, exploiters. Columbus Avenue still runs through Grant Park.

On the eastern side of Grant Park lies the Art Institute next to which the Old Route 66 started or ended. If the shore of Lake Michigan is considered the starting point of the road, 66 will become longer by the length of Grant Park, but many people consider Route 66 to begin at Adams Street, at the main entrance to the institute. The matter is confused by the fact that the streets in this area later became one-way. There are only vague memories concerning the site of the first shield-shaped Route 66 sign.

At its earliest stage the Road did not begin until Cicero, eight miles west of the Loop. In 1933 the terminus was moved to Chicago at Jackson Boulevard and Michigan Avenue, although some say it was Jackson Drive and Lake Shore Drive, because in that same year Jackson was lengthened through Grant Park because of another World's Fair. When Jackson Boulevard became one way in 1955, the beginning of 66 moved a block north to Adams and Michigan Avenue. So actually going west, Route 66 is a bit shorter than when coming east. Since 1995, Historic Route 66 signs have been documenting the various routes.

According to the Illinois Route 66 Society, the Road starts from the shore of Lake Michigan and runs through Grant Park along Jackson Drive, splitting into two by the Art Institute. From the front of the institute, the Road continues along Adams Street almost straight west to Ogden Avenue, where it turns southeast towards the town of Joliet, partly along the street named after the town.

At its beginning in Chicago, Route 66 is really a road of culture, art, and literature, both American and European. The Chicago Art Institute has paintings by famous Americans and works by such European artists as Monet and Chagall. In Cicero, on the northern side of the Road, lie Oak Park and the former homes of Frank Lloyd Wright, Ernest Hemingway, and Edgar Rice Burroughs, the creator of Tarzan.

In the history of Chicago, Route 66 can claim only a small chapter; the Road never had the kind of significance to the city it had to the smaller towns along its trail. In Chicago, US Highway 66 was only part of the city's many streets. Only after the Road reached the prairies, linking towns together and not merely running through them, did the tales begin to travel it.

The Pontiac Trail

According to Tom Snyder: "Of the Midwestern states, Illinois has always been the champion trader, track layer, and road builder." A long time before anyone even dreamed of Route 66, the road from Chicago to St. Louis, Missouri, was an important part of the Illinois area road network. It connected the Great Lakes and the Mississippi River, forming the western link between the North and the South. The road had as many names as a beloved child. The East St. Louis-Springfield-Chicago trail only listed the most important cities along the road. The Mississippi Valley Highway referred to the fact that along this road it was possible to reach the Mississippi Valley area. The Greater Sheridan Road got its name during the Civil War when General Philip Sheridan's troops used it as their supply line. As the road continued south from St. Louis, the Texas-bound travelers named it the Lone Star Route.

The road was officially named the Pontiac Trail in 1915. The name was justified by the fact that Pontiac, the Ottawa chief who led a rebellion against the English in 1763, had frequently traveled in the area, spent his last years there, and eventually died near St. Louis at the southern end of the Road. The town named after him was also located on the Highway.

In 1918 the state of Illinois started to sell bonds for road improvements. Within three years the Pontiac Trail became SBI 4 (State Bond Issue Road 4) according to the number of the bond sold for the improvement of this road. With the help of the bond money, the entire road was paved by 1926. When SBI 4 became US 66 in the following year, all cars of the time could drive on it. The sections made for the new road were paved immediately, and since 1930 Route 66 practically never lacked an all-weather covering in Illinois. At the time, the road was completely surfaced only in Illinois and Kansas—but the Kansas section of Route 66 was less than 15 miles long, while there was some 350 miles of it in Illinois.

As elsewhere, the trail of 66 varied in Illinois. Initially, it ran from Chicago through the "prison city" of Joliet, but later it passed Joliet to the west, although not quite as far west as the present Highway I-55. Many of the road signs for the old, as well as the new, highway were made at Joliet prison. The town has appeared in at least two films: *The Sting*, directed by George Roy Hill and starring Paul Newman and Robert Redford, begins at Joliet. So does *The Blues Brothers*, before it moves on to Chicago.

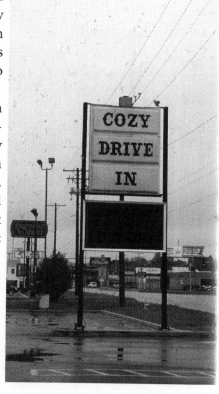

Joliet was founded by Charles Reed in 1831 and named perhaps for the French ex-plorer Louis Jolliet, who traveled in the early 1670s with Father Jacques Marquette from the Great Lakes to the Mississippi River. When they returned, they probably passed by the area of Joliet, after discovering that the Mississippi does not run to the Pacific Ocean.

For some obscure reason, Joliet was called Juliet for a number of years, and a village called Romeo, now Romeoville, was estab-lished north of the town. Perhaps the town was not named originally for the French explorer but for somebody's wife, lover, or daughter. Mother-in-law? Or maybe after William Shakespeare's *Romeo and Juliet*.

The Illinois state prison on its high hill can be seen from Highway 66 after the traveler has passed the center of Joliet. The sights of the city center may be somewhat harder to locate, although there are enough signs of the historic highway everywhere in Illinois. The now silent Ri-alto Theater on Chicago Street belongs traditionally to the milestones of the roadside. The casinos by the river seduce people who want to become rich quickly but often become poor instead.

Going to Joliet, Historic 66 ran sometimes quite close to the west-ern bank of the Des Plaines River, one of the tributaries of the Illinois River, and then crossed it south of Joliet as I-55 does today. The head-waters of the Des Plaines are northwest of Chicago, and one stretch of the river runs less than ten miles from Lake Michigan. It does not empty into the lake, however, but continues south, joins the Illinois River, then the Mississippi, and finally empties into the Gulf of Mexico in Louisiana. A canal that is still passable links the Des Plaines to the southern branch of the Chicago River. The Historic 66 runs a long way beside the canal. Those interested in the canal can leave the road for a moment and cross the canal in Lockport, a town named appropriately for a canal feature.

After leaving the Windy City, Historic 66 runs through rustic settings. On the left the trees at times hide the view to the Des Plaines and the Illinois-Michigan Canal. Green fields open to the right. In places the road deviates from the old trail where new roads and buildings have destroyed the foundation of the old highway. At times the Old Road, its asphalt crumbled and over grown with weeds, can be seen next to the new road. This is the case all the way to Los Angeles.

South of Joliet the hilly plains of Illinois begin, already giving clear signs of the prairie landscapes west of the Mississippi River. Corn is the most important crop here, although everything from tobacco to alfalfa is also cultivated. Much of the corn is used as pig feed. This is the zone of pork and corn reaching from Ohio to Iowa.

Along the Road, we pass small towns like Diamond and Pontiac. The Historic 66 winds through downtown Joliet, downtown Elwood, and downtown Wilmington, although the centers of the latter two towns are barely noticeable. In Wilmington the 66 crosses the Kankakee River and runs along its bank. Then on to Braidwood, Godley, and Braceville, where the closed Riviera Restaurant stands to the left of the road immediately after the river bridge, nearly hidden by bushes. Then Gardner, Dwight, and the Carefree Motel.

Yes, Godley. "You drive Route 66 and missed Godley!" The late Tom Teague, formerly a teacher and later a Route 66 booster has marked down these words of Bob Bolen as a part of the Route 66 legend. Godley was originally built as a place of entertainment for miners, and truck drivers later joined in. Then the mine was exhausted, and the new highway took away the truck drivers. We, too, would have missed Godley, had we not been aware of the town. And still—my apologies, Bob Bolen—would it have made any difference? Godley doesn't even appear on the *Rand McNally Road Atlas*, although it can be located on the 2002 *American Map Road Atlas*, and you can also find it in the Google Maps on your internet.

A church moved from Gardner and a coal mine office building moved from South Wilmington were combined in 1928 to become the Riviera Restaurant, where we would have stopped had it not been closed, possibly for good. Originally, it was surrounded by a small zoo, a picnic park, and a swimming place. In the spring of 1996 the brush around it was growing in the rain and the paint was peeling off. Interstate 55 passes the restaurant only a few miles away but passes it nevertheless. Later I learned that the building burned down but, apparently, was reopened for business a few years ago.

South of Dwight the next town is tiny Odell with a church, a couple of houses, and a gas station surrounded by fields of corn and other plants. But what a gas station! It is a landmark of the Old Road, bearing the logos of Standard Oil and Shell, still in good shape and painted, although a couple of windows may be broken. Probably no use trying to get some fuel, though—or should you try, anyway?

After Odell, the Road connects a number of places that have taken their names from American Indians. Cayuga refers to an Iroquois people, whose principal living area was far northeast but who also wandered around Illinois, conquering and later fleeing. The Old Log Cabin Inn appears to date back to those times. Its more modern version, the New Log Cabin Inn, also seems to have seen its best days a long time ago.

Since 2004 Pontiac has been the new home of Illinois Route 66 Hall of Fame, having moved here from McLean further south down the Old Road. Baby Bulls Restaurant connected to a service station and a shopping mall represents a more modern highway tradition in Pontiac; it is neat and ordinary, and it serves good common food. The owners, Jim and Janice Letsos, advertise their restaurant in the traditional American way. The license plate on their car reads "Baby Bulls." Restaurants belonging to the same chain also serve customers in Gilman and Petersburg, but those towns are not located on the Old Road.

Past Pontiac the Indian names continue. First there's Ocoya, then Chenoa and, after Lexington, Towanda. Then it's about time to get back to Normal, which happens to be the name of the next locality, nowadays practically a Bloomington suburb.

But before that, please, make the side trip to Chenoa. It really is a nice little town just east of Route 66. There's a good-looking mural of Route 66 right downtown and a fine cafeteria at the intersection of Highway 24. Enjoy the charming atmosphere of a small city with interesting houses.

Maple Syrup and Pig Hip

The first major town after Joliet is Bloomington. The town has two college campuses, but it should not be confused with the town by the same name in Indiana, the neighboring state, a town of smaller size but more students and greater fame. A few famous Americans, however, have their final resting-place in the cemetery of Bloomington, Illinois. Adlai E. Stevenson (1900-1965), who was influential in politics during the early Cold War era and served as the American United Nations ambassador, has his monument and grave here. As a Democratic candidate in 1952, he lost the presidency to Republican Dwight D. Eisenhower.

Another tombstone marks the grave of an earlier politician, David Davis (1815-1886). He worked as a judge in Illinois and became friends with Abraham Lincoln. Davis led the Lincoln supporters in the Republican Party Convention in 1860, where Lincoln was chosen as the candidate for the presidency. As president, Lincoln rewarded Davis by appointing him judge of the U.S. Supreme Court in 1862. Davis's loyalty to the Republicans was not impeccable though, and he represented the Democratic Party as the Senator from Illinois from 1877 to 1883.

Next to the cemetery gate stands a tiny wooden house belonging to the cemetery's historical society. No matter whose grave you are looking for, these people can help you. One seldom finds such friendly and informed service. In a short time you can learn a lot about the history of Bloomington and its surroundings as well as the celebrities of its past and perhaps the present. You can think about them while trying to wind your way out of the town along the Old 66 or its remains and past the Beich candy factory, owned today by the notorious Nestle Company, on the right side of the road. On the left, trucks roar down Interstate 55.

Bloomington cemetery has many tombstones reading Funk. Only a few miles south of Bloomington, there is a small natural wonder, hundreds of years old: Funks Grove, a stand of maple trees in the middle of the prairie. The family of Isaac Funk, who lent his name to the place, moved into the area sometime in the 1820s, soon after Illinois joined the Union in 1818. The Funks had previously moved from Kentucky to Ohio, where they continued their westward journey. In Illinois they worked as farmers and cattle breeders. Before the completed railroad stopped cattle herding, the Funk family often drove their cattle as far as New York. The railroad took cattle only to Chicago, but a member of the Funk family established his own slaughterhouse there.

Because the Funk farm was located near maples, maple syrup was on the family's menu. Gradually, it became a large-scale business, especially after cars started to travel on Route 66. In 1948 six hundred buckets were hanging in the trees collecting the sap; in 1988 there were some four thousand buckets. The price of maple syrup had simultaneously increased from seven dollars a gallon to twenty-nine dollars. The Funks sold maple syrup by the roadside and still do, although most of their syrup is now sold directly to merchants. Interstate 55 has diverted many customers. Despite the Funk Sirup Company ads along the new highway, few drivers make the side trip to the Old 66 for syrup. If they'd tasted it, they would.

The Funk syrup farm is worth seeing. The syrup is good and the reception warm, at least when Glaida Funk herself stands behind the counter. Mrs. Funk was ready to tell many stories both about the Funk family and the Old Road. Susan, the daughter of Stephen and Glaida Funk, has written more than thirty romance stories and many children's books. With the new 66 nostalgia, new editions of her children's books have been published in a series dedicated to the Old Road.

Syrup is spelled "sirup" everywhere at the Funk farm. According to an old dictionary, there is a definite difference. "Sirup" means pure natural product, whereas the syrup spelled with a "y" can also refer to industrial products with preservatives and chemicals that make storage easier.

After Funks Grove the maples vanish and the cultivated prairies continue. Just south of Funks Grove is the small town of McLean, whose service station became an important resting-place for truck drivers during the Golden Age of Route 66. Since the new highway is close enough and there's also an intersection close to the station, the Dixie Truckers Home, established by J. P. Walters and John Geske in 1928, has survived. The station got its name because trucks stopping there often came from, or were headed to the South, to Dixie. Dixie Truckers has the best buffet on Route 66. McLean was originally the home of the Illinois Route 66 Club, and the club operated a Route 66

Hall of Fame at the Dixie Truckers Home. It was not a large museum featuring, only a couple of walls full of photographs. Since the Hall of Fame moved to a more spacious building in Pontiac, the rather spacious mall of the service station holds little paraphernalia or trinkets related to the Old Highway.

Atlanta, Illinois, is a town on the Historic Road whose name is older than that of its Georgia namesake. Nobody knows anything about the town, even though it boasts an octagonal library building with a clock tower and a wooden grain elevator. Now there is a little Atlanta Route 66 park right across the street from the library.

Traveling southwest from Atlanta, we reach small Lawndale and then the bigger Lincoln, obviously named for the great Illinois president of the Civil War period. Unfortunately, we find nothing special in either town. Maybe a couple of decent eateries and the old Postville Courthouse in Lincoln are worth a brief stop.

Approaching Broadwell, the Old Road runs side-by-side with the newer and broader Interstate 55, which seduces the driver to take the bigger highway. This detour has to be done for some distance, as 66 is in no shape to be driven. Glaida Funk had warned us not to miss Ernie Edwards's Pig-Hip Restaurant, but we almost did, looking at the grain silos, cement factory production lines, or whatever it was, on the left side of the road. We had to turn the car around and drive down into the yard of the dilapidating restaurant in the fork between the two roads.

We had hardly gotten out of the car to take photographs when Ernie himself came almost at a half-trot to greet us. My brother became the first Finn ever to sign the Edwards's visitors' book. Many Germans had visited the place, and Ernie presented several German and American newspaper clippings where he was mentioned as part of the Route 66 revival. One of the clippings was written in Japanese. By now he should also have a copy of my Route 66 book in Finnish, and I know some Finns have visited him since 1996, as my wife and I did in 2002. This happened to be on Mother's Day, and families had gathered to celebrate. Nevertheless, everyone welcomed us with open hearts, and we had more than our share of a good tasting cake. Ernie looked at his files and easily found the photo of my brother and me from 1996. We updated our photos, and I took one of the Edwardses by the wall with the old bluish wallpaper adorned with ships. I wonder whether this was what was left of the original wallpaper so relevant to the Pig-Hip story.

Founding the restaurant in 1937, Edwards got cheap wallpaper with pictures of ships and named the restaurant Harbor Inn, although there are no harbors, sea, or ships anywhere near Broadwell. Sometime later, a local farmer came in to buy a sandwich. Ernie was roasting a ham, and the farmer pointed at it and said he wanted a slice of that pig hip. Ernie believes that he never met the farmer again, but the restaurant took its new name from him. In the best of times, Ernie Edwards had a couple of other restaurants nearby, a gas station next to the Pig-Hip, and a tiny motel. It was all in the family. Ernie ran the restaurant, his brother the gas station, and his sister the motel. "It did not make you rich, but most of the time it was fun," said Ernie.

After closing the business in 1991, Ernie spent his retirement days with his wife in a house behind his restaurant, mainly gardening. And of course telling stories to bypassers if they bothered to stop here, be they Americans, Germans, or Finns traveling in the area. The sign "tourists welcome" showed you the way. In 2007 the original Pig-Hip building caught fire and was destroyed. A stone marker now stands on its place.

After my first visit, I urged everybody to visit Ernie as soon as possible as he was approaching eighty at the time, and the Mrs. was only five years his junior. No reason to haste anymore; Ernie Edwards died in April of 2012 at the age of ninety-four.

Car Tops and Cozy Dogs

The grave and museum home of President Abraham Lincoln lie in Springfield, the capital of Illinois, where tourism centers on the Civil War president. At the cemetery north of downtown, the Lincoln family burial chamber's obelisk towers high above the other tombstones. The chamber itself holds not only graves but also statues portraying Lincoln and a number of quotes from his speeches or writings. According to a legend, touching the nose of Lincoln's statue that stands in front of the burial chamber brings good luck.

Lincoln moved to Springfield in 1837, and the only house he ever owned has been turned into a museum in a residential area close to the city center. The law firm of Lincoln and his associate also remains. Not all tourist attractions in Springfield relate to Lincoln, however. There are no less than two capitol buildings, the old one and the new one, only a third of a mile apart. A magnificent example of Frank Lloyd Wright's Prairie School architectural creations is the Dana-Thomas House, built in 1902.

The Highway's route through northern Springfield varied over the years. Before we have to make up our minds about which route to take, we find Shea Tops. There Bill Shea sells tops for small trucks, pickups and platforms that help people, if not to travel on the back of the lorry, at least to sleep there or protect the goods they carry. Shea is as small, merry, and energetic as Glaida Funk and Ernie Edwards had told us he would be. Shea has been a part of Springfield business life for almost seventy years. Most of this time he ran a service station on Highway 66. After his return from World War II in 1947, he managed a Texaco service station by the roadside. His rapid and friendly service once earned him the "Texaco service man of the month" title. Later he bought his own Marathon station, also on Route 66. When the 66 was dead and gone, Shea took up selling "tops."

His store displays a versatile collection of things related to the Old Road and old service stations: all kinds and sizes of road signs and gas pumps, an ancient jukebox, a Coca-Cola machine from the 1950s . . . Bill Shea is exhilarated when he turns on the miniature model of the gasoline pump for my video camera. Shea's Tops is a living museum and a still functioning car repair shop. Bill no longer sells gas, but all kinds of apparatuses and especially old cars are being repaired and painted in his shop. In spite of many visitors, Bill Shea states that we were the first Finns ever to stop at his place.

In his *Route 66 Remembered*, Michael Karl Witzel writes that "Sometimes, along the forgotten miles of old road—where weeds have grown high and the memories of yesteryear move along the whispering wind—one can almost hear the sounds of old attendants gassing cars. Unfortunately, the recollections grow quieter with every passing year." With Bill Shea you can still see the real thing, but if you want to meet him, you might want to hurry, as Bill is already over ninety.

We leave Springfield by way of the Cozy Dog Drive-In. Nearly everybody has tasted hot dogs; some have even tried corn dogs. The hot dog was introduced to the world at the St. Louis World's Fair in 1904. The corn dog was introduced at Springfield, Illinois, or maybe Muskogee, Oklahoma. Around the end of World War II, Edwin Sutton Waldmire, Jr., took a fancy to hot dogs sold inside waffles in Muskogee. Preparation of that treat took twelve to fifteen minutes. Waldmire figured that he could do it more quickly. He put the sausages on sticks, rolled them in corn-flour dough, and fried them in hot oil. The technique has since been improved to make several corn dogs at a time. He called the corn battered sausages "Cozy Dogs." After establishing Cozy Dog Houses in two spots in Springfield, in 1950 Waldmire finally opened his own café on the south side of town in the same house as a Dairy Queen ice-cream parlor on Highway 66. A new legend of the Road had been born.

Ed Waldmire's Cozy Dog Drive-In did not segregate customers according to color. A long time before the 1960s Civil Rights acts, white and black people could sit where they wanted at the Waldmire Drive Inn, as long as they sat on chairs. When the Dairy Queen put a sign on its door stating that it reserved the right to place their customers at whatever table they wished, Ed Waldmire tore up the sign. Several times. Finally, the company learned and removed the sign. Later Ed became Springfield's first Commissioner of Civil Rights.

Ed openly opposed the Vietnam War. He even closed his restaurant for a couple of days and served free coffee to everybody who promised to write to their congressmen to put an end to the war. In 1971 Ed and his wife Mary sold the company to their son Buz, who managed it with his wife Sue for over twenty years. In 1995 the Dairy Queen sold its share, and Buz Waldmire was also forced to sell his share to the Walgreens chain. Writer Tom Teague predicted that by the summer of 1996 the place would have a shopping mall, and the Cozy Dog would be gone. It stood stubbornly there in May, however, and Buz Waldmire promised to build a new café by Highway 66 as close to the old site as possible if he had to.

And indeed he did. The new place stands only some three hundred feet north of the old place, which is now occupied by a Walgreens drug store. The new Cozy Dog has no drive-in window, but the restaurant is there, and the Edwin Waldmire Memorial Library has been moved there from Arizona together with Bob Waldmire, another of Edwin's sons. The place is now run by Sue Waldmire and Ed Waldmire IV.

Corn dogs are cheap at the Cozy Dog. On a May day in 1996, two tasty Cozy Dogs encrusted with corn dough, together with a huge portion of French fries with the skin on cost only one dollar five cents, tax and all. Six years later the price had gone up a few cents, but the taste was the same and the portion as generous.

At the Cozy Dog Inn, each visitor receives a small notebook. Bob

Waldmire has decorated each notebook's back cover with a map of the Old Road, and the front has a picture of the old Cozy Dog building and Bob's old place in Hackberry, Arizona. Nowadays, the drawings may have changed.

The philosophy of the place may have changed also since Ed Waldmire's death in 1993. A newspaper clipping pinned to the wall argues against restrictions on weapons.

Written by Walter Williams and published in Springfield's *State Journal Register* on July 6, 1995, the article argues that the number of weapons diminishes crime. One wonders. This type of logic does not always open to a European. The waitress sighed, singing about how many guns a man must shoot before people believe that it hurts. In the words of songwriter Bob Dylan, she also believed that the answer was "Blowin' in the Wind."

In Springfield, Route 66 in its Golden Age was mainly the road to St. Louis, not farther. It ran a part of the way across downtown as St. Louis Street, in fact. Originally, that section of road was built from planks covered with a coat of asphalt. On a hot day the street would swing. Literally.

From 1926 to 1931, Federal Highway 66 faithfully followed Illinois State Highway 4 from Springfield to Staunton. In 1931 the Road was changed to run through Litchfield and Mount Olive and west of Livingston. During the next couple of decades, the trail varied and ran through different small towns or past them. In one version, Livingston was on the northern side and Staunton on the western side of the Road.

Floods and Mounds

Weather in North America can be as strange as anywhere. Droughts in some parts of the United States are balanced with floods somewhere else. In my travels, I have often found both these extremes on and around Route 66. The year 2002 was no exception. While most of the Southwest was suffering from drought for want of snow the previous winter, the Midwest saw much of May from a watery perspective. We had just arrived at Divernon, a small town south of Springfield. Even the interstate was closed because of flooding.

Route 66 passes Divernon on the east side, as does I-55. Because of the flood we found ourselves exploring the little town and found it quite similar to many others along the Old Road. The tiny railroad station has some historical value. A relatively large park marks the town square with the bandstand and all, and a few shops and bars and a family restaurant surround the square.

If you wanted to avoid Divernon, you could take the western branch of Route 66 from Springfield through Chatham, Auburn, Thayer, Virden, Girard, Carlinville, Gillespie, and Benid to Staunton. There is no guarantee, however, that you could avoid the flooding. If you chose to try via Divernon, you would continue south via Waggoner and Litchfield.

Ariston Café in Litchfield is still in business. Pete Adam opened the first café as early as 1924 on SBI4. A new diner was built in 1931, and a third one was opened on the 66 in 1935 between the first and second cafes. This café—where celebrities like the governor of Minnesota, the 1968 Democrat presidential candidate Hubert Humphrey, and musician Jimmy Dorsey have dined—continues to serve good food to passers-by. Particularly their dessert tray is worth a look if not a taste for those who are afraid of becoming fat.

Only a block from Ariston's "aristocratic café" is a 66 inn and motel. Probably, anyway. Different traveler's guides recommend different routes through Litchfield. It is also confusing that two roads running close to each other are called "Road 66" and "Old Road 66," and the "Historic 66" signs point in a completely different direction.

Worker unrest is part of Litchfield area history. Mining has gone on here for way over a hundred years. There have been disputes between employers and workers for almost as long. In 1898 these disputes led to the so-called Virden riot. In 1936 the United States Union of Progressive Miners erected a large monument at a cemetery south of Litchfield to commemorate the victims of the riot and their "hero," Mary "Mother" Jones, who allegedly asked her followers to "pray for the dead" and "fight like hell for the living."

Past the cemetery, the Road soon veers left and after a while passes another of its old landmarks, another service station on the right side of the road. The village is Mt. Olive, "mountain of the olive tree," a name that describes the Biblical hopes of its founders more than the reality of the landscape. The service station is a tiny Shell station that Russell Soulsby and his father opened in July 1926, only four months before 66 was opened to travelers. The story is familiar: the Highway and Soulsby's station succeeded and perished together. When there was plenty of traffic on the Road, the Soulsbys sold milk, ice cream, and other merchandise in addition to gasoline. In 1991 the station was closed because it no longer met new environmental standards.

From Mt. Olive, the Old Highway crosses the new highway on a new bridge. The old Mobil station in Staunton opened and saw its best days during the golden era of the Old Road. After Hamel, population 550, there is Edwardsville, population 21,550. Two options of Route 66 connect these two places. The 1940 to 1977 alternative runs right by Interstate 55.

Edwardsville's sole claim to fame is that it has given Illinois no less than eight of the state's governors. Some of their homes are now museums. In Edwardsville, Route 66 ran quite a distance west of the present I-55 before turning directly westward toward Pontoon Beach and Mitchell. The Hen House at the corner of Illinois 111 and Route 66, and most importantly for business, right on I-270, provides standard food, which is always better than the standardized food of chain restaurants. The nearby Bel Air Drive-In still seems to be in good shape.

Visible giant mounds of Cahokia, an Indian city once inhabited by more than thirty thousand people, remain far southeast of the Road. The new 55 passes close to the mounds. Cahokia was perhaps the most important center of the Mississippian culture that flourished widely in the southeastern parts of present-day United States from roughly AD 900 to 1500. Largest of the mounds in Cahokia is about one hundred feet high, seven hundred feet wide, and one thousand feet long. It is the largest manmade earthen structure in the Western Hemisphere. A two-mile long palisade with watchtowers surrounded that and sixteen other mounds. Outside the palisade were perhaps an additional hundred mounds.

By around AD 1200 Cahokia began to decline and was totally abandoned some two hundred years later. Nobody really knows why. Perhaps it faced hostilities from surrounding Indian groups that eventually made it impossible to live in Cahokia. Perhaps the fields became overused and barren, or perhaps the climate became colder. Perhaps the deterioration of public health brought down the city. Little pebbles in the corn flour destroyed the teeth of Cahokians. Smoke from firewood and garbage contaminated the center of the city. Malnutrition was common, as people ate too many carbohydrates and too little protein. Many diseases followed, tuberculosis being the worst. Who knows? When the Spanish conquistador Hernando de Soto traveled through the area in 1539-1543, Cahokia was gone, but he met some Indians who still followed the customs of the Cahokians. In 1989 the United Nations Educational, Social, and Cultural Organization (UNESCO) made Cahokia a World Heritage Site.

In Mitchell, the Historic Route still runs through the shade of trees, far from the world of haste speeding a few miles south of the town along the new highway I-270. Finally, the 66 joins it, crosses it, and begins to search for a bridge over the Mississippi River from Illinois to Missouri.

There were, and are, many bridge alternatives to cross the "Old Man River." The most famous of them is the Chain of Rocks Bridge. It crosses the river over rapids full of stones, making a bend in the middle. Nowadays, however, it is forbidden to drive across the bridge. It has been turned into a state park and is open to hikers and bikers. Good signs guide the way to a lookout where you can marvel at the bridge. There are always large birds to be seen on the swampy terrain.

Crossing the river over the same bridge as the 66 is probably easiest south of the Chain of Rocks. The road follows the Chain of Rocks Canal to Venice. There are no gondolas here, but there is plenty of marshy terrain. At the edge of town, the road running by the river suddenly turns to a bridge and crosses it. Those who wish to avoid bridge tolls should cross the Mississippi still further south and come to downtown St. Louis on the new I-55/I-64. After the side trip to Cahokia, of course.

3

Land of the Muddy River

Gateway to the West

Michael Wallis, the writer that really began the new boom of Route 66 books wrote of St. Louis that "after the Louisiana Purchase extended the boundary of the nation to the Rocky Mountains in 1803, all travel to new frontiers began in the city. It was considered a major destination. St. Louis was an open door to the virgin West."

Many things can be linked to St. Louis, and it has made many things famous. But as *The Rough Guide to the USA* says: "Any city capable of producing two of the twentieth century's greatest poets—T.S. Eliot and Chuck Berry—must have a lot going for it."

At the St. Louis World's Fair in 1904, the audience was introduced to ice cream cones, iced tea, and hot dogs. In 1944 Vincent Minelli set his film *Meet Me in St. Louis* at the fair. It starred the director's wife, Judy Garland. Margaret O'Brien received a special Oscar for her charming interpretation of the little sister. I can still hear the title song in my mind every time I am even close to Missouri's largest city. "Meet me in St. Louis, Louis, meet me at the fair . . ."

At the St. Louis World's Fair, an ice cream stand stood right next to Ernest A. Hamwi's place of Persian waffles. One day the ice cream man ran out of dishes, so Hamwi rolled one of his waffles into a cone and offered it to his neighbor as a substitute dish. Soon everybody wanted ice cream from a waffle cone, or cornucopia, as it was originally called. The term "ice cream cone" does not seem to have entered the language until 1909.

A nice place to have ice cream in St. Louis is Ted Drewes's ice cream parlor on Chippewa Street. The parlor is a white house whose outer walls are decorated with wooden icicles. The employees wear daisy-yellow shirts and caps, with small 66 signs at the end of their sleeves. Especially in the summer, there may be long lines of people outside the parlor. Ted Drewes's father, whose name was also Ted Drewes, opened an ice cream parlor in St. Louis in 1927. The younger Ted Drewes grew up surrounded by ice cream and inherited the company from his father. Travis Dillon, one of Ted's sons-in-law, took the company over after Ted. Chris Beckemeier is the company's present manager.

Despite many temptations to sell out, Ted Drewes has kept his frozen custard a family business. The business has also outrun its competitors. In 1996 a Baskin Robbins chain kiosk sold thirty-nine flavors of ice cream practically next door. In 2002 it was gone, but Ted Drewes was still there with lines outside its windows—and still is. This is custard worth waiting for. Even my wife, who is not that keen on sweets, always has two portions of Drewes's ice cream: one of cherry and one of pistachio. The Chippewa Street business has been expanded a number of times; Drewes has tried to keep the original style. He says that both the house and his company are a part of history—an institution of Highway 66. And you cannot argue with that.

St. Louis, located on the western side of the Mississippi River a short distance south of its confluence with the Missouri, is the third largest city on Route 66, after Los Angeles and Chicago. With the present population of some 2.3 million people, it is about the twelfth largest metropolitan area in the United States. In 1850 it had 50,000 inhabitants. At that time, the city was the eighth largest in the United States, bigger than Chicago and Los Angeles combined. In 1900 St. Louis boasted some 612,000 inhabitants. Chicago was already larger, but St. Louis was still five times as large as LA.

St. Louis is a very central city in American history and culture. It is located practically in the middle of the United States and halfway down the Mississippi River from north to south. It has always been on thoroughfares from all directions and continues to be even in the age of overland roads. I-55 runs north from there towards Chicago, roughly following the Old Route 66, and south to Memphis and New Orleans almost on the Gulf of Mexico. I-70 runs northeast to Indianapolis, Pittsburgh, and New York. Interstate 64 runs east to Louisville,

Kentucky, and Richmond, Virginia, and finally to Norfolk on Virginia's Atlantic coast. Interstate 70 goes straight west from St. Louis across Missouri to Kansas City, Denver, and the mountains in Utah. And I-44 follows the traditional 66 southwest to Oklahoma City.

St. Louis was founded as a town by the Frenchman Pierre Laclède in 1763, when the territories east of the Mississippi were lost by the French to the English in the Seven Years War. Soon it was a new center of the fur trade, whether upstream or westward to Santa Fe. In European maps, St. Louis was in Louisiana, a territory belonging to Spain. The Native American peoples inhabiting the area hardly recognized either Spain or France as the owner of their lands.

When Napoleon conquered Spain, ownership of the wide Louisiana territory passed from Spain to France. Napoleon was short on money in 1803; he offered the entire area to the United States for some three cents per acre, and President Thomas Jefferson was willing to buy. St. Louis quickly became the gate through which the Americans traveled west. The expedition led by William Clark and Meriwether Lewis left from St. Louis and charted a trail across the Great Plains and the Rockies all the way to the Pacific Ocean from 1804 to 1806.

St. Louis became the center of the American fur trade. Manuel Lisa, William Ashley, and John Jacob Astor all operated out of St. Louis. During the latter half of the nineteenth century, there were claims that the whole world passes through St. Louis, when huge caravans of settlers started from there on their journeys to Oregon and California each spring.

A big museum and research center in St. Louis is dedicated to the name of Thomas Jefferson to commemorate the westward expansion. The most visible part of it is the Gateway Arch, designed by the Finnish architect Eero Saarinen and built in the mid-1960s. It is the largest arch of steel in the world, rising on the bank of the Mississippi River to an amazing height of 630 feet. It is the tallest national monument built since Robert Mill's Washington Monument in 1884. A special elevator with small cabins inside takes tourists to the top, bending with the arch at times and finally righting itself back to horizontal again.

When I first visited the Gateway Arch in the spring of 1975 during my first trip to America, I asked the lady at the ticket counter, the poor student that I was, whether Finns would get a discount. Unfortunately, no such thing, and indeed, it took me a long time to explain why being Finnish should have entitled me to anything. Eero Saarinen (1910-1961), however, is one of the most famous Finnish architects in America. In addition to the arch, he has designed several other great works, including General Motors Technical Center in Warren, Michigan; Columbia Broadcasting Company Headquarters, the 38-story tower in New York; and the Trans-World Airlines terminal at John F. Kennedy Airport symbolizing the spirit of flight.

In Finland, however, Eero is perhaps not quite as famous as his father Eliel Saarinen (1873-1950), the designer of the Helsinki railway station, dormitories at Yale University, and many other buildings around the world. He moved to America in 1923 and taught for several years at Cranbrook Academy in Michigan.

The views through the small windows of the Gateway Arch are breathtaking, both over the Mississippi to Illinois and from the other side to downtown St. Louis and beyond to Missouri. Most of the old Highway 66 bridges can be seen from the arch. Only the Chain of Rocks is not visible from here.

In the Shadow of the Gate

St. Louis Union Station was opened in 1894, and it is still an important tourist attraction, although railroad traffic has grown quiet since those days. Once the busiest passenger-rail terminal in the whole United States, the restored station today is a big mall with a hotel, a ten-screen movie theater, shops, and restaurants. Before the bridges were built across the Mississippi, five ferryboats carried whole trains across.

Another mode of traffic today even more quiet than railroads, passenger traffic on the Mississippi River is clearly recovering. In cargo traffic, the river never stopped being an important route. Now tourism and gambling are bringing the old riverboats back.

Gambling is an old specialty of the Mississippi and Missouri riverboats. During the past few years, there have been attempts to revitalize this tradition, especially after certain states and local businessmen had had enough of Nevada's exclusive right, as well as the "money plundering" of Indian casinos founded all around the country. Regardless of state laws, American Indians have been able to open casinos inside the reservations in whatever state their reservation happens to be in. Indian casinos, however, take less than 10 percent of the total business.

In addition to riverboats, the heart of St. Louis belongs to the fur trade, Western expansion, and jazz music. Brass horns and ragtime have been St. Louis's special trademarks since the beginning of the twentieth century, when riverboats carried Dixieland music between New Orleans and Chicago and always stopped at St. Louis. St. Louis hosts the national ragtime festival every year around midsummer. Many famous jazz musicians have considered the city their home; they include Lester Bowie and Miles Davis. Bowie was also a member of the Art Ensemble of Chicago, an avant-garde ensemble and for decades the "flagship" of the "great Black music." Although founded in the late 1960s in Paris, France, it nevertheless took its name after the end—or beginning-city of our Route.

The most famous of the Route 66 town songs is also dedicated to St. Louis: the "St. Louis Blues." Black cornet player William Christopher Handy composed it in 1914, adding the "tangana" (the habanera rhythm) to more traditional black music. Handy had already composed and played the blues for a long time and contributed greatly to its popularity. According to his autobiography, he was the "Father of the Blues." Handy played in different orchestras mainly in Memphis, Tennessee, St. Louis, and later New York; he even played for some time in Chicago as a stand-in for Louis Armstrong.

If there are many different versions of Bobby Troup's "Route 66," the same is true of "St. Louis Blues." One of the most famous early blues singers was Bessie Smith, whose version of the St. Louis song is sometimes seen as the best single example of blues in its sophisticated but still relatively pure stage of development. No one, especially no white person, could possibly imitate Bessie Smith. But popular songs have a life of their own, and so does "St. Louis Blues."

The trumpet of Louis Armstrong blows it with a rhythmic bubbling, and halfway through the song a hoarse voice comes in searching for a lady. Benny Goodman's horns play equally fast, but the sound is different, backed by a deep groove by the bass and drums. Bing Crosby's slow and swaying singing tells another story altogether. If Armstrong's version was created on the boardwalks of the Mississippi and Goodman's almost under them, Crosby takes his interpretation from the classiest nightclubs of the city's wide Park Avenue. Not everybody, however, likes St. Louis. Julie Christie sings to a Missouri resident who got out of town in "You've Come a Long Way from St. Louis."

The St. Louis music tradition has fared almost as badly as riverboat gambling. In this cradle of blues, jazz has been stuffed into small and remote suburban clubs that few know about, or it has been tamed and turned into family entertainment performed at big festivals and concerts, the way everything exciting can, with the power of money, be flattened to triviality and digestible by everybody, a process quite common in the United States. Michael Saffle, professor of music at Virginia Polytechnic Institute and State University, thinks that this is mostly what has happened to jazz everywhere in America.

St. Louis has other musical offerings besides jazz. The city has its own symphony orchestra and opera. But one should not forget Scott Joplin and his tradition. Joplin and his bride Belle Haden lived at the beginning of the twentieth century in St. Louis in a house that has now become a state historic site. The master of ragtime composed perhaps his most famous piece, "The Entertainer," here. The piece was used as the tune for the 1973 film *The Sting*.

Reverend William Eliot, the grandfather of T.S. Eliot, co-founded a college that became Washington University, which is among the best in America. The poet Thomas Stearns Eliot, who moved to England as an adult, was born in St. Louis on September 26, 1888. He took his elementary schooling in the city and lived there for his first seventeen years. Eliot won the Nobel Prize as an English citizen in 1948. One of his most famous poems is "The Love Song of J. Alfred Prufrock." Prufrock was the name of a St. Louis furniture merchant.

Blues and rock singer Chuck Berry also saw the light of day for the first time in St. Louis. He was born on October 18, 1926, on Goode Avenue; no wonder one of his most famous songs tells the story of a boy named "Johnny B. Goode." Berry began his artistic career on the Illinois side of the river at the East St. Louis's Cosmopolitan Club and went on to contribute many songs to the American canon of cars and mobility.

St. Louis has a place in comic strip history as well, since Geo Mc-Manus was born in the city around 1883—the artist was unsure about the year: he was too young then to remember. His *Bringing up Father* introduced Maggie and Jiggs in 1913 and brought the rags to riches dream onto newspaper pages. By then, Maggie and Jiggs and McManus had moved to New York.

St. Louis people have attempted to cheer up the riverbank milieu of the Mississippi in downtown St. Louis, next to the Gateway Arch and the riverboats, with an area called Laclède's Landing. Old customs warehouses have been turned into beer halls, microbrewers, restaurants, and jazz clubs. Most evenings the place is quiet, though. Live music is rare there except on weekends. The locals have gone home to the suburbs and the tourists have gone to bed, having spent the day taking in the city sights. Restaurants start to empty soon after 7:00 p.m. The riverbank is not the only place to find good restaurants. Pleasant experiences are in store for people who like Italian food at Charlie Gitto's place just a couple of blocks away from the Old 66, right in the center of the city. No wonder athletes, actors, politicians, and other celebrities of Italian descent have dined there and left a wall papered with their photos to prove it.

The Anheuser-Busch brewery lies south of the city center, in an area that once was home to German and East European immigrants. Many of them worked at the brewery. For those accustomed to British ales, Czech pilsners, and German or Finnish lagers, the product of major US breweries falls short. For a good beer, try the microbreweries at Laclède's Landing.

Athletics is an essential to a community's culture, and St. Louis is no exception. The city hosted the Olympics in 1904. The National Bowling Hall of Fame is here. The hockey team is called the St. Louis Blues. The baseball team is the St. Louis Cardinals, a name referring to birds not to the Catholic Church hierarchy. And why not birds? Aviation has long been part of the town's experience. In 1927, early in aviation's history, Charles Lindbergh made the first solo flight across the Atlantic in the "Spirit of St. Louis." For years the city has been home to the Mc-Donnell Douglas Aerospace Corporation; and since its sale to Boeing in 1997, the latter aviation giant keeps offices and factory here. More planes have been built in St. Louis than in any other city of the world.

St. Louis is an excellent place to disprove the idea of a "one and only genuine 66." Old Route 66 alignments through the city are, as Tom Snyder says, plentiful but serpentine. In different years, Route 66 took several different routes through St. Louis, and at any given time several simultaneous alternatives existed. This is also the case with the present interstate highways. The normal interstate highways at places are joined by business roads or other alternative routes marked by the letters I, BR, BUS, ALT, or something similar.

Originally, Old 66 crossed the Mississippi north of St. Louis across a bridge named after President William McKinley. The route ran south of the present I-55 from Edwardsville, Illinois, to Venice, and then across the bridge to St. Louis on the Missouri side of the river. In Missouri the journey continued to Manchester along Manchester Road and from there to Gray Summit. The McKinley Bridge is the only one of the Route 66 bridges still in use, but nowadays there's a fee to cross it. Charging fees goes against the spirit of the old Federal Highway, however.

In 1933 or 1934 a Municipal Free Bridge, built in 1917, was chosen as the Route's path across the Mississippi. In Illinois, it took 66 from Edwardsville to East St. Louis and across the river to downtown St. Louis. Twelve blocks away from the river, 66 turned south along Twelfth Street, ran along it to Gravois Avenue and Chippewa Street, near Ted Drewes's ice-cream stall. Watson Road led the Route out of town to Crestwood on the south side of Manchester Road. The Municipal Free Bridge has been renamed after General Douglas MacArthur, the hero of World War II, and for some, perhaps, of the Korean War. No longer is the bridge free; it, too, is closed.

When the speed of the cars grew and the traffic increased, St. Louis might have formed a bottleneck on Highway 66. A detour was constructed, therefore, in the late 1930s so that travelers would not be forced to confront the downtown traffic jams among railroads and merchandise shipments. In this routing, 66 ran from Edwardsville only to Mitchell before crossing the Mississippi River to Glasgow Village north of St. Louis via the Chain of Rocks Bridge. It was also thought that the new, broader bridge would provide a better image for the city. This new Route 66 bypassed St. Louis completely from its northern and western side and joined the old route in Kirkwood between Manchester and Crestwood.

The changing of the traffic stream naturally guided the related business activities. Motels were born and died according to the location of Route 66. There are plenty of such memories of the Old Road's golden age in St. Louis: the Wayside Motel, La Casa Grande Motel, and so on. A theater was even named after highway 66. At its peak, the "66" Park Theatre included an indoor parking lot, a Ferris wheel, a carousel, and circus bears.

The Coral Court Motel in Marlborough, a southwest suburb of St. Louis, is almost as famous as Drewes's ice-cream parlor. It was a round-cornered, yellow-brick motel built in 1941. Each room had a garage of its own with an indoor entrance to the room, so passersby might not see who went to which room and with whom. In the late 1960s the traffic moved a few blocks north on Interstate 44, and it seemed that the Coral Court was doomed. A preservation society was founded to cherish the past of the motel, but despite the struggle, it was demolished in 1995. One wall was saved, however, and moved to the Museum of Transportation in Kirkwood. It stands in the corner of the museum's hall for automobiles dedicated to Route 66. The museum collection includes an airplane, but most of its vehicles are trains, their number illustrating the importance of this first really mass transportation device. One can easily spend a full day at the museum.

In Marlborough, earthmovers have shaped the neighborhood of the Old Road into something quite different from just a few years ago. By the roadside, only haphazardly erected signs marking the historic Road serve as reminders of the past. A few shops and cafés advertise themselves with the magic number. George's Bar and Grill serves drinks and snacks to travelers and locals.

Just west of St. Louis but still part of its city parks lies the newly established Route 66 State Park, a nice little park more for bikers and birdwatchers than for motorists. It has a short stretch of the Old Road left to see before the grass covers it all.

Little Towns beyond the Sunset Hills

Missouri is in the middle of the United States, and this, perhaps, has made the people to be cautious. Tom Snyder claims that "Missourians, hands thrust securely into their pockets, can stand for an hour while they wait for you to state your case, make your best offer, or ask directions. In the end, they'll know all they need about your business and you'll know nothing more than you did an hour ago. Some say that comes naturally to folks of solid mining-farming-mountain stock who had to contend with riverboat gamblers, Damn-Yankees, Kansas guerillas, and the weather hereabouts."

In Missouri Route 66 runs diagonally across the state from St. Louis to the uplands southwest of Springfield. According to Nick Feet's *Traveling Route 66*, running close to I-44, Route 66 "continues the journey away from St. Louis through the Sunset Hills District; it then crosses the Meramec River, heading towards the town of Eureka." The Road mainly follows old Indian paths known in the early nineteenth century as the Great Osage Trail, named after the Osage Indians. In 1857, after the federal government gave John Butterfield the license to carry mail from St. Louis to Los Angeles, the Indian trail in this area became a stagecoach road.

During the Civil War the Osage Trail became an important military route that both warring parties strove to use. The Union equipped the trail with a telegraph line, and the Confederate troops tried to cut the line. The road became known as the Great Wire Road. Major roadside telegraph offices were built in St. Louis, Rolla, Lebanon, and Springfield. After the Civil War, the telegraph line lost most of its importance, but the many towns along the road stayed alive.

Southwest of St. Louis, after Gray Summit, Route 66 followed the route that is now I-44 with relatively few deviations all the way to Springfield. I-44 has in essence replaced the 66 between St. Louis and Oklahoma City. For some thirty miles from St. Louis, the Henry Shaw Gardenway escorts I-44. The Gardenway was lined with various Missourian trees in honor of the founder of the Missouri Botanical Garden, which had been a major St. Louis tourist attraction since 1858.

The small town of Eureka was a trading post before the Civil

War. Eureka's most famous sight today is probably Six Flags over Mid-America, an amusement park on the west side of town. It has taken its name from the flags of the six nations in control of Mid-America at one time or another: Spain, France, England, Mexico, the Confederacy, and the United States. Here the Old Route 66 runs north of Interstate Highway 44 mainly as its frontage road with service stations, restaurants and stores. At Eureka, Route 66 crosses under the new highway to its southern side and finally separates from it so that it can't be seen from I-44, as there are high cliffs between the two roads.

The prison town of Pacific lies less than five miles from Eureka. Route 66 runs through it, but I-44 circles the town from the north. Just before downtown Pacific, a historic monument by the roadside commemorates a Confederate guerilla band's visit to the area. The monument marks the northernmost place the guerillas came to rest after having destroyed the town's railroad station, railroads, and bridges on October 2, 1864.

West of Pacific both I-44 and its frontage road, Route 66, climb out of the valley with Route 66 reaching all the way to the top of Gray Summit. After crossing the new Interstate, Route 66 curves by the nature reserve of the Missouri Botanical Gardens. The area was formed in the late 1920s from abandoned farmlands. It recently changed its name to Shaw Arboretum in honor of the botanist Henry Shaw. Just across Route 66 from the Arboretum is a modern Best Western Diamond Inn providing overnight sleep at reasonable prices.

Gardenway Restaurant, also on the Road at Gray Summit, used to be one of the original Route 66 restaurants. Unfortunately, it has been closed for years. The sign is still there, but even most of the ruins have gone. The motel of the same name, however, operates right on 66. On the other side of I-55 you can still eat at Road House 100, as road 100 here is the Old 66. The roadhouse is a local honky-tonk, but the food is reasonably good.

St. Louis is not yet far away, but maybe the inns of the area are still in business precisely because of it. They are probably cheaper than those in the big city, after all. Many travelers on Route 66 know Pacific's Red Cedar Inn and Gray Summit's Garden Way Motel. West of I-44, a short distance before Stanton, the Arch Motel has erected a small arch reminiscent of the St. Louis Gateway Arch to tempt tourists.

The Caveman's Family

After Pacific, signs advertising the Meramec Caverns begin to appear. After Villa Ridge the roadsides of Interstate 44 are full of them, as well as ads for a couple of motels, the Jesse James trading post, and a toy museum. The caverns and hollows near Meramec River south of Stanton are among the most famous sights along Old Route 66. Lester B. Dill developed them into a commercial tourist attraction in the 1930s. He bragged about not only having taken more people underground than anybody else, but also having brought them back alive.

The Meramec State Park was founded in 1928, and Thomas Benton Dill, Lester's father, became its first director. Lester signed an agreement with the state and started his cave guide business, which soon included selling homemade food and souvenirs. A couple of years later the agreement expired, and when the Great Depression began, the agreement lapsed. Dill decided to open a cave of his own and rented the Salt Peter Cave a few miles downstream from the State Park. The cave had received its name in the nineteenth century when saltpeter miners used it for storage and shelter. The Salt Peter Cave was indeed a good choice for the tourists. Legend has it that Hernando de Soto visited this large cave in 1542. Jacques Renault, a French miner, was reputed to have visited the cave some two hundred years later. Further, local tradition claimed that runaway slaves had used the cave as their hideout on the run north via the Underground Railroad. No doubt many outlaws had also sought shelter in the cave, among them perhaps even Jesse James himself. Some people still believe that James hid a part of his loot in the cave.

The stories and legends were important to the cave's success, but Route 66 was more important still. Dill realized that the tourists could be tempted to the cave from the Route, renamed his cave the Meramec Caverns, and launched a massive advertising campaign by the roadside. During the Depression, the traffic was not always reliable, and for three years the Dill family lived in a tent near the caverns and worked hard to keep the road to the caverns open in the winter and the floods out of the caverns in the spring. Dill also arranged dances in the cave to get additional income. During World War II he tempted the Army to conduct training exercises in the caverns and gave GIs discounts to the evening dances. One of the soldiers married Dill's daughter. After the war, the son-in-law, Rudy Turilli, became the managing director of the cavern company.

Almost from the start, little signs or plates advertising the caverns were attached to the fenders of visitors' cars. This custom became easier in the 1950's, of course, when bumper stickers appeared. The stickers also announced that highway patrols didn't harass cars bearing a cavern sticker, because patrolmen could see the drivers were tourists bringing money to the region.

In 1940 Dill found in a previously unexplored nook of the cavern some rusty guns and a small casket that he claimed had belonged to Jesse James. Ads immediately referred to the caverns as Jesse James's hideaway. Nine years later in Oklahoma, Rudy Turilli met a hundred-year-old J. Frank Dalton, who claimed that he was the real Jesse James, and the man shot in 1882 as Jesse was in reality a fellow named Charlie Bigelow. Turilli at once hired Frank Dalton, or Jesse James, as the drawing card of the Meramec Caverns. Dalton died in 1951 while traveling in Texas, just three days before his 104th birthday.

Dill's right-hand-man and Route 66 activist Lyman Riley traveled along the Road. All the businesses along Highway 66, from Chicago to California, knew him because he was putting out cave folders in the motels. In an interview with Michael Wallis, Riley was very frank: "Make no bones about it, our main purpose was to get more business on the highway." Riley retired in 1967, Dill himself died in 1980, and his grandson Lester Turilli took over the cavern. Recently, it has become big-time business. Connected to it are a restaurant, a souvenir shop, a motel, and a camping site. Visitors may fish or go canoeing on the river. A small paddleboat helps tourists admire the Missouri landscape from the Meramec River.

Young members of the family and relatives are still mostly guiding the cavern tours. A tour lasts an hour and a half with enough time to visit many corners of the caverns. The figures of Frank and Jesse James pursued by a sheriff had been placed in the river streaming out of the cave to feed the imaginations of the tourists.

Today dances and festivals are still being arranged in the big cave. Deeper inside the cave visitors can see all the typical features of a limestone cavern: stalagmites and stalactites, underground ponds, and crystal stones. The tour ends by praising the United States with colored lights reflected on the cave wall and a recording of "The Star-Spangled Banner." Kate Smith's performance of "God Bless the America" reverberates off the cave walls while the guide presses light switches to create a show of colors, still using the technology of 1946.

The Meramec Caverns have brought other entrepreneurs to the location. A very nice toy museum stands on 66 just before the turn-off to the caverns. A Jesse James museum is right next to it. One of the worst tourist traps on the entire Route 66 is located between the cave and the Road itself. Jesse James Trading Post and the Riverside Reptile Farm stand there, side by side. The trading post sells all kinds of "Indian jewelry," mostly manufactured in Asia, and other trinkets. The reptiles have been stuffed into small glass cabinets where they can barely move, and the tourists get to see them for a few bucks. The alligators, acquired in the spring of 1996, have been named Frank and Jesse after the James brothers, although one of them is female.

Battle Road

Southwest of Meramec Caverns, both Route 66 and Interstate 44 approach the northern projections of the Ozark Mountains, skirting the northern edge of a forest area dedicated to Mark Twain, the Missouri writer who used to live in Lebanon. In Stanton, we are already on the section of road between the small towns of St. Clair and St. James, known before World War II as the "red light zone" of Route 66. During Prohibition, "girl places" sold spirits in this section. Townspeople with sacks of money came from Chicago, Detroit, and St. Louis. Usually, they headed back home with empty pockets, as well as "all their sacks."

The tradition of distilling alcohol is not forgotten in Missouri. Vineyards can be seen on both the old and the new highway. The name of the small town Bourbon doesn't necessarily refer to the corn whisky of the same name. It is true, though, that corn is grown nearby. The Old 66 is the town's Main Street.

Cuba is another town the 66 splits right in the middle. Cuba is a daughter of the Old Road. In summer, the lampposts of Main Street are decorated with canvas flags to show where the historic road runs. For a person willing to take a break here, I can recommend the Chandler Café in the heart of Cuba. It is on the Road and serves delicious old-time homemade food in huge portions, cheap and fast. For free, you can also hear local stories and meet other travelers of the Road. This is something different from the ubiquitous hamburger, Chinese, Indian, Mexican, and other eateries littered along the roadsides.

With its population of some three thousand, Cuba may not be an important tourist town with plenty of sights to see, but there are a few interesting little things right on Route 66. At Macinnis Wood Products at the eastern end of town you can view enormous timber. Big wood has also been used to build the Naygree Whale Motel and the Hick-Ory Bar-b-q next to it, both on the north side of the Road—if they still exist. And don't miss the beautiful mural of the apple pickers on a wall near Chandler Café on the other side of the highway. The townspeople are believers, as a shield-shaped sign will tell you, that Jesus is the King of the Road.

After Cuba comes Fanning and an old car museum. The Old 66 has received new numbers, or more accurately letters in the form of county roads like KK or ZZ. There are also disputes about the location of the true 66. Signs pointing to the historic Road lead the driver almost by force to the southern frontage road of I-44, although the traveler's guides claim the Old Road runs north of I-44. In this confusion, one is likely to miss both the 66 Motors on Kings Avenue and the Rolla campus of the University of Missouri, if not the whole of Rolla.

One of the darkest moments in the history of the United States was the Japanese surprise attack on Pearl Harbor in December 1941. It brought the United States into World War II, but at the same time dealt a severe blow to American morale. The following spring, morale was boosted when the aircraft carrier *Hornet* and her sixteen planes bombed Tokyo, led by Jimmy Doolittle. The raid restored American faith in their chances and eventual victory, although the Allies were by no means winning the war in the Pacific. The town of Doolittle, by the Old Road, is named for the ace pilot.

Travelers must use the new highway between Doolittle and Arlington, as the Old 66 is no longer passable there. In Jerome, however, you can get back to the feeling of the Old Road for a moment, if you get off the interstate and drive through the town. Here we are at the northern edge of another section of Mark Twain National Forest. Beautiful forested hills reach out in practically all directions.

In this area lies that section of Route 66 known as Devil's Elbow. To find it, choose the roads marked J and Z, turn left by a white and yellow building to the first two-lane road going left, and cross the Big Piney Creek on a rusty steel bridge built in 1923. Hardly any traffic follows this section, so you can enjoy the singing of the birds in peace. From the top of a hill, you can see Missouri countryside for miles around and some of the distant Ozarks. Some well-kept houses sit near the hilltop. No fields are in sight and industrial plants are far away. How on earth do people live here? Why does the place have such a horrible name? Originally, because of its location by a particularly bad place in the river known as a "devil of an elbow."

The place is so beautiful I find it hard to believe it has anything to do with the devil. Properly, the next town is called St. Robert after the saint by the same name.

Leonard Wood was a soldier, a physician, and an administrator. He participated on the campaigns against the Apache leader Geronimo in 1885 and 1886. He was the US military governor for Cuba (the island, not the town) from 1899 to 1902, commanded forces in the Philippines in various ranks and roles from 1903 to 1908, and returned to the islands as the governor-general in 1921. In 1917 at the beginning of World War I, President Woodrow Wilson passed him by as leader of the European Expeditionary Force and gave the task to John J. Pershing. In 1920 Wood was about to become the presidential candidate for the Republican Party, but in a "smoke-filled room" the party regulars chose Warren G. Harding instead. Wood died in 1927 at the third operation of his brain tumor. He is remembered by Route 66 with a relatively large piece of land south of St. Robert. Fort Leonard Wood was built in 1941 on the eve of World War II.

Then on to Waynesville, whose Main Street is called Historic 66. A Phillips gas station is located conveniently on it. There is a Family Restaurant at the intersection on both sides of the new interstate serving sandwiches, which are nothing much but sandwiches. After Waynesville, follow Buchorn and Laquey. Then Hazelgreen, a small village north of the Gasconade River. Route 66 crosses the river on a handsome bridge. Often the river itself is not too full, but with the flooding of 2002, it was a mighty handsome stream. Water prevented public access to the public fishing place. Flooding waves had even forced some fish to the road, where they were fighting for their lives with too little water to swim back. We were able to return some to the river, but many fled to the ditch on the other side of the road, and I doubt if they ever made it back to safety.

After Hazelgreen and uphill, Lebanon soon follows. It is a relatively large town stretched along the northern side of the Interstate. There is the Satellite Café, or what's left of it. There is the Midway Speedway track. Also the Route 66 Antique Barn, a barn made into an antique shop, on the right, and the Munger Moss Motel on the left with some special Route 66 theme rooms available for real lovers of the Old Road. And disputes about where the 66 runs, or ran. Disputes even within the Missouri 66 Society. Choose a new road commissioner! The old one is good! Some of the roadside inhabitants are so fed up with tourists gawking at the road that they tell passersby to stay away from their yards. You'd better obey.

South of Lebanon are plenty of ruins of bankrupt inns and cafés. All that is left of some service stations are the rusted gas pumps. This is part of the historic Road landscape and atmosphere and, unfortunately, also part of its everyday life. Phillipsburg, Conway, Niangua, Marshfield, Northview, and Strafford, which is a small congregation of buildings.

Before we enter Strafford, billboards tell us that we are approaching an exotic zoo. Buena Vista's Exotic Animal Paradise has built itself a handsome gate, complete with flags of various countries. Of course, there is no mention about what it costs to visit the animal paradise, until the girl selling tickets at the counter tells us. By then it would be too embarrassing to turn back, and the long queues of cars behind us prevent it anyway. In 1996 we were lucky. We got there late in the afternoon, and there was not a single car behind us. There were several cars ahead. They did not turn around; instead, the four-member family dutifully paid $8.50 per adult and whatever the children were charged for the joy of driving for a few minutes and gazing at exotic animals like bulls, ostriches, peacocks, and water buffaloes. We thought the price was too high to pay for a short visit to the tiny zoo. After all, we were neither rich nor your typical Ozarks hillbillies. By 2002 the price had gone up to cover the TV commercials the zoo now used to lure more visitors. We drove by on a darkening night.

Springfield, "the Queen City of the Ozarks," in southwesten Missouri is the third largest city in the state after St. Louis and Kansas City. It is a gateway to the recreational areas of the Ozark Plateau. The Ozarks Mountains, mostly in the state of Arkansas, are an old and eroded remnant range. The area is considered beautiful wilderness but also the backwoods of the United States. Country yokels inhabit the Ozarks. The name Ozark Plateau sounds like an exciting and mystic old Indian name from the times when the Osage, Quapaw, and Missouri Indians still roamed the thick forests or paddled the rivers in canoes. The name is French in origin, however, as the French called their local fur trading post in the area Aux Arcs, something like "on the arches" or "by the arches," possibly "by the bends of the river."

Springfield itself is a relatively old Euro-American city west of the Mississippi River. The first white settlers came there in 1829. It is the southern terminal of the old telegraph line and is related to Civil War events in several ways. A relatively important battle took place at Wilson's Creek on August 10, 1861. Maybe as many as 2,500 soldiers died in the battle. To commemorate it, the road crossing the southern branch of Wilson's Creek is named Battlefield Road. The supermarket by the same name along the road lies seventeen miles from the actual battlefield. For Civil War buffs, or for anyone interested in military, or just US history, those seventeen miles are worth driving.

Wild Bill Hickok was one of the heroes of the West who stayed in Springfield for a short time. In 1862 he shot a man named David Tutt at the Town Square for gambling debts. Later, Hickok ran for sheriff and came in second. Besides the West and the Civil War, the city is tied in tightly with the history of Highway 66. There in 1947, Sheldon "Red" Chaney and his wife opened the first drive-in restaurant in the world. Historic Route 66 still cuts right through the industrial outskirts and the heart of Springfield. It passes by the city hall, but other than that the scenery is nothing special.

From Springfield Route 66 continued to Carthage, roughly following the same route as the present roads 266 and 96. Carthage is another old town, founded in 1842. It is located in one of the best farming areas of the Ozarks and the only area in the United States producing gray marble. The new Interstate Highway 44 passes the town far to the south. The Civil War did not pass Carthage, however. In the battle of Carthage on July 5, 1861, some 4,000 Missouri State Guard troops together with 2,000 unarmed recruits gave a thorough beating to some 1,100 Missouri volunteers fighting for the Northern side. Today the field is a state park. There were many fights in Carthage even after 1861, since some Missouri people supported the South and others the North. In September 1864, however, the Southerners burned down the town.

The most famous Carthage woman has to be Belle Starr, nee Myra Belle Shirley, who spent her childhood in Carthage. Later she assisted the notorious, but efficient, Southern guerrilla troops led by William Quantrill. After the war Belle led her own band of outlaws, headquartered at the farm of her second husband Sam Starr in what is now Oklahoma.

North of Carthage lies Kellogg Lake, on whose northern shore road 71 coming from the north joins the old Historic 66, Missouri Route 96 in these parts. Norman and Wanda Jackson used to run a motel at the crossroads with competition from a couple of hotels belonging to major hotel chains. Luckily, the traffic is busy, and so the Jacksons also managed. It is true that nobody's getting any younger, though. Norman suffered a stroke in 1995 and "got to take a short walk each day."

Previously, the 66 ran on the southern shore of the lake until a new bridge straightened it. Norman Jackson recalled how the road used to run where nothing but fields are today. He traveled from Springfield to California on the old highway as a young man in 1946, having returned from World War II. It felt like a fine way to see one's own country after the battlefields of Europe. Many people did that, Jackson reminisced.

The last of the Missouri towns is Joplin, near the border of Kansas and Oklahoma. It is an important production area of zinc, but lead and limestone are also quarried there. Here Route 66 took three different trails. Seventh Street, dividing the town from east to west is also still Route 66, although its status has dropped from federal highway to state road. On the southern side of the road, a speedway track proudly bears the number of the Old Road. The new I-44 passes Joplin in the south and goes on southwest to Oklahoma, missing Kansas altogether. The Old 66, however, runs through the town straight west and crosses the Kansas border. Route 66 Carousel Park and Paddock liquor store are there to provide you entertainment just before you cross into Kansas.

4

Land of the South Wind

Mining Country

Kansas is named after the Kansa Indians living in the area. The word means "people of the south wind." Indeed, there is a southern wind here that has forced the trees to lean north both in Kansas and Oklahoma.

The Old Highway US-66 made a Kansas bend only some thirteen miles long. It ran, and still does with the same number, from Joplin to Galena and Lowell, after which it veers sharply south to Baxter Springs and across the Oklahoma border to the small town of Quapaw. The Kansas bend was originally made in order to create a transport route from the zinc and lead mines in the southeast corner of the Sunflower State.

The new interstate does not make the bend. As the late Tom Teague so aptly described it in his *Searching for Route 66*: "In carving their smooth and true channels across this country, interstates bypassed thousands of towns. But in Kansas, they bypassed an entire state. The new road takes a hypotenuse southwest from Joplin straight into Oklahoma. Southeastern Kansas is off its map all together."

Possibly due to its short length and definitely because of the Road's importance in the area, Route 66 was paved throughout Kansas by 1929, as it was in Illinois. In Missouri, at that time, less than two thirds of the length of the road was paved, and in Oklahoma less than one fourth. Route 66 ran in New Mexico, Arizona, and California over 1,220 miles, only 64 of which were paved in 1929. By this date in Texas, plans to pave the road hadn't even begun.

Before the Missouri-Kansas border the Old Road offers two alternatives again: Road 66 and the Old Road 66. Only the latter will nowadays take you to the border; it turns right after a green sign and then veers to the left and crosses a railroad bridge. At some point it also crosses the state border. Where? There's no sign revealing that.

Galena in Kansas does not appear a wealthy town. The lush farming areas of Illinois and Missouri are gone. Surprisingly, few cars drive the streets of the town. Many of the houses are crumbling. Abandoned railroads crisscross everywhere. Signs pointing to the Historic 66 lead to a sharp bend to the right. In an abandoned railroad station we find the Museum of the Road, the Railroad, and Mining. One of its treasures is a Nazi banner snatched from Hitler's Eagle's Nest by a local Edward Beyer.

The southeast corner of Kansas is both a mining and a farming area. The white community that settled here halfway through the nineteenth century was already leaving the town when the mining operation started to grow quickly around World War I. When Highway 66 was opened, the area produced about half the world's lead, zinc, and cadmium. The Eagle-Pitcher lead mine and smelting plant in Galena was at times one of the largest in the world. Gigantic refuse heaps offered children good sliding in winter and summer. No one realized that the heaps were filled with poison.

In 1935 a strike at the mine resulted in bloody confrontations between strikers and police. The miners went as far as closing Route 66, after which the Governor of Kansas declared martial law in the whole state. The miners did not break, although the road was reopened. The strike was broken only after no less than nine miners were shot in a skirmish on April 11, 1937. No monument commemorates them or the event.

The amount of metals in the mined rock dropped to 8 percent in the 1960s, and mining became largely unprofitable. The population of Galena has dropped from more than fifteen thousand to some three thousand. All that remain are silicosis, heart diseases, paralyses, and kidney failure. The appearance of these diseases is 50 percent more likely in southeast Kansas than elsewhere in the United States.

When the mines were closed, the refuse heaps stayed. When the pumps stopped pumping, the water leaked back to the mining shafts, rivers, and groundwater. Nearby Tar Creek has been declared one of the most polluted sites in the United States.

Despite cleansing efforts, much of the groundwater is still severely polluted in places, and the foundations of buildings crumble into underground cavities. Some of the refuse heaps are still there. So are silicosis, cancer, heart diseases, and kidney failure. The brick houses in downtown Galena are ruins. Very few cars are on the streets. No lively diners or cafeterias to stop for.

Luckily, but not quite. There is the Four Women on the Route on Main Street. Renee Charles, Betty Courtney, Judy Courtney, and Melba Rigg have changed an old abandoned gas station into a diner and souvenir store. The International Harvester L-170 that became the inspiration for the character Mater in the Walt Disney movie *Cars* is their local mascot and can be seen in front of the Snack Shack.

Cattle Town Road

Route 66 leaves Galena for greener landscapes. It crosses the Spring River. The thick-growing oaks and cottonwoods on the bank hide an inn. The river gives a name to the locality: Riverton. Road 66 ends and joins road 69. Ahead is the Eisler Brothers store, which also has seen better days. Or maybe not, as it once was elevated to house the headquarters of the Kansas Historic Route 66 Association. It's a place to enjoy an old-fashioned deli sandwich and a cold soda or to add trinkets to your Route 66 souvenir collection.

The Rainbow Bridge has been elevated to glory as a landmark of the Old 66. It is one of the so-called Marsh Arch Bridges, named for their designer James Barney Marsh. Road 69 has been straightened out to cross the river a few yards downstream, and driving a car on the old arched bridge is now prohibited. Walking is permitted, though. The arches have rusted, but the bridge older than 66 itself is still undemolished and probably will stay so. The Kansas 66 Association will see to that. Rainbow Bridge is its most important preservation item. Below the bridge the river is usually small, but floodwaters can rise dangerously close to the bridge level, not to mention the nearby sections of the Road that are lower than the bridge. This happened in the spring of 2002. At times, you could not get to the Rainbow Bridge from the east, since all the road was under water. Upstream, the fields and pastures suffered much from the flood. One night on the bridge we spoke with some local folks about this. Because the road was covered by water, they could not get to their property. This is how much we understood of their talk and could also see with our own eyes. The rest of the conversation was held in language unintelligible for us.

"If you've ever wondered why all the old timers seem to have huge, nautical compasses mounted in their cars or camper cabs, one look at the map for this part of Old Route 66 will provide the answer," claims Tom Snyder in his *Route 66 Traveler's Guide*, and he is right. From the bridge we turn left along Willow Avenue. Then left a few blocks later between wooden houses, right along Military Avenue. But how do roads come, go, and continue in Baxter Springs? There is a definite need for a compass around these parts. Luckily, the signs for Historic Route 66 seem to get better year after year. Some are nothing but handmade signs on heavy paper, probably put there by some 66 aficionado who did not have a compass.

However the roads run, Baxter Springs is one of the two in any way important centers of population along Route 66 in Kansas. It is the first cattle town in the state. The first settlers came there in 1858, and ten years later the area was organized into a town. Baxter Springs had, of course, been an important trading center and resting place along Spring River before any white man saw it. Indians had been in the area for who knows how long, and Osage Chief Black Dog gave his name to the trail through the place, the Black Dog Trail. The town got its name from John J. Baxter who founded a trading post there in 1858 but died the next year.

During the Civil War, Quantrill's guerrillas destroyed a Union garrison and killed most of its men in the Baxter Springs Massacre in 1863. When the railroad reached the area, Baxter Springs became the northern terminus of the Shawnee Trail cattle route coming from Texas. And cattle are still the town's pride. Bill Murphey's restaurant on Road 66 has extremely good and relatively cheap steaks. His restaurant operates in a house that used to be a bank. It's no surprise that it was the very bank Jesse James and Cole Younger robbed in May 1876. Murphey's restaurant has now relocated across the street, and the bank is occupied with Café on the Route and the Little Brick Inn.

In Kansas, Route 66 enters the Great Plains states. For some, everything between the Mississippi Valley and the Rocky Mountains is referred to as the Great Plains, but for others the term is reserved for the area west of the hundredth meridian. We are not that far west yet, and the scenery in Galena or Baxter Springs does not look like the

Plains. The climate is still too moist here, even flood-prone as we have seen. Winfred Blevins's *Dictionary of the American West* puts a lot of emphasis on the moisture: "If there is enough moisture for farming, it isn't the Great Plains."

Due to the lack of water, the whites originally did not give much for the Plains. Major Stephen H. Long called the area a Great American Desert after exploring large portions of it in the 1820s. Less than fifty years later things changed when immigrants from Ukraine brought with them the seeds of hard winter wheat. Today, regardless of Blevins's definition, the Great Plains, from Texas to the Prairie Provinces of Canada, is the largest wheat producing area in the world. According to the 1991 edition of *Let's Go: The Budget Guide to USA*, every Kansas farmer feeds you and seventy-five others. Kansas is the chief wheat producer for the United States and also supplies bread for Russia, ironically, with the same hard winter wheat immigrants brought there in the 1870s.

Route 66, however, does not cross the Great Plains in Kansas. It turns south instead and crosses the Plains via a southern route. We don't have to continue much farther across the Oklahoma border before reaching the Plains.

5

The Home for All Indians

Mr. 66 and William Rogers, Sr. and Jr.

In Oklahoma Route 66 returns home. Cyrus Avery created it here; Lon Scott and Andy Payne made it famous; Jack Cuthbert, Will Rogers and Woody Guthrie traveled it to introduce Oklahoma to the world.

If Cy Avery is considered the founding father of Route 66, Jack Cuthbert, a barber from Clinton, Oklahoma, must be the godfather. He was nicknamed Mr. 66. According to his wife Gladys Zobisch Cuthbert, "Jack dedicated his life to route 66."

Originally, however, Cuthbert was not particularly keen on Highway 66, although Clinton was on it. He became interested in the Road only after World War II, goaded by Clinton's postmaster Frank Smith. The old National Route 66 Society founded by Cy Avery and Lon Scott in the 1920s had, for all practical purposes, ceased to be after the war. When the traffic on the Road resumed after 1945, local societies were founded in Arizona, New Mexico, Texas, and Oklahoma, and soon they got a national organization to unite them.

In 1947 Jack Cuthbert became the secretary of the Oklahoma society and Frank Smith became its chairman. Seven years later Cuthbert was nominated as chairman of the Oklahoma society and the secretary of the national society. He held this position for the next twenty years. Chairmen came and went, but the secretary stayed on, and, therefore, Cuthbert got his nickname. He toured the country advertising the Road and lobbying for small towns so that the new routes of 66 or other highways would not skirt the small towns to whose economic life the Road was essentially important. The National Route 66 Society suffered its worst defeat when it was not able to get I-66 as the number of the new highway replacing the Old Road, not even where it was replaced by I-40 between Oklahoma and California.

William Penn Adair Rogers is an even more famous Oklahoman. Rogers was born in Oologah, Cherokee Country, in present Oklahoma, on November 4, 1879. As a young man he cruised the eastern parts of the United States with traveling theater companies. When he was about forty years old, he got a contract with Sam Goldwyn and started to act in silent movies filmed in California. Soon the movies made Rogers famous as a comic cowboy character and a great lasso artist. "We loved Will Rogers, we loved his smile, we went to the movies Will Rogers to see. We follow him now for many a mile from old Oklahoma to Los Angeles," sang Woody Guthrie in a song he dedicated to Rogers and Route 66, the "Will Rogers Highway."

Rogers's hometown was Claremore in northeast Oklahoma on Route 66. It had been the first capital of Oklahoma Territory but later lost the position to Oklahoma City. Rogers was so interested in the Road running through his town that in the Bunion Derby of 1928 he promised an extra prize for the competitor who would reach Claremore first.

Rogers was about to become a silent screen star but never really made it. He kept up his popularity with writing humor columns in the newspapers. Then his first real talkie, *They Had to See Paris*, in 1929 was a hit. Soon he was a Star with a capital S. His support of Franklin Delano Roosevelt was generally credited with helping Roosevelt get into the White House. FDR allegedly offered to help Rogers become governor of Oklahoma, but he refused to run. Later, he did, however, serve as an honorary mayor of Beverly Hills, California.

Rogers died unexpectedly at the peak of his popularity in an air crash while on tour in northern Alaska near Point Barrow in 1935. The recovered body of the Oklahoman pilot Wiley Post was buried in Edmond near Oklahoma City. In May 1944 the body of Will Rogers was moved to a memorial center built in Claremore. His wife Betty Rogers, who died in June, is also buried there.

The Will Rogers Museum and Memorial Center was founded in Claremore in 1938, only a mile from Route 66. The museum holds Rogers's saddle collection and prize collection as well as all kinds of material related to his life and career: stage garments and so on. One of the rooms is dedicated to the memory of the air crash; in another there's a continuous show of Rogers's movies. In a third room you can listen to Rogers's radio programs. The center portrays Rogers as an Indian, humorist, philosopher, father, cowboy, and pilot. The place of honor is reserved for Jo Davidson's full-size duplicate of Will Rogers's statue. The original decorates the Capitol Building in Washington, DC.

Will Rogers, Jr. (1911-1993) was the oldest son of Will and Betty Rogers, who to some extent followed in his father's footsteps. He worked mostly in California as a journalist, actor, and politician. In May and June 1941, he spent his honeymoon driving with his bride from Las Vegas to New York, mainly on Highway 66. In 1951 Warner Brothers made a movie about the older Rogers (*The Story of Will Rogers*), and Junior acted as his father in it. Jane Wyman, Ronald Reagan's first wife, played the role of Betty Rogers.

Around the time of the filming, the idea came up to name Route 66 the Will Rogers Highway. It is possible that Lester Dill's business associate Lyman Riley had the idea or at least proposed it. In any case, the National Highway 66 Society began to promote the idea. The road between St. Louis and Santa Monica got Will Rogers's name officially in 1952. A long caravan traveled the Road to California and set up memorial plates and Will Rogers Highway signs along the way. The caravan naturally had great publicity value for the movie. Jack and Gladys Cuthbert, Lyman Riley, and Lester Dill, among others, participated in the procession. Riley commented that actually the Will Rogers Highway was only the road between the Meramec Caverns and Needles, California. "Nobody at St. Louis hotels cared anything for the Road, nor anybody in California, but it was important to the people living between them."

With the new interstate highway system, Route 66 and the Will Rogers Highway were left to play second fiddle, but the name of Will Rogers was also given to the Will Rogers Turnpike, the new I-44 running from the border of Oklahoma to the vicinity of Tulsa. The Old 66 is also still being used and the state of Oklahoma has even allowed it to keep its old number all the way to El Reno.

Dust Bowl Writing and Singing

In Oklahoma the East meets the West. Route 66 runs mainly across roaming plains inside the old Indian Territory. From Springfield to Tulsa the Road passes through fewer hills than in the Ozarks. They are also lower and somewhat more densely populated. Mining goes on in the farthest northeast corner of Oklahoma, but from the Highway you mainly see farming, cattle, and oil wells.

Route 66 made Oklahoma a part of the United States, but it was also the road out from Oklahoma. During the Depression, some 330,000 Okies, 15 percent of the state's population, moved out, mainly to California, along Route 66. One of the worst draughts of the century coincided with the Depression in the early 1930s. A bushel of wheat that had cost $1.16 in 1925 was worth only $0.33 in 1931. The cultivation methods that relentlessly exhausted the soil served to complete the devastation. The topsoil was gone with the wind. As dust it invaded all nooks and crannies. A dust bowl was created on the Southern Plains. People died of silicosis; cattle died of thirst. Many left.

In 1936 the *San Francisco News* asked John Steinbeck, then a young novelist who had just gained some fame with his *Tortilla Flat*, to write a series of articles on migrant workers. These articles led Steinbeck a few years later to describe the fate of one of the migrant Oklahoma families in *The Grapes of Wrath*. The Joad family leaves their home in Oklahoma, crams into their overloaded rattletrap of a car, and heads for California in search of better luck. Steinbeck's description is ruthless: "The dawn came, but no day. In the gray sky a red sun appeared a dim red circle that gave a little light, like dusk; and as that day advanced, the dusk slipped back toward darkness, and the wind cried and whimpered over the fallen corn." The movie based on the book leaves no doubt about the road the family takes: Route 66 signs are clearly visible on the screen.

On April 14, 1935, in the midst of the severe Depression, a massive dust storm spread from western Kansas across Oklahoma to the Texas Panhandle. To many it seemed that the end of the world was at hand. Woody Guthrie, living in Pampa, Texas at the time, wrote a song called "So Long, It's Been Good to Know You." It is a farewell to the people forced by the storm to abandon their homes, and it became the Okies' unofficial national anthem. Nowadays many singers perform it as their final song of the evening, perhaps unaware of the tragic background of the song, drawn only by the words of the chorus: "So long, it's been good to know you."

Woody Guthrie continued the themes of the Depression, the Dust Bowl, and Okies on the road in many of his songs. One of his tunes is called "Talking Dust Bowl Blues." Another is "Do-Re-Me," which in Guthrie's composition refers to money the travelers should have on them already upon entering California; otherwise, they will not be welcomed. "California is a Garden of Eden, a paradise to live in or see," sings Guthrie, "but believe it or not, you won't find it so hot, if you ain't got the do-re-me." Then you better go back to your "beautiful Texas, Oklahoma, Kansas, Georgia, Tennessee."

Guthrie was among many readers impressed with Steinbeck's novel. He devoted a long song (or a song in two parts) to young Tom Joad, the hero of the book. The song is clearly inspired by both the book and the movie. The movers and their route are also well described by "Will Rogers Highway," whose title refers to Route 66. Perhaps Lyman Riley got the idea for the name of the highway from this very song by Guthrie.

Woodrow Wilson Guthrie (1912-1967) was the popular favorite of the Great Depression. His most famous songs probably include "Union Girl," and the patriotic story about how the land belongs to you and me "from California to New York Island and from the redwood forests to the Gulf Stream waters" ("This Land Is Your Land"). He became a famous radio star in the 1930s, but later his reputation as a leftist sympathizer eroded his popularity during the Cold War and the McCarthy era.

Guthrie's recordings were mostly recorded by Columbia Broadcasting System (CBS), whose radio stations also played them and in whose programs he performed on a regular basis. The story has it that all the CBS secretaries fell in love with him. During the Depression he was involved in a federal employment program meant for artists, and due to this program the Library of Congress has preserved his interviews and a bunch of his songs in its archives. Of course, the library also holds recordings by other artists from the same unemployment program. Woody Guthrie's son Arlo has continued in his father's tradition and was relatively popular in the 1960s and 1970s. Arlo continued his career in television and, for example, played an overage pupil in a school series located in Hawaii.

The Dust Bowl made the Franklin D. Roosevelt government focus on land management and ecological balance. The Department of Agriculture sent advisers to the area to teach the farmers better techniques for tilling the soil. Some 220 million trees were planted as a windbreak running roughly along the 99th meridian from Abilene, Texas, all the way to Canada. The "Shelterbelt" crosses Route 66 pretty much on the Oklahoma-Texas border.

Many other New Deal programs tried to help both the farmers and workers. Special loans were provided and special unemployment programs created. One program whose mark on Route 66 is still seen in some sections of Missouri and Oklahoma was the Civilian Conservation Corps. They planted many trees, built fire towers, and managed and constructed sites related to preserving nature.

The Works Progress Administration project known as Federal One employed many writers, actors, and artists. It included the Federal Art Project, the Federal Music Project, the Federal Writers' Project, and others to fill the New Deal alphabet soup. Many familiar names worked with these programs, including Aaron Copland, Saul Bellow, Ralph Ellison, Arthur Miller, John Huston, and Orson Welles.

The government also hired photographers. Their photos were collected by the Historical Section, which in 1937 became part of the new Farm Security Administration. Particularly, Dorothea Lange's haunting images of Dust Bowl migrants have become classic depictions of the Great Depression. The pains of Steinbeck's writings or Guthrie's songs have their match in Lange's photos.

The Dust Bowl days bring bitter memories for many Oklahomans, and, therefore, many people still hate Route 66 in its home fields. For those who took on the Road as part of the American exodus, the end was not necessarily bitter. Many of them did eventually find jobs in California and elsewhere in the West. Also their music and their folklore became somewhat of a dominant culture of the times. But, yes, they were not in Oklahoma anymore, and the relationship with the Road didn't start to become positive until after World War II, when Route 66 began to bring money into Oklahoma. This change made it easier to romanticize the reputation of the Road. A new culture entered Oklahoma via Route 66 with its hitchhikers, neon advertisements, cafeterias, and service stations. Now it is even possible to listen to Woody Guthrie's songs with a positively nostalgic attitude.

The dust storms have not stopped, however. More people live in the Dust Bowl area now than ever before. More fields of wheat and other non-native crops have replaced the original grasses that tied the soil together better than the new and alien species. Farming techniques have developed, but still the wind occasionally destroys the harvest almost totally. Some of the storms since World War II have actually been worse than those of the 1930s. Luckily, they have occurred during times of prosperity rather than depression, and no new Dust-Bowl ballads are needed to comfort modern-day Okies.

Indian Country Road

"Ridiculed by the rest of the nation as boring, and forever the butt of jokes at the expense of the 'Okies,' Oklahoma has had a traumatic and far from dull history. In the 1830s all this land, held to be useless, was set aside as Indian Territory; a convenient dumping ground for the so-called Five Civilized Tribes, who blocked white settlement in the southern states," explains the 1996 edition of USA, the Rough Guide. Another guide book, Fodor's USA from 1992 continues: "The name Oklahoma came from two Choctaw words meaning land of the red people, and today there are about 67 Native American tribes represented in Oklahoma's population. Much of the state's outlook evokes memories of its two most familiar elements, the Indians and the cowboys."

Like all land in the Americas, Oklahoma originally belonged to Indians. It remained theirs longer than most other regions in the United States. The experiments of the US government's Indian policy included forced removals of Indian nations and tribes living east of the Mississippi River to an area west of it with the aim of creating there a permanent territory where white people could not settle. The white settlers, however, did not pay much heed to such law, nor did Congress, which was soon ready to change its Indian policy. Many times.

The present area of Oklahoma was nevertheless made into an Indian Territory, and white people were banned from going there until the 1890s. Indian tribes were transferred to the territory from all around the United States, east and west. In 1889 a small part of an area previously reserved for the Cherokee Indians was opened to white settlement, and soon other parts of the Indian Territory experienced the same fate. The areas inhabited by white people became Oklahoma Territory, and in 1907 all of the old Indian Territory lands were combined with it to create the new state of Oklahoma.

In Illinois, Missouri, and Kansas the Indian presence on Route 66 is small and almost nonexistent except in place names, including all of the three state names and historical markers and remnants of the past.

In Oklahoma, New Mexico, and Arizona, however, Route 66 continues to be an important Indian road. More than 400,000 American Indians reside in the Sooner State. Living Indian communities dot the roadside together with memories of the past long before whites ever wandered lost into America.

California has the largest Native American population with 738,976 Indians, and Texas the seventh largest, more than a 100,000, although Route 66 does not go through the most Indian populated areas in these states. In New Mexico and Arizona, however, the Road passes through several Indian reservations. Arizona has the third largest Native American population, and New Mexico the fourth largest; 275,000 and 195,000 respectably. Navajos are the largest of the Indian nations inside the

United States. More than 300,000 of them reside on their reservation along the Old 66 in New Mexico and Arizona. In the Southwest, American Indians are an essential and still a visual part of the Route 66 environment.

Indians have influenced many aspects of Route 66, and the Road has revolutionized their lives. Route 66 brought many whites to the Southwest and made indigenous peoples part of its tourist and entertainment activities. Route 66 brought southwestern Indians into the American cash economy. This does not necessarily mean that American Indians have forsaken their traditions and Indian-ness. Navajos and Hopis receive much of their income from mining activities, but agriculture, sheep herding, and cattle ranching remain important sources of income, supplemented of course by tourism. Hopis still believe in katsina-spirits, and most Indian Nations organize traditional rituals according to their old calendars. American Indians have adapted to the Euro-American way of life in order to survive, but many of them have also preserved their identities as the indigenous peoples of America. Route 66 is a visitor, too, on Indian land.

Along the Old Road from Kansas, the first Oklahoma town is Quapaw on the former Quapaw Reservation. The Quapaws were removed to Oklahoma in the 1830s from their old homesteads in Missouri. The town itself was founded in 1897. Route 66 reaches the town almost stealthily on nearly level ground, drives through it as its Main Street, then veers right, and disappears into the Plains. A good fifth of Quapaw townspeople are American Indians. Some of them have become wealthy by leasing their land to lead and zinc mining companies. The murals along Main Street, however, portray railroads, horses, and, of course, Highway 66. Immediately south of town is a Phillips Petroleum Company sign almost as old as the Road.

In the United States, business is valued perhaps even more than elsewhere in the world. President Calvin Coolidge said: "The business of America is business." After the Indian town of Quapaw, the next locality on Route 66 in Oklahoma is Commerce. The Road runs again across this town right in the center as its Main Street, but here it is named Mickey Mantle Boulevard to commemorate one of America's greatest baseball players. Son of a miner, Mantle grew up in Commerce in the 1930s and 40s.

The Road goes on while the towns change. The next town is again strongly Indian. Miami got its name from the Miami Indians, removed here from Ohio. The Americans searched this area for lost Spanish gold mines, which were, according to legend, used by the first Europeans in the sixteenth century. These mines were never found but zinc and lead were.

On the eve of the Civil War, Congress looked into opportunities to promote equal education in the West. When war broke out, Congress passed a law proposed by Senator Justin Morrill in 1862, according to which each new state would receive from the federal government a land grant that it could sell for money to found and maintain agricultural and engineering institutes of learning. The law was later extended to involve all states west and even some east of the Mississippi River. This is how the so-called A&M (agriculture and mechanical) colleges and universities came to be. One of these land-grant institutions is Northeastern A&M in Miami.

The center of Miami, as in bigger cities, emphasizes the pedestrian opportunities for shopping. Extensions of the sidewalks changing from one side of the street to the other force the Old Road to wind its way between parking spots and flowerbeds past the memorable Coleman Theater built in 1929 for the local mining magnate George L. Coleman. Despite having every possible food chain represented from McDonald's to Kentucky Fried Chicken, surprisingly none of the hotel chains have found their way here. Perhaps they are all stuck closer to the interstate.

After Miami, the trail of the Old Road disappears. People disagree on its route, now under the sod. Plenty of roadwork and new bridges have lost the original route, and detours serve to make finding it even more difficult. Buffalo Ranch in Afton, one of the Old Road's legendary institutions, is unfortunately also gone. An old gentleman bid his visitors welcome at the Ranch trading post in 1996 and was delighted when the visitors' book did not receive a new German autograph but that of a citizenship heretofore unknown. The conversation was factual, even formal, considering we were in the United States. The shop was full of paraphernalia but also quality Western shirts and trousers. The guests were informed where the best chances were to find the ranch's herd of buffalo.

After World War II, Allene Kay and her husband looked at the map for a place where they could establish a tourist trap. Ogallala, Nebraska, seemed like a suitable place, as the highway across the Great Plains ran through it. Nowadays, I-80 has replaced the Highway. The stream of traffic in Ogallala was not busy enough to maintain the Kay business, and so they moved to Afton, Oklahoma, on the edge of town on Highway 66, and built their small buffalo ranch there. Initially, the ranch boasted only seven buffaloes. Later, they added llamas, deer, and exotic hens. Seeing the animals cost nothing, but the Kays hoped that visiting tourists would spend money at the Buffalo Ranch Trading Post.

Also at the Buffalo Ranch were an ice cream parlor and a restaurant specializing in buffalo burgers. The food was sold in a separate building. The other house was the actual souvenir and Indian goods store. The big trading post, which offered a variety of Indian jewelry and tourist junk, was centered mostly on selling clothes, although the visitors' book was there, and on its windows a couple of Old 66 signs had found their last resting-place. Seeing the animals was still free of charge. The atmosphere was different from that at Strafford's Exotic Zoo in Missouri. The Buffalo Ranch animals were at least as exotic. A herd of buffalo fed far out in the pasture. A corral held a live buffalo to delight the tourists, and there was also a hybrid of a buffalo and a beef cow, a beefalo, as some Americans call it. There were a llama and a yak. Exotic hens ran at our feet.

In 1997 Buffalo Ranch Trading Post was closed with both the Kays gone. Seven years later the remains of the ranch were demolished to make room for a convenience store that now bears the name of the Buffalo Ranch. You can spend the night in Afton at the Palmer Hotel or go into a saddle store across the street and admire an entire wall full of matchboxes.

After Afton, there are a couple of small but significant Route 66 towns. Vinita was Cy Avery's hometown before he moved to Tulsa. The town is named after sculptor Vinnie Ream. The most famous of his works is certainly the statue of Abraham Lincoln in Washington, DC. Southwest of Vinita lies Chelsea, one of Oklahoma's first oil towns. One of the few remaining detached houses that Sears Mail-Order Company sold after World War II, mail-ordered in parts and assembled on the spot, still stands in Chelsea.

The oil pumps started to produce black gold in Chelsea in 1889. Sallie McSpadden, Will Rogers's sister, once lived here. So did the famous cowboy singer Gene Autry. He used to work at the railroad station prior to his career in singing and movies that later took him to California. If you continue to Texas and California, you will come across Autry again.

The next town on Route 66 is Bushyhead, named after a Cherokee chief whose feathered headpiece was particularly magnificent. Andy Payne's home is in Foyil. From Foyil, Road 28A runs about five miles from the Old Highway to a totem pole park that had become one of the attractions of the Old Road. Folk artist Edward Nathan Galloway built the world's tallest totem pole there from concrete and wire. This oddity, some eighty-eight feet high, is a wonderful mixture of white concepts about American Indians and their totem poles. In reality, Oklahoma Indians did not traditionally carve totems; instead, totem poles belonged and still belong to the culture of American Indians living far in the Pacific Northwest.

The big concrete totem pole has a couple of smaller neighbors, and a team of volunteers maintains the park. For those really interested in American Indians and those knowing something about them, the park is a definite disappointment. The road leading there is all the more interesting. It is like an asphalt-covered rollercoaster where you can step on the brake yourself.

There is no avoiding Indian names in Oklahoma. The name of the state itself is, after all, a distorted form of the Choctaw Indian words meaning "home for Indians." The next town after Foyil is tiny Seqoyah, named for the Cherokee who developed a syllabary for the Cherokee language. This old coal station is hardly more than a memory. However, the Seqoyah alphabet has lasted, and Cherokee is still a living language in both its spoken and written forms. The *Cherokee Phoenix*, published both in Cherokee and in English, is probably one of the oldest continuously published newspapers or magazines in America. It began in Georgia in 1828 and moved to Oklahoma with the Cherokees. Nowadays, it is published monthly in Tahlequah, the Cherokee capital on the former reservation.

The next town after Sequoyah, Claremore, was a roadside town long before Highway 66. The old stagecoach trail from Vinita to Albuquerque, New Mexico, ran through it. The town got its name from Osage chief Clermont or Clermos. When the Cherokee Indians were brought there from the Carolinas and Georgia, they soon clashed with the Osages in a bloody battle nearby. Claremore is the seat of Rogers County. The name of the county commemorates Clem Rogers, the father of Will Rogers, the "great son" of county and town alike. Will Rogers claimed that he was born "between Claremore and Oologah before either of them was a town." Rogers chose Claremore as his official birthplace, because only Indians could pronounce the name of Oologah. Whatever the birthplace, the burial site is at Claremore's Will Rogers Memorial Center on land once owned by Rogers. Claremore continues to cash in on, even to live by, Will Rogers's fame and name. The road leading to the Memorial Center is called Will Rogers Boulevard. A Will Rogers Hotel is on the left and a Will Rogers Best Western Motel on the right, or was it just the opposite? All possible businesses use the name of the beloved cowboy artist.

But Claremore is also the home of writer Lynn Riggs. The Richard Rogers and Oscar Hammerstein musical *Oklahoma!* is based on Riggs's play *Green Grow the Lilacs*. The musical made its debut in 1943 and is still one of the most famous musicals in the history of Broadway, New York's theater district. This romantic story from the times of early white Oklahoma was later filmed as well. Fred Zinnemann directed the 1955 movie.

Will Rogers was a distinct character of the West, perhaps more skilled at lassoing than shooting, but guns are naturally an essential feature of the West. One of the largest, if not the largest, collection of guns in the world is to be found at 333 Lynn Riggs Boulevard, which is Route 66, at J. M. Davis Arms & Historical Museum. It exhibits the gun of Pancho Villa, the Mexican revolutionary hero, as well as guns of Emmett Dalton, Henry Starr, Cole Younger, and other outlaws.

Lilacs may grow green and copper too turns green with age, but river water can also be greenish. Past Verdigris, Oklahoma, the old Highway 66 crosses the Verdigris River on four lanes and a pair of bridges. For some reason these two arched bridges, Felix and Oscar, are not identical twins. They are, rather, an "odd couple." The nearby railroad bridge joins this complex of bridges, crossing the river east of the twins.

Southwest of Verdigris is Catoosa, another Indian name. The word is believed to derive from a saying meaning "people of the light," although the language of origin is unknown. Nor is it certain whether the Cherokees saw the same light as the Quapaws or whether they meant the same people. Be that as it may, Catoosa was nevertheless organized as a post office by John Gunther Schrimsher, Will Rogers's uncle, after the American Civil War.

North of the bridges at a crossroads stands Lil' Abner's Dairyette Café. It is an original Route 66 institution and has stood on the Road for more than fifty years. The books written about the Road neglect to mention it, however, and, therefore, it has not become one of the Road legends. Why? Maybe the owner hasn't wanted it to, or maybe writers didn't get free meals there. Nor did we, but the helpings of salad were generous, cheap, and tasty, and the other items looked delicious. We'll definitely stop there next time, too.

Oil on the Road and in Towns

The coast-to-coast bunion derby in 1928 made the Double-Six famous before it was even passable by car from one end to the other. The term "double-six" became "sixty-six" mainly because of the Phillips Petroleum Company and, eventually, the song by Bobby Troup. Phillips Petroleum is one of the most important service station chains in Oklahoma and its neighboring areas. Frank Phillips set it up in 1917. The Federal Highway 66 ran across Phillips's key marketing area.

Several stories purport to explain the name of the Phillips Petroleum Company. According to one that is usually believed to be true, two high-ranking workers of the company, Salty Sawtell and John Kane, were on their way from Oklahoma City to a meeting in Bartlesville, driving a car with the tank full of the company's new high-octane gasoline. Near Tulsa, Kane, behind the wheel, noticed that the car picked up a lot of speed with the new gasoline, "at least sixty miles per hour." Sawtell replied: "Sixty nothing? We're doing at least sixty-six!" The men stared at each other and realized approximately at the same time that they were driving sixty-six on sixty-six.

In Bartlesville, Sawtell and Kane told the other participants in the meeting about their discovery, and it amused everybody, including Frank Phillips. The company's chain of service stations was soon named Phillips 66 and the name has lasted, although nobody remembers the original connection to the name of Route 66.

Michael Karl Witzel has another story in his *Route 66 Remembered*. According to this one, prior to founding the company, Frank and L. E. Phillips had only sixty-six dollars left when their first successful oil well struck black gold. Because of the timing of their lucky strike, they decided that if they ever marketed gasoline to motorists, it would be christened Phillips 66. Since then, Phillips 66 has spread its service stations far from Oklahoma and Texas. The company's gas pumps are found as far as North Carolina on the East Coast of the United States.

The Phillips 66 Petroleum Company is by no means the only company with the magic double-six in its name. Some other service stations in North Carolina use the number 66 in their names, although they have never had anything to do with the Phillips company. And of course a large number of old and new gasoline business entrepreneurs on the Old Road have the number 66 printed on their badges.

In northeastern Oklahoma, the central area of the Phillips company, the Old 66, whose number here is unchanged, runs alternatively on both sides of the new I-44 highway, here named the Will Rogers Turnpike. All roads join in Tulsa. It is the second largest city in Oklahoma with almost half a million inhabitants. The town was founded in the Indian Territory but really started to grow in the 1920s with the oil industry. It is still known as the oil capital of the world.

Tulsa is also a city of education and culture. It boasts at least two university campuses. The buildings of Oral Roberts University are almost postmodern. Its space age prayer tower provides a splendid view over the city. At the gate of the university, a bronze statue of hands clasped in prayer, nearly forty feet tall, greets visitors. The founder was an evangelist minister, who began preaching in the 1930s and built up his own Pentecostal Holiness Church, which he united with the United Methodist Church in 1968. With radio and TV stations, and with the university, Oral Roberts started a worldwide evangelistic movement.

Right on the western edge of Tulsa, on the border of Osage land, lies the world-famous Gilcrease Museum. Its treasures consist mainly of Indian-related and other Western paintings. The Philbrook Art Museum also houses a large exhibition of Indian works, although most of the collection is European and American art from the nineteenth and twentieth centuries. The museum itself is located in the ninety-thousand-square-foot abode of the late oil king Waite Phillips.

Tulsa has also made it to both the silver screen and the playing disk. Gene Pitney is still "24 Hours from Tulsa," as his song recounts. "Take Me Back" to Tulsa plead Bob Wills and his Texas Playboys in 1941. The movie made of Tulsa in 1949 as well as its theme song are simply called *Tulsa*. A more modern film with the same name was made in the 1990s. In it, however, Tulsa was nothing but the locale where some of the movie took place, as the old movie was truly of the town, its people, and its oil.

Of course, Tulsa is also a Route 66 city with many relics from the golden age of the Road. New landmarks have appeared by the Old Roadside even during recent years. On Eleventh Street near Tulsa University was a Metro Diner. It benefitted from the university's students, but in 2006 it was torn down to make room for the university expansion. Somewhat further there was a Route 66 diner, which, I believe, still exists. The Road climbs across the city to its central hill and finds a bridge to cross the Arkansas River, possibly a different bridge than before.

Down the Arkansas River, some fifty miles southeast of Tulsa, off 66, which goes the opposite direction, is Muskogee. An important center of Indian history, it is worth the side trip for everyone interested in American Indians. Cherokees, Creeks, Choctaws, Chickasaws, and Seminoles were among the many Nations who were forced to leave their homes in the east and move to Oklahoma. In their new territory, they were so quick to reorganize their lives that they have been known ever since as the Five Civilized Tribes. In Muskogee is the Five Civilized Tribes Museum. Further northeast is the Cherokee capitol Tahlequah. The nearby museum village of Tsa-La-Gi features a pageant every summer of the Cherokee removal from Georgia and North Carolina. When the Cherokees proved unwilling to leave their homes, they were transferred by force to Oklahoma in the spring of 1838. During the move, one fourth of them died of the cold, hunger, and diseases. Thus, their journey became known as the Trail of Tears. In Oklahoma, Route 66 is also a trail of tears for white folks as it took so many Okies from their homesteads.

From Tulsa the old and the new highway turn southwest and follow the railroad tracks. Frankoma Pottery is located near Sapulpa on the Tulsa side. The pottery business was set up in 1933 by John Frank, a young ceramics teacher at the University of Oklahoma, who had been educated at the Chicago Art Institute, the very place from which Route 66 begins its wandering across the country.

Sapulpa is rich in both Indian and pioneer lore. It was founded in 1886, and like its neighbor Tulsa, it began to flourish with the discovery of oil. Today, oil is routine business in Sapulpa. The glass industry is important here in addition to natural gas and oil. Many American

Indians still live in the area. To "help" them and other people with their unexpected financial difficulties, the Apache Pawn stands right on Route 66, although rumors claim that it might be closed. Further downtown on the right side of Dewey Avenue, which is 66, stands one of the many public libraries that the railroad and steel magnate Andrew Carnegie helped to fund in the early nineteenth century.

Between Tulsa and Oklahoma City, small towns have given way to the bigger cities. Kellyville, Bristow, Depew, and Warwick now serve mainly as service stations for the roads passing through them. Most of these towns have their origins in the land rushes of the 1890s. Depew has a small stretch of very Old 66 alignment serving as an entrance to some of the housing lots. Flowers cover the western end of this section. Kellyville was founded in 1893. Cotton Gin Diner provides a nice stop on Route 66.

In Stroud, we enter the lands of the old Sac and Fox Nation Indian Reservation. There still is a marker for that. The Sac and Fox originally did not live in central Oklahoma, but far in the north, just south and west of Lake Michigan in present-day northern Illinois and southeastern Wisconsin. They were more used to woods and rivers and the big lake than the southern plains of their present home. I am sure that they did not move here voluntarily. Remember the Sauk leader, Black Hawk, who fought back in the 1830s west of Chicago?

In Stroud the Old 66 is the Main Street, just as in so many towns before it and after it on the Road. Right in the center on top of a hill we find the Rock Café. In 1996 the flags of the United States, Germany, and Switzerland swayed in front of the building. The owner of the café was in fact supposed to be German. His neighbors told us that once upon a time he worked as a cook on a ship on a lake in Switzerland, where a Stroud woman found him, married him, and brought him to Oklahoma. Despite its rough name and stony look, the Rock Café was a quiet and peaceful place. But so are all of Stroud, and the Oklahoma countryside as a whole. Even the Rock Café lights went down soon after 10:00 p.m.

The website of Rock Café, however, does not verify the above story. Perhaps the locals in 1996 were only pulling our leg. According to more reliable sources, the rocky building was constructed in 1939 by Roy Rieves and originally run by Miss Melma Holloway. Between 1959 and 1983 Mamie Mayfield took care of the place and became a legend among truck drivers and others passing by. She gave up because of her old age, and, apparently, the building was out of business for a few years. In 1993, however, the present owner, Dawn Welch, took over and uplifted the old place to its present glory. But why in 1996 was there a German flag and a Swiss flag? In 2002 they were gone. Instead of them, the pink Route 66 flag flew next to Old Glory. Was this perhaps because of the Pixar film crew, who visited the site in 2001 while making the animated film *Cars* and modeled the character of Sally in the film after Ms. Welch?

The youngsters in Stroud amuse themselves by driving back and forth through the town on the section of Route 66 less than a mile long. But what else is there for them to do, unless they are interested in watching television? The Cue & Draw Bar at some time at least used to offer refreshment for nightwalkers. The bar boasted a jukebox and a couple of pool tables. You could have American beer in pints or bottles. The bar sold no strong spirits. A mix of beer and tomato juice seemed to be a popular drink.

When the going—or not going, really—in Stroud gets boring, it is possible to spend the night at the Holiday Motel, managed by Dan and Carolyn Guthrie. It proudly announces its owners as American citizens—no offence, but what foreigner would be crazy enough to buy it, anyways? Registration is quick, insofar as Carolyn has time to do it, what with the flock of children and a dog twirling at her feet. Furthermore, the hotel urges travelers to "stay with the winner" and charges an according price for the room. Well, cruising around the world one has sometimes had to sleep in even shaggier premises—seldom, though, thank God.

We bid farewell to Stroud at a Double-Six carwash. Next we encounter sparsely populated countryside. Was there really no room here for the Indians? Was it really necessary to deprive them even of this land? And where are the deprivers of the land now? The rain beats against the windshield, corn keeps growing, and the pumps keep pumping up the black gold. As Jack Rittenhouse wrote already in 1946 in his guidebook to Highway 66, "the route is through rolling countryside—once the haunt of Indians, later the territory of cowmen and 'bad men,' but now devoted principally to oil and agriculture." Davenport Cemetery in my opinion is one of the most beautiful resting places along the Old Road.

Cowboy Towns

In Chandler Route 66 is First Street. At a curve is a Phillips 66 service station and on the right, the Lincoln Motel. There soon follow the Steer Inn Family Restaurant and the Lincoln County Museum, or was it the other way around? Well, if you want to find whether they're still there, that is not a problem. All the four places are so close to each other, and Chandler is such a small town.

Then Wellston, where the Road crosses beneath the new I-44. More fields of corn, sugar beets, and whatnot. But why not? A man has to eat, and a woman, too. We are after all in Arcadia. According to the Roman poet Virgil, Arcadia somewhere in Greece was a place that contained almost everything. Arcadia, Oklahoma, is nevertheless a small place. The governing feature of the landscape is a round barn on top of a hill, a Route 66 landmark even before it was repaired. Just before, on the opposite side of the Road are the Oklahoma Route 66 Association and Hill-Billee's Café.

East of Arcadia is a monument to the poet Washington Irving, who traveled the area and then wrote his *Tour of the Prairies* in 1832. On the Oklahoma prairie, Route 66 also tours from Arcadia to Edmond, now a northern suburb of Oklahoma City. The beautiful campus of the University of Central Oklahoma is in Edmond. At the cemetery lies Wiley Post, Will Rogers's co-pilot on the fateful flight in northern Alaska. Of the three airports in Oklahoma City, the southernmost is named for Rogers, the northwestern for Post.

The West begins at Oklahoma City. The town was built in the middle of the Indian Territory in an area not specifically designated to any Native American group. Therefore, it was also one of the first areas to be opened to whites on April 22, 1889, and some ten thousand settlers peopled the area on the first day. A number of them had sneaked across the border before its official opening. These premature people have earned Oklahoma its nickname, the Sooner State.

Oklahoma City became the state capital when some of its citizens stole the governing paraphernalia from the original capital city, Guthrie. Most of the original settlers gained their livelihood from agriculture, and the city is still an important agricultural center. The oil boom began here in 1928, and the pumps haven't stopped pumping since. There is an oil well even under the state capitol. None other than the

Phillips 66 Company pumps the black gold from it, as Route 66 barely manages to skirt the corner of the capitol square.

Oklahoma City is distinctly Western, but many cultural achievements of the East have found their niche here, too. The city boasts a relatively famous symphony orchestra and theater. The theater is famed for its peculiar architecture. Oklahoma City University is here, but the best college of the state lies further south in Norman. Western phenomena, however, are a governing feature of Oklahoma City. Even the amusement park is built around Western themes as a Frontier City. There's a long hill with persimmon trees, rising in a gentle slope from the Old 66. On top of Persimmon Hill stands the National Cowboy and Western Heritage Museum, originally founded in 1955 as the Cowboy Hall of Fame and Western Heritage Center. Both real rodeo riders and cowboys from the films have their pictures and stories collected there. John Wayne has a corner of his own with its collection of katsinas and Bowie knives. Some thirty-five years ago the corner exhibited a big diorama presenting the life of Oklahoma Indians, but since then the Indians have had to give way to Wayne. But then, isn't this what happened in the movies as well?

On the grounds of the Cowboy Museum, William Frederick Cody, a.k.a. Buffalo Bill, sits on his horse and waves to the tourists, bidding them to follow him West. A replica of the same statue is located in his namesake town of Cody, Wyoming, in front of the Western Research Center and Museum dedicated to Buffalo Bill. In Oklahoma City the four riders of *Coming through the Rye* keep Buffalo Bill company. The statue by Frederic S. Remington portrays four cowboys: two of them on their way to a whorehouse, two returning from it. It is left for the spectator to guess which two. Possibly the most famous of the statues is inside the Cowboy Museum, *The End of the Trail*, sculpted by William Earl Fraser, originally for the 1904 St. Louis World's Fair. Subsequently, this Indian, sitting on his horse looking depressed, has become a symbol of the defeat and nineteenth-century destruction of the Indians.

With cowboys and Indians it is easy to forget the African Americans of Oklahoma, many of them cowboys and Indians. It may even be that the term "cowboy" was originally used in the East for black herders of cattle in the Carolinas. The first blacks arrived in Oklahoma in the 1830s as slaves of the Five Civilized Tribes. By 1907 there were more blacks living in Oklahoma City than Indians and whites combined. After the Civil War, many blacks from the old South had wandered west. By some estimation, a third of all the cowboys were black during the golden age of cattle drives.

For some years, Oklahoma was very segregated. There were separate Indian towns, white towns, and black towns. Relations between the races were not always harmonious. Many blacks served as "buffalo soldiers" in the Indian wars, a name they earned from Natives because of the texture of their hair to that of the buffalo. In 1921 as many as thirty-six people were killed in race riots in Greenwood, now a district of Tulsa. The Oklahoma Jazz Hall of Fame now stands on the location. Many black jazz and bebop musicians started off with the Oklahoma City Blue Devils, including vocalist Little Jimmie Rushing and pianist William "Count" Basie.

The early times of Oklahoma Territory are portrayed by the Harn Homestead and 1889ers Museum in Oklahoma City. The modern space age has its place in the Kirkpatrick Science Center. The National Softball Hall of Fame amuses playful sports enthusiasts. Even firemen have a museum of their own. At an angle opposite the Oklahoma Capitol House is the Oklahoma History Center, the state museum. The collections include a rare painted buffalo hide, a genuine pioneer wagon, and other articles from the Indian and pioneer days. A group of rooms represents a cross section of Oklahoman life until the present times. Paintings by Kiowa Indian artist Monroe Tsatoke decorate the walls of the museum, depicting the Indian tribes removed to Oklahoma. A large painting of the Cherokee Trail of Tears dominates the staircase.

In Oklahoma City Route 66 itself did not affect the city's street scene much during the Depression or even during the years of plenty following it. The same is true in Chicago, St. Louis, and Los Angeles—all of them too big and self-sufficient to feel the Road's impact. In all of them, however, Route 66 delved right into the heart of the city; it still makes a U-shaped arch deep inside Oklahoma City almost scratching the capitol's wall. Some downtown buildings have become landmarks of the Mother Road. One of them is a cupola resembling one half of a pineapple sliced in two, another the huge milk bottle of Townley Dairy, and a third the Classen Grill. Perhaps it's time to have lunch, to stop and park the car; after all, it was somewhere around here where the first parking meters were installed just before World War II.

Cavalry Road

Route 66 finds its way out of downtown Oklahoma City along a beautiful six-lane avenue. Finally, it joins the traffic stream of the new Highway I-44 where the Old Road is crammed under and on it. The first encounter between I-44 and Route 66 is short, as the Old Road turns west before the new one does. West of Oklahoma City both roads head West side by side, not far from each other, and sometimes together. The small town of Yukon was built toward the end of the nineteenth century, while gold rushes tempted people to Alaska and Canada and the Yukon River, the source of the town's name. The yellow we see here, however, is only golden grain, wheat, and corn. Large mills and silos line the roadsides. The cultivated fields go on until the horizon and probably even beyond it.

But Yukon is also on a cattle trail. The Cherokee trader Jesse Chisholm used this route in his pre-Civil War travels. After the war, his name stuck as cattle drives widened the trail from San Antonio in Texas to the railroad depot in Abilene, Kansas. At Yukon the Chisholm Trail from 1860 followed, generally, the present Ninth Street. Chisholm is buried only a few miles north of El Reno.

El Reno got its name from nearby Fort Reno. The fort was founded in 1876 in Indian country at a time when Major Marcus Reno waged war against Indians in the north. Initially, the fort operated as a training center for army horses, and during World War II it was a POW camp. When the railroad was built on the southern side of the Canadian River, many inhabitants of Reno City on the northern side of the shallow river moved their houses and belongings to the southern side. Due to a whim of somebody with a command of Spanish, the name of the town was given a Spanish masculine definite article. Canadian County Museum is located in an old Rock Island Railroad building there. The museum area also contains Darlington Indian Prison and the cottage used by General Philip Sheridan during the Indian Wars. Both were transferred here from their original sites. So were the Cheyennes and Arapahos, whose tribal offices are in nearby Concho, Oklahoma.

Part of the 1988 movie *Rain Man* was filmed in El Reno. Dustin Hoffman played the role of the autistic savant brother of Tom Cruise. Hoffman had fought for years to make the movie, and his efforts paid off. He won his second Best Actor Oscar and Barry Levinson the Best Director Oscar for their work on this film. It must have felt good, as

Levinson was the fourth director of the movie, after three had quit the project.

After El Reno, Route 66 crosses the South Canadian River on a bridge with no fewer than thirty-eight arches. The river is usually only a couple of arches wide, sometimes even less. During flood season, however, it can fill the entire riverbed and all the arches are necessary. Fields and pasture on both sides of the river make use of the water. The nearby town is called Bridgeport.

An interesting side trip for everyone interested in Native American history and culture is south from Bridgeport to Anadarko. The Native American Hall of Fame is there with small busts of famous Indians. Right next to it is a small but interesting museum. Further down the road, or actually up the hill, is Indian City USA, one of the saddest examples of how the many American Indians have been subdued by white tourism. There are "replicas" of villages of different Indian cultures that you can ride to see on a special train. The visitors' center is filled with junk.

Back to Route 66 and west, we drive through a number of small towns, insignificant to the rest of the world. These towns were, of course, never insignificant to the people living in them, nor to Route 66. The Road was the backbone of these towns and existed precisely for them. Several small bridges cross several small rivers on the stretch between Bridgeport and Weatherford. Whenever the Road goes down, you learn to expect a tiny creek and a bridge, and your expectation is usually fulfilled.

Lucille Hamon from Hydro had done everything you're supposed to do on Highway 66: she had managed a café, a grocery store, a gas station, and a motel. Sometimes all of them at once. When the officials removed the numbers of the Old Road in the mid-1980s, Lucille put up a new sign to replace the one gone with the wind to state that the Old Road is still alive. No wonder many still stop at her place even since her death in 2000. There is a little memorial on a wall across the road from her place, which has become almost a shrine dedicated to the "Mother of the Mother Road."

Before Clinton there's the Cherokee 66 Museum. It unites the Indian and Highway traditions, even though we are already far from the heart of Cherokee country. Clinton once was the home of Jack Cuthbert, Mr. 66. No wonder that the Oklahoma Route 66 Museum is there.

The museum claims that both Will Rogers and Route 66 are symbols of American optimism. Furthermore, they have become internationally known, sharing Oklahoma with the world. Please, step in and spend some time at the museum to pick up part of that optimism. When you get hungry, there is a Route 66 restaurant across the street.

Coming to town from the east, Route 66 climbs to the hill in the center of town. The historic Calmez Hotel soon appeared on the left, although it too, already in 1996, had seen better days and was demolished in the fall of 2000. On the right there used to be a landmark of the Old Road and a source of legends: the Pop Hicks Restaurant, owned by Howard and Mary Nichols. Definitely worth a stop. In 1996 we did stop. The food was good, the helpings were generous, and the price was reasonable. A small side room was dedicated to the Historic 66. After 1999 no need to stop anymore: Pop Hicks has burned down.

Going further up the hill the Old Route 66 goes here, there, or that way, depending on the narrator. One traveler's guide tells us to turn left along Fourth Street. The signs guide us to the curve a block further. Right along Frisco Avenue. Now where was Road 183? The town hall is on the same street as Pop Hicks was, just up the hill. Once the town housed a big tuberculosis hospital for American Indians. After confusion, you're back on the right road, or at least we were.

Elk City is bigger than it appears on the map. While Clinton is relatively compact, perched upon its hill, Elk City spreads in a ribbon on both sides of the Route, which makes a gently sloping S-shaped figure in the center. Nearby, to the left, traffic thunders on the new I-40. The museum complex of the old town of Elk City is located, amusingly, in the corners of Museum Drive and Pioneer Road with Route 66. Old Town Museum is one part of the complex. National Route 66 Museum another.

Elk City is also a cattle trail town and a railroad town. In these parts, what else could it be? Once the Great Western or Dodge City Cattle Trail moved cows through here from Central and West Texas to meet the railroad cars in Dodge City, bound for the slaughterhouses in Chicago. Eventually, the railway came to Elk City and ended the drives further north.

Elk City became a townsite in 1901 as a shipping center at the end of the Choctaw, Oklahoma, and Gulf Railway Line. Originally, the railhead was called Crowe, but to please the beer baron Adolphus Busch with hopes that he would establish a brewery in the town, it was re-named Busch. With no such luck, the town was renamed again after Elk Creek which runs through the city. The creek itself was named for an Indian chief, Elk River.

On both sides of Route 66 running across the town as its Main Street are various businesses and stores, including liquor stores and kiosks. Some of them are closed, though, and the paint is peeling off others. Have the good people of Elk City lost their appetite for booze? Dave Warren, now residing in Santa Fe, reminisces that when he worked in Oklahoma as a teacher, the state was completely dry. You were never-theless allowed to take your own bottle to a bar. They labeled the bottle with your name and kept it in the bar. When the need arose, the bar-tender would pour a drink for the owner of the bottle.

The situation has not improved drastically, as we experienced in Stroud. The same happened again at the Country Palace on the edge of Elk City, where we found plenty of live music and American beer. There were rows upon rows of bottles on the wall behind the counter, much as in any similar watering hole anywhere in the world. Howev-er, the Palace does not serve spirits. Well, in that case what are those bottles doing on the back wall? And why does the clientele sitting at ta-bles licking their lips drink something from small glasses next to their beer? The substitutes for spirits around these parts are various essences and juices. Yep, on closer inspection, that's what the back wall bottles contain. After all, they did mix tomato juice and beer at the Cue and Brew, didn't they? The Country Palace also has these cocktails.

At least two Oklahoma TV channels show nothing but country music or related programs. One of the channels concentrates on vid-eos by various artists, the other shows actual dancing. You can hardly talk about dancing to the music, however, as certain figures learned by heart clearly seem to be more important than the rhythm. This is also the case at Elk City's Country Palace, particularly when the live music stops and the players take a break. When the music starts coming off a record or television, people rush to the dance floor like groups of performers. The line dancing begins. The music and rhythm are not of much consequence. When the song is slower, we make these fig-ures; when it's faster, we dance like this. The correctness of the figures seems to be important, not keeping time with the rhythm. Is this type of line dancing another example of American individuality? A foreigner sometimes wonders if there is such a thing? Really?

A little more than twenty miles north of Route 66 on the shore of the Little Washita River is Black Kettle Park, nowadays Washita Battlefield National Historic Site. At this spot in 1868 George Armstrong Custer confronted the November frost and, with his regimental band accompanying him, led an attack on a peaceful Indian village. The cold froze the notes and the Indian corpses. The music stopped short, but the shooting went on until more than 100 people—90 of them women, children and old people, of course—and 875 horses had been killed. Black Kettle, the leader of this band of Southern Cheyennes, was among the casualties. Fifty-three imprisoned Cheyennes were force-marched almost a hundred miles to Fort Supply. Among the prisoners Custer found himself a woman to console him, on long journeys where his white wife Elisabeth could not follow. The Cheyenne woman gave Custer a son. He might have had children with other Indian women as well, but he had none with Elisabeth.

There we have another Dustin Hoffman connection. In 1970 he played the role of Jack Crabb in *Little Big Man* from early boyhood to an old age of 121 years. The movie turns western facts, or should I say myths, upside down in a hilarious manner. As a good comedy, this one also makes you not just laugh but also cry and, perhaps most importantly, think. One of the great scenes depicts the Washita River Massacre with the pompous Custer and the deceived Indians. In the film, Crabb became the real hero of the battle, not Custer, but Crabb was on the Indian side.

Sayre is a town on the Red River, although the present town center lies quite a distance from the water. The Beckham County Courthouse has become world famous after appearing in John Ford's film version of *The Grapes of Wrath*. After Sayre, the 66 and I-40 cross the river. It's said that an Indian uprising of 1959 happened on the Old Route 66 bridge. The bridge itself was burned and barricades blocked the way there. When travelers slowed down to take the detour, Sayre high school students advised them to shut their car windows and head west as fast as they could, as the "bloodthirsty" Indians who had burned the bridge were on the "warpath". It took the highway patrolmen the better part of the day to calm down the tourists who were breaking speed limits and to convince them that the Indian uprising was nothing more than a high school gag.

At one time speeding was also a problem in the town of Erick. Around World War II, a policeman named Elmer excelled at slowing down the cars driving through the town. Some young people tried to escape, but their cars were no match for Elmer's black 1938 model V-8 Ford. Elmer was so efficient that tourists began to steer clear of Erick. Comedian Bob Hope, who had received a speeding ticket from Elmer, announced in his radio show that from now on he would only go through Erick on the back of a donkey. Finally, Elmer was transferred to other duties so that the town's tourist business wouldn't go completely bankrupt. But even today some travelers on the Old 66 tell how they have seen a black Ford appear from out of nowhere in their rearview mirrors on black nights when their speed is about to hit the limit.

However fast we travel, we eventually get to Texola. Unfortunately, there is no activity there. The town is almost already in Texas, wherever the state line may go. No sign marks it on the Old Road. Maybe the border has also been buried under the new interstate highway.

6

The Panhandle

Still on Cattle Town Road

When there is no river to cross or any other clear natural borderline, moving from one state to the next often goes unnoticed. Who would bother to register each sign by the roadside—if they even exist in the first place? The border between Oklahoma and Texas can nevertheless be determined, if not by the inch, at least approximately. A natural line, as it was, something abstract and invisible, has always separated the states. Politicians and registered land surveyors need draw no line since the wind would soon erase it anyway. The borderline is noticeable because the real West begins on the border of Oklahoma and Texas. In the minds of the ordinary people, "West" means barren plains, tall mountains, Mexicans, and Indians. At least the dry plains begin on the Texas border, and the other phenomena of the real West are quick to follow.

Here Route 66 really is the road to the West. It ran from east to west and its remains still do. The length of the highway across the second largest state was 178 miles from Texola to Glenrio. No less than 91 percent of this highway is still used, mainly as a service road for the new Interstate 40, or as local branch roads. The Old 66 serves as the frontage road along the southern side of the new highway for roughly eighty-eight of the eastern miles and along the northern side for the rest of the miles. Often the 66 ends in a cul-de-sac, and some of it is unpaved dirt road.

"Interstate 40 spans the Texas Panhandle like an endless airport

runway. Cars and trucks hurry east and west and disappear into infinity," writes Michael Wallis in his *Route 66: The Mother Road*. "Heat
waves rise from the pavement and hang over water mirages pooled
across the width of the road. In these parts, when it gets very hot or,
in the dead of winter, when blizzards howl out of the north, drivers
often wish the linear interstate were just an illusion and that the old
highway—U.S. Route 66—would reappear."

Only a small nook of big Texas is affected by the Old 66 or the new
I-40. The highways split only the northwestern corner of Texas, the Panhandle, as they run on the northern edge of the Staked Plains or Llano
Estacado. Some say that landform was named for the fortress-like appearance of its escarpments, but there is also a more interesting story
behind the name, and more likely true. This wide plains area in western Texas and eastern New Mexico was in the opinion of the Spanish
invaders so void of landmarks that, in order to keep from losing their
way, they would drive stakes into the ground to mark where they had
come from and thus be able to find their way back. Later, European settlers built villages and towns on the plains. Despite today's landmarks,
the Staked Plains still appears entirely empty in places as far as the eye
can see. And here it can see further than in most places. The Lubbock
singer/songwriter Butch Hancock has said that the Llano is so flat that
you can see for fifty miles in any direction, and if you stand on a tuna
can, you can see for a hundred miles.

From an American Indian point of view, the area has never been
empty. Before the arrival of whites, thousands of buffalo wandered
across the Panhandles of both Texas and Oklahoma, followed by
groups of Apaches and other Indians. The Mexican sheepherders
coming from the south built the first European villages, often right in
the middle of Indian country. When American cattlemen arrived, the
sheepherders and Indians withdrew, the latter often only after resistance.

The climate of the Panhandle varies, but it is almost always windy.
An old saying has it that before going out, you had better stick an iron
bar out the door. If the bar does not bend, it's okay to go out. If the
wind is hard enough to bend the bar, you should stay inside.

The summers are hot and dry in the Texas Panhandle and most of
northern Oklahoma. Early drivers always packed extra cans of water.
If the children didn't need it, the car did. It is still a good idea to pack

plenty of water. The wind can bring in thunderstorms and even floods from the Gulf of Mexico. A wind coming from Hudson's Bay far up north may also create rather nasty surprises in the form of dust storms or even blizzards that can drop temperatures by dozens of degrees in a moment. Woody Guthrie himself witnessed a fierce dust storm in Pampa, in the Texas Panhandle, in 1935. In the summer of 1996, we escaped a hurricane east of Vega by half an hour, and, in the spring of 2002, we experienced a tornado watch that covered the Texas Panhandle and most of Oklahoma.

The most magnificent thunderstorms are reputed to be seen on the Llano Estacado. I have experienced thunder there twice and can validate the stories. In my first storm, the lightning in the northern sky was breathtakingly beautiful. The lines of light were sharp between the sky and the earth. The second time I awoke in Vega in the middle of the night, aroused by a strange light streaming in from the open bathroom window. For a moment, I thought that something was burning behind the motel. I heard no sound of thunder and no sound of rain hitting the roof, and I saw no sharp flashes of lightning, only the strange changing light. The rains didn't come until early in the morning. Heavy, violent, Texan. The rain ceased for a moment and the next minute our car was battered by such a hailstorm that my brother and I seriously thought the windshield would shatter at any second. We were both protecting our faces with our hands in case it really did shatter. After the storm had passed, my brother tried to regain his composure by smoking a cigarette in the parked car—with the window open, true enough, although he had promised not to smoke inside the car.

Due to the north wind, winters are frequently cold and sometimes snowy in the Panhandle. The wind will whirl even a small amount of snow so violently that snow fences line the roads; people plant hedges and trees to block the wind. Of course, the trees also help bind the soil threatened by erosion. The fruitful topsoil is as loose today as it was during the Great Depression. The soil itself is rich on the northern side of the Staked Plains, however. It produces plenty of good pasture for cattle but also—at least when there's enough water—corn, wheat, and vegetables. There are also riches underground, oil and natural gas in particular.

The oil town of Shamrock is located on the spot where the Old 66 and the new I-40 meet Highway 60/83 running from Mexico to Canada. At the crossroads, there's the most famous sight of the town, Nunn's Café, with its rather tall art deco tower. J. M. Tindall, the founder of the café, named his restaurant the U-Drop-In on April Fool's Day, 1936, but it soon became simply Nunn's Café. The story has it that Tindall's friend John Nunn, who designed the house, drew the plans in the sand with a nail and left the nail sticking out of the ground. The builders took the nail to symbolize a tower—and so the café got a tower, and Route 66 a landmark. The café was for sale in the summer of 1996. Six years later we still found no activity in it. Nowadays, however, the Shamrock Chamber of Commerce occupies this famous landmark.

The area around Shamrock is seldom green. Once a year, on St. Patrick's Day, the people of Shamrock celebrate the patron saint of Ireland so enthusiastically that all the other Panhandle towns turn green from envy. And why not? An Irish immigrant, George Nickel, named the town Shamrock, in 1893.

West of Shamrock old neon signs are reminders of livelier days on Route 66. A big Texan sign announces the greatness, maybe even megalomania, of Texans. (Don't take this wrong; I am proud to be an adopted Texan, after living deep in the heart of the state several times.) What is big in the Panhandle today is the all-embracing, all-covering monotony and similarity of the interstate highway concrete belt bypassing almost all of the towns. It urges you to drive across the Panhandle quickly, to a place sheltered from scorching sun, treeless plain, thunder, and hailstorms. The Old 66 visited each village and town. Each village was different. And as national radio commentator, writer, public speaker, and politician Jim Hightower says in the title of his populist critique of American politics, there's nothing in the middle of the road (in our case I-40) but yellow stripes and dead armadillos.

On the Old Road, even animals had enough time to cross safely. Sometimes you can still see rattlesnakes, prairie dogs, and jackrabbits. Someone even claims to have met a jackalope, a horned jackrabbit, the most wonderful animal of the wide West, and—according to legend—the result of a love affair between a jackrabbit and an antelope. On the new highway the thunder of the trucks numbs the ears. Under a full-moon night on the Old Road, those with keen ears can hear the jackalope's song. Or is it just the wind, carrying a melody into the dreams of a lonely cowboy?

The road preceded the railroad in the Texas Panhandle, and, when the rails were laid on the prairie, they required several crossings. The railroad became the Texas Panhandle's link to the East before Route 66, however. At the turn of the century, the town of McLean was built as a Rock Island Railroad cattle-loading station. The English rancher Alfred Lowe split enough land from his ranch to house the town and named it after Railroad Commissioner W. P. McLean in 1903. Nine years later, Rowe decided to visit his homeland. He returned—or rather did not return—on the *Titanic*.

Initially, cattle and the railroad nourished McLean. Then oil was found nearby in 1927, and Route 66 came to town. An unprecedented boom lasted until the new highway was constructed to pass the town on the south side. The townspeople opposed the construction of the new highway, but there was no stopping the residents elsewhere or their interests. In the summer of 1984 the traffic lights were removed from the new highway, and I-40 was now free to carry both travelers and goods past McLean and also from McLean.

The Devil's Rope Museum recalls the heroes of the Old Road at the Route 66 Hall of Fame. In front of the museum more than a bouquet of barbed wire tells the ignorant what devil's rope is. The ranchers who were proponents of open fields and opponents of the farmers' desire to fence their cultivated fields and vegetable gardens considered barbed wire the devil's gift to humanity. There is a map on the wall of the museum where visitors from around the world can attach pins to mark their hometowns. There were plenty of pins from Germany and elsewhere in central Europe, even four pins from Sweden. In 1996 we were there too early to see the museum open, but in 2002 we made sure that there is also now a pin from Finland.

In the middle of McLean, the Texas 66 Society has restored the first Phillips 66 service station in Texas to delight tourists and townspeople alike. Elsewhere in the town, murals remind us of the town's past heydays.

Some twenty miles west of McLean lies Allanreed, yet another town repelled by the new highway. It is true that Allanreed was not one of the absolute favorites of the Old Road either. Although the 66 originally ran through the town, it was relocated to pass the town on the northern side in the 1950s. Motels advertised Allanreed as a place where you could sleep undisturbed by the noise of highway traffic. Allanreed was born with the railroad when the team building it reached the place in 1902 and erected a water tower for the train to collect water from nearby springs. Originally, the town was even called Springtown or Spring Tank. Some people called it Prairie Dog, because there were plenty of those little rodents around. Finally, the present name combined the surnames of two businessmen, Allan and Reed.

The next town on the Old Road is also a railroad town. It, too, was founded in 1902 and got its name from Colonel B. B. Groom who, like Alfred Rowe, was a wealthy rancher. The land was cheap and the soil rich, and thus many other farmers of wheat, corn, and cattle moved there within a few years' time. Eventually, Highway 66 arrived to complete the connections with the railroad and the telegraph.

One of the pioneers in the area was Henry S. Boydstun, who moved to Texas from Illinois in 1890 at thirty-two years of age. His small son died in the same year and was buried on the family's farm. In 1898 Boydstun donated the two acres of land around his son's grave for a public cemetery. A small farming community with a school and a post office was already growing around the farm. The post office operated from 1891 to 1940, when it was closed and Boydstun was annexed to Groom.

Just outside Groom, religion on the Old Road grows to Texan measurements. The Cross of Our Lord Jesus Christ is the largest cross in the Western Hemisphere and shows off to some fifteen miles. Its total height is 190 feet, its arm span 110 feet, its weight 1,250 tons. Around the cross there are statues depicting the thirteen stations of Christ's Via Dolorosa. There is a visitors' center and a museum housing a life-size copy of the Shroud of Turin, the piece of cloth that supposedly was on Jesus when he was buried.

West of Groom there are more of the dying, and even dead, small towns. Grain is still being grown here. Windmills pump water from deep artesian wells in the fields, and mills and warehouses line the road. For a short time in the late 1920s, the 66 ran to Washburn as a dirt road until it found a more northern route to Amarillo. Before Amarillo, however, we drive past the slanting water tower of Britten and the big grain silos of Conway, both famous landmarks of the Old Route 66. In Conway, there's also the Bug Ranch, modeled after the more famous Cadillac Ranch yet to come further down the Road in western Amarillo. Here half a dozen Volkswagen bugs are standing partly underground. Right next to it is the Conway Restaurant. It's a nice family place. You should try their soup of beans. That will keep you going for a long time, probably through all the Texas towns mentioned in the

Grapes of Wrath: "And this day the cars crawled on and on, through the Panhandle of Texas. Shamrock and Alanreed, Groom and Yarnell. Then went through Amarillo in the evening, drove too long, and camped when it was dusk. . . . The land turtles crawled through the dust and the sun whipped the earth, and in the evening the heat went out of the sky and the earth sent up a wave of heat from itself. . . . The land rolled like great stationary ground-swells. Wildorado and Vega and Bosie and Glenrio."

Yellow and Red Land

Texas Panhandle is a land so strange. "People who live on this land are afflicted either with the fierce loyalty known only to those who

have learned to hold adversity lightly in their hands, or the equally burning desire to get the hell out of here," claims Tom Snyder and the *Route 66 Traveler's Guide*.

Some thirty miles south of Amarillo runs the Palo Duro River, formerly the scene of frequent skirmishes between Indians and settlers, which is not surprising. While the plains are nothing but emptiness and desolation all the way to infinity, it is as if God wished to create an opposite precisely to emphasize the emptiness. Palo Duro Canyon, the canyon of the hard wood, is beautiful. Trees, water, flowers, cliffs, colors. The dream of the West at its best. It was a place worth fighting for in the middle of the Staked Plains.

Once, this was the heart of the Comanchería, the empire of the Comanche Indians. Palo Duro Canyon provided shelter, water, and grass for their many horses. In hard winters, it was one of the few places for that in the southern Plains. But Comanche trading and white commercialism could not work together for more than a century. The Indian horses and trading had to give way for white business, ranching, and farming. The Comanche territory was reduced first to an area in southwestern Oklahoma south of

Route 66, later to a small reservation around Fort Sill. The reservation is gone, but the Comanche Nation is still centered there.

Two confrontations in Palo Duro Canyon have been preserved in white annals more accurately than others. In 1868 a team of white buffalo hunters were ambushed by Indians and suffered a defeat. Six years later Colonel Ranald McKenzie beat a band of Comanches almost in the same place, and Chief Quanah Parker was forced to capitulate. Now the canyon holds a state park, a visitors' center, a store, and a museum of the Plains Indians. In the summertime there are outdoor performances of the romantic musical "Texas."

Amarillo has almost two hundred thousand inhabitants, and after the small Panhandle towns, it seems really big. Freeways crisscross east, south, and west. The new I-40 runs past the city on the southern side in an almost metropolitan multilayered crossing with highways I-27, 60, 87, and 287. In downtown Amarillo several blocks of tall buildings break the monotony of the flatlands. If not for the buildings, one could see two days away. That's how flat the terrain is. Even the singer is lost and short of landmarks while begging: "Show Me the Way to Amarillo."

But if you are not lost, you will find your way to the heart of the city on Old Route 66. You can find many fine and uplifted 66 places here. Southwest Sixth Avenue is one of the best remaining city sections of the Old Road, superseded perhaps only by a similar section in Albuquerque, farther west. Park your car and walk for a while. Drop in to the many stores and cafés along the street. You'll soon find that the word "Texan" does indeed mean "friendly."

Amarillo is an old cattle town. Large roasts and T-bone steaks are still the pride of Amarillo restaurants. The Big Texan promises a free four-and-a-half pound piece of beef—if you can eat it in one hour. The appetizer is a shrimp cocktail, and, of course, there is also baked potato, salad, and wheat bread to consume with your meal. If you can't eat it all, the meal will cost more than seventy bucks.

The founder of the Big Texan is R. J. "Bob" Lee from Kansas. In the 1950s, he was disappointed to find that the kind of real Western restaurant he had imagined and hoped for couldn't be found in Amarillo. So he founded one himself, on Route 66, of course. When I-40 was opened in 1968, Lee moved his restaurant there, and the business is still going great. But can anybody eat beef weighing four and a half pounds, plus all the fixings? According to Big Texan's Book of Fame, some five thousand people have.

If you are following the Old Route 66, and even if you are not lost, you may not find the Big Texan. There are signs well before the place, but when you get closer, the signs disappear, particularly if you follow the Route 66 signs. I think you can actually ask whether the Big Texan really is still a Route 66 restaurant; if it's not on Route 66, how can it truly be a famous Route 66 business? Perhaps the Big Texan once was on 66, and we can think about it as one of the legends of the Old Road, but when it moved next to I-40, did it not give away its birthright? Money, I am sure, is better on the new interstate, and the Big Texan has, indeed, prospered, but those traveling on the Old Road will not go by it. In the countryside the sphere of 66 reaches wider in all directions, as it still provides the road you need to take. In cities, where you have other options, I think that only those right on 66 can claim to be Route 66 sites and businesses.

Amarillo used to be a collecting place for buffalo hides before the arrival of the ranchers. With the arrival of cows, the city's leather industry has grown even more. The city is also the largest helium producer in the world and a center of the nuclear-weapons industry. The end of the Cold War caused economic problems as Amarillo switched from making nuclear weapons to taking them apart. The Catholic bishop of Amarillo became a national celebrity in the 1980s for his sermons against nuclear weapons in a city making its living from them.

Spaniards gave the place its name "Amarillo," meaning "yellow," because of the yellow beaches of a lake south of the city. When the town was organized in 1887, its initial name was Oneida. The name was changed when the town became the center of the county. Anglos claim that the name is due to the fact that so many of the houses in Amarillo had yellow paint at the time. In that case, why didn't they call the town Yellow? Would it perhaps have been too cowardly?

In Amarillo the 66 once again takes several routes. Even before the introduction of the federal highway system, the Ozark Trail highway from east to west ran through the city. Later, it became a part of the paved 66. At that time the route suggestion of the 66 had already been changed five times. In 1938 many people spoke of the Road as the Will Rogers Memorial Highway, although the name was not officially changed before the caravan of 1952. Route 66 changed its path once more after 1952.

The most famous sight in Amarillo, also firmly connected to the history of Route 66, is the Cadillac Ranch on the western edge of the city. The founder, Stanley Marsh 3 (three, not third), was born in Amarillo on January 31, 1938, and calls himself a dust bowl baby. Highway 66 is an important part of Marsh's childhood. The dream of his youth was to drive a pink Cadillac down to California along Highway 66 in the company of a beautiful blonde. Having had enough adventure, Marsh founded the Cadillac Ranch in 1974 and staked ten Cadillacs representing models from 1948 to 1964 upright into the ground. In the summer of 1997 the Ranch moved some two miles west in order to avoid the expanding Amarillo city limits.

The Cadillac Ranch is so famous that you would think there had to be a visitors' center and souvenir shop there. This is (fortunately) not the case. The Cadillacs just stand there in the middle of a field. Tourists wandering in to have a closer look have trampled a hard-packed path all the way from the highway. There is hardly anything as important and at the same time as unusually noncommercial on Route 66. Once and for all, a downright charming place.

A couple of miles west, there's a Love's Travel Stop with a gas station and the Texas Trading Company beside it. The Trading Company sells everything, of course, but it also tries to maintain the fame of the Old Road, not only as America's Main Street but also as the Main Street of the Texas Panhandle. There is a big difference. The Texans of course feel the latter to be the greater honor.

Next on Route 66, come Bushland, Wildorado, and Vega. Water-pumping windmills stand by the roadside. In Wildorado there at least used to be the Tumble Weed Café, which is only fitting. The wind has teased the cars by moving this barbed weed bush of the West on the road for some time already. From here on, we saw some tumbleweed every day.

A film with the name *Tumbleweeds* first appeared as a silent in 1925 starring perhaps the first of the celluloid western heroes, William S. Hart. Although he had an excellent speaking voice, he decided to retire when the talkies began, as he was tired of the movie business. He appeared once more, however, in an introduction to the reissue of *Tumbleweeds* in 1939.

One of the now traditional songs of the West also relates to this weed, "Tumbling Tumbleweeds." Bob Nolan's lyrics are a brilliant description of the American ideal and national character, "lonely but free." The most famous singer of the song, Orvon Gene Autry, was even nicknamed "the Cowboy." Autry, however, was not just an ordinary cowpuncher. He made his first record in 1929, when he was known as the "Yodeling Cowboy." He moved to motion pictures after having

a popular music program on the radio. In 1934 Autry played a singing cowboy for the first time in *In Old Santa Fe*. His real break came a year later in—what else?—*Tumbling Tumbleweeds*, in which he appeared with Roy Rogers. Autry sang the song again in the 1945 western *Don't Fence Me In*; Rogers sang it in *Silver Spurs* in 1943 and also in *Hollywood Canteen*. The Sons of the Pioneers, founded by Rogers, made the first commercial recording of the song in 1934. Bing Crosby made it a hit in 1940.

All and all, Gene Autry recorded some six hundred songs, mostly westerns, but also "Rudolph the Red-Nosed Reindeer." The latter has sold more than ten million copies and has had probably as many versions and translations into foreign languages as Bobby Troup's "Get Your Kicks." Nevertheless, the cowboy image was what Autry liked and wanted to preserve. Even in the army during World War II, he wore cowboy boots with his uniform. After 1956 he dedicated his life to his many businesses. He owned several radio and television stations, hotels, oil wells, and even the California (nowadays the Anaheim) Angels baseball team. It was not usually a winning team and Autry's widow, Jackie, later sold the team to Disney. In 1988 Autry established the Gene Autry Western Heritage Museum in Los Angeles. He was "Back in the Saddle Again," a song that hit the charts once more in 1993 with the movie *Sleepless in Seattle*. Autry died in 1998 at the age of ninety-one, only three months after Roy Rogers.

On Route 66 in the Southwest, the tumbleweed truly is a ubiquitous friend to cowboys on horses or in cars. Not too many of the wandering cowboys or their fans are likely to know, however, that the tumble-weed is an old Russian thistle and was brought to North America by immigrants sometime during the nineteenth century. This symbol of the West then is really an eastern product—but aren't they all? Isn't the West really a product of the hopes and wishes of easterners? Perhaps of their fears, too.

Vega is in the middle of the plains. On the Old Road, the Sands Motel is operated by the Best Western chain as the Best Western Country Inn. It offers the traveler tidy accommodation at a reasonable price. There's a restaurant next to the Sands, and the motel guests get a discount. The friendly dynasty of the Hall family used to govern the locality, maybe still does. Gerald was the manager of all Best Western Hotels in area 5-2, Stephen R. was the managing director of the motel, and Michael managed not only the motel but the restaurant as well.

West of Vega, many towns on the Old Road are already dead. The wind wiped away Ontario a long time ago. (Perhaps carried it far north and made it the central province of Canada.) Landergrin was never more than a few shacks between the road and the railroad anyway, yet George Rook's Route 66 Antiques, dedicated to the Old Road, used to hang in there. Adrian is also left. There, too, a landmark of the Old Road called the Bent Door Café is breathing its last. The window has already been shattered for years in this restaurant, originally put together from the remains of an old flight control tower. Some efforts seem to be underway to uplift the roadside. A new opening day for the Bent Door Café was planned to be June 1, 2007. It seems as the planning still continues.

Some people think that Vega is the center point of Route 66, and that belief may underlie an effort to revitalize the town. Others are of the opinion that Adrian, just short of the New Mexico border, is the halfway point. At least there is a small marker and the Midpoint Café across the street from it. Regardless of which direction you may be taking, at some point near here you have traveled half the journey. Both Chicago and Santa Monica are a good 1,100 miles away. You may be correct, whether you pick Vega or Adrian. The United States is a free country, and Route 66 is a free road.

Glenrio is also on the Texas side of the New Mexico border. Or is it? There is a difference of opinion, but in reality the town is divided between the two states. Does it matter, anyway? To Texans it does matter, to Glenrio people maybe not, whether the townspeople of Glenrio are true Texans. No sign marks the state line on the Old Road.

Some people feel that the West begins at the eastern border of Kansas or Oklahoma. Others think that the West begins after Oklahoma City and the real West, with a capital "W," only on the border of Texas. Some people include Texas in the Southwest. Those who think they know better claim that the Southwest won't start until the New Mexico border. The 1992 *American Southwest* edition of the *Inside Guides* has an opinion of its own:

> Makers of maps like to keep things orderly and tend to define the American Southwest in terms of state boundaries. But those who live in it, and love it, and consider time spent elsewhere a sort of exile, know another type of boundary must be applied. The Southwest begins where the land rises out of that vast ocean of humid air which covers Midland America and makes it the fertile breadbasket of half the world. And it ends along the vague line where winter cold wins out over the sun, and the valleys—as well as the high country—are buried under snow. There is one more ever essential requirement. Wherever you stand in the Southwest there must be somewhere, on one horizon or another, the spirit healing blue shape of mountains.

7

Land of the Zia Sun

The Land of Enchantment

According to Tom Snyder, "New Mexico is descended from the sky." His guidebook for the Road claims that "other places along old Route 66 have been formed from rivers, mountains, and plains. Other states have been forged by iron-willed men meeting in urgency behind closed doors to make a truce, a compromise, a set of defensible boundaries. But New Mexico has no door on its history, no roof on its being. The first allegiance of most people here is to the land and to the generous sky above."

The sky and the earth meet on the Great Plains. But in western New Mexico and Arizona the Plains do not reach the horizon. Cliffs eroded by the wind, rain, and sand, or snow-capped mountains cut the journey of the Plains short. The sky and the earth never meet, but their yearning for each other creates the tension and the enchantment, the charm of the American Southwest.

New Mexico truly is a land of enchantment. Its symbol is the Zia Indian sun figure with golden or orange rays. New Mexico is the heartland of the Southwest. It is the land of Indians, Hispanos, and Anglos. New Mexico has always been Indian country. In relation to Route 66, the Apaches are in the south, the Comanches are in the east, the Pueblos are in the middle, and the Navajos in the west.

New Mexico has been Hispano or Chicano country for a long time, too. The expedition of Francisco Vásquez de Coronado sought golden cities from this area between 1540 and 1542 and had to confront Pueblo Indians defending their possessions. As a result of Coronado's excursion, Catholic priests stayed in the area and new Spanish expeditions followed one another. Gradually, the area became Spanish. Or so it appeared until in 1680 when Indians from several pueblos rebelled and drove the Spaniards all the way back to El Paso. New Mexico belonged to American Indians once more, but only for twelve years. In 1692 Spain sent a strong military detachment that suppressed the rebel Indians and reestablished Santa Fe as the capital. When Mexico declared itself independent in 1820, New Mexico became its northern province.

Texas, the northeastern province of Mexico, declared its independence in 1836, and demanded New Mexican territory east of the Rio Grande. Texans even set out to conquer Santa Fe, but the attempt came to nothing, even before Mexican soldiers had beaten the would-be conquerors. In 1845 Texas joined the United States. This led to a war between the United States and Mexico. In the war, the US conquered almost one third of Mexico's territory. In the Treaty of Guadeloupe Hidalgo in 1848, Mexico ceded most of New Mexico, Arizona, and California to the United States. This is how New Mexico became Anglo country.

In the Southwest, everybody but the Indians and Spanish-speakers are Anglos, not merely white people speaking English. This means that in New Mexico, blacks and Asians are also Anglos. After the Anglo conquest, New Mexico and Arizona were made into territories, and they became states in 1912. Today, New Mexico has more than two million inhabitants; some 195,000 are American Indians and a good 600,000 are Spanish-speakers. Probably several thousand illegal Spanish-speaking aliens also live in the state.

New Mexico is mainly dry plateau, but particularly in the north pine trees provide wood for forestry. There are tall mountains up north; Wheeler Peak reaches an altitude of more than thirteen thousand feet. The Continental Divide formed by the Rockies runs through western New Mexico. East of the divide, the waters run to the Gulf of Mexico; west of it, to the Bay of California.

The old Highway 66 ran all the way across New Mexico. From the Texas border to the Pecos River, the country is still the northern edge of the Staked Plains. This plateau is some sixty square miles of very rough terrain. Comanches once hunted buffalo here. Coronado called the area America's great desert. In 1849 Captain Randolph B. Marcy described the Llano Estacado as the great Sahara of North America, as wide as an ocean, where even the "savages" dared travel only along well-known trails certain to have water.

During the California gold rush, Marcy looked for a trail from Fort Smith, Arkansas, to Santa Fe. Navy Lieutenant Edward Fitzger-ald Beale believed the image of the Sahara, and nine years later, in 1858, before searching for a suitable cart road from Fort Smith to the Colo-rado River and California, he had camels brought from Africa for use by the US Army. This experiment did not work out. A few camels es-caped and bred in remote regions. Some people claim that offspring of the beasts are still wandering in the most distant and deserted areas.

The cart road explored by Beale created the foundation for later roads, Highway 66 and the present I-40 among them. Beale predicted that the route he charted would be-come a major migration route to California, and that is exactly what happened. Almost all traffic on 66 during the Depression was headed toward California. Between the Texas border and Tucumcari, Route 66 was a very dangerous road. It was narrow, full of holes, and badly maintained. According to Michael Wallis, many inhabitants of the area considered the construction of I-40 a blessing.

In the Footsteps of Indians and Spaniards

Glenrio is half in Texas, half in New Mexico. The road headed west from the town changes immediately into a gravel road not very tempt-ing to follow. There is no sign bidding you welcome to New Mexico; only a small pole by the roadside marks the state line. On the Texas side, the ruins of the last or the first motel in Texas, depending on whether you come from east or west, stands as a reminder of days gone by. A few other buildings repeat the message. The only intersection leading to Glenrio from the new highway is on the Texas side of the border. We have to return there to continue our journey west.

No matter where Glenrio is, Endee, Bard, and San Jon are definitely

New Mexico. At the crossroads in Endee is a forsaken Café & Motel on what used to be Route 66. In San Jon, Country Crossroads sells Route 66 trinkets. Nearly thirty miles from the state border a monument states that Comanches once hunted buffalo in the area. Later, their trails were followed by Santa Fe Trail merchants, and Pedro Vial probably returned this way to St. Louis from the first American trading trip to Santa Fe around the year 1790.

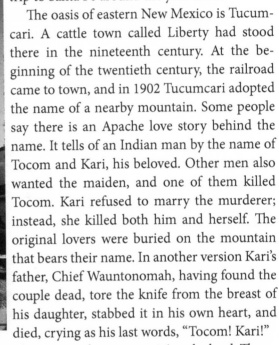

The oasis of eastern New Mexico is Tucumcari. A cattle town called Liberty had stood there in the nineteenth century. At the beginning of the twentieth century, the railroad came to town, and in 1902 Tucumcari adopted the name of a nearby mountain. Some people say there is an Apache love story behind the name. It tells of an Indian man by the name of Tocom and Kari, his beloved. Other men also wanted the maiden, and one of them killed Tocom. Kari refused to marry the murderer; instead, she killed both him and herself. The original lovers were buried on the mountain that bears their name. In another version Kari's father, Chief Wauntonomah, having found the couple dead, tore the knife from the breast of his daughter, stabbed it in his own heart, and died, crying as his last words, "Tocom! Kari!"

Tucumcari is Comanche country, however, not Apache land. Therefore, it may be that the love story of Tocom and Kari is an Anglo product, although the Apache leader Geronimo himself reputedly recited the tale. In the Comanche language "tukumukaru," or something like that, means a place to rest or lie while waiting for someone to approach. In other words, a lookout point. The mountain of Tucumcari, rising 4,967 feet above sea level, is a good place from where to observe the surrounding plains.

Tucumcari is a Route 66 town to the core and in the full meaning of the word. The new interstate slaps it in the face, but it has nevertheless remained an important farming town and a significant tourist center. The roadside signs that urged travelers to stay in "Tucumcari tonight" have become a Southwest legend. The Blue Swallow is one of the Old Road monuments related to this slogan. Lillian Redman, for years the owner of this 1939 motel, was born in Texas but traveled to New Mexico in a wagon with her father in 1915. She later worked in various parts of the Southwest as a Harvey Girl. In 1958 her husband Floyd gave her the Blue Swallow as a gift. In the late 1990s she began to consider retiring, and eventually she did. New owners Dale and Hilda Bakke installed new telephones in every room, but of the old round dial mode instead of the more modern touchdown keypad machines. Recent owners Terri and Bill Kinder kept the tradition of hospitality alive, although the motel was closed for the winter months. Currently, Nancy and Kevin Mueller manage the Blue Swallow in a true 66 fashion.

Almost opposite the Blue Swallow is Tepee Curios, a shop specializing in souvenirs and especially in Indian jewelry. The tepee picture of the shop's advertisement links Tepee Curios to the long tradition, according to which all Indians are alike, and to the Route 66 tradition, according to which the Road opened the market to Southwest Indian products. Attracting the passing tourists is vital to business. In this sense the picture of the tepee is efficient, because everybody knows it means Indians. And, in Tucumcari, why not? The Comanches used to live in tepees.

In Tucumcari, Route 66 travels right through the town on Tucumcari Boulevard and on Old Route 66 Boulevard. It is lined with motels and cafeterias. Blue Swallow, Apache Motel, Palomino Motel, Paradise Inn, Ranch House Café. If you want Mexican food, you can always make an appointment for a date in La Cita. On the western end of the boulevard stands the convention center with a stylized 66 monument in front.

Nevertheless, the 66 Boulevard is not the Main Street of the town, although you are easily inclined to think so. The real Main Street and the actual downtown are some six or seven blocks north on Highway 54 and closer to the railroad. The train station is of Spanish style, but the passenger train seems not to have stopped there for ages.

West of Tucumcari the Road begins to rise higher from the Staked Plains. Montoya, Newkirk, and Cuervo ("little raven") are hardly anything but names on a map. Even the new church in Newkirk was destroyed a long time ago, and the church built to replace it is not very new either. In Cuervo a gas station is still open, however, and even the church looked better preserved.

The famous Goodnight cattle trail used to run north between Montoya and Newkirk. This trail, opened in 1866 and used for some twenty years, steering clear of the most dangerous Indian areas, went from the cattle herding area in Texas to the railroad in the north. That is where rancher Charles Goodnight drove his cattle, loaded them in the train, and delivered them to Chicago slaughterhouses and the meat packers in the East.

The land in eastern New Mexico is rich with Western lore and early American history. The trail that Captain Marcy and Lieutenant Simpson took from Arkansas to Santa Fe in 1849, "opened" in 1840 by Josiah Gregg, runs parallel with Route 66 and I-40. Some sixty miles south by southwest from Tucumcari is Clovis, which gave its name to a certain type of arrowheads believed to be some eight to ten thousand years old. The actual discovery was made still another ten miles south at Blackwater Draw in 1932. For decades it led scholars to believe that humans had entered North America only around the time of the Clovis Point or maybe no more than two thousand years earlier. Recently, new discoveries and new scholarship have challenged the Clovis Theory. Many scientists believe that humans have inhabited the Americas at least forty thousand if not sixty thousand years. Some talk even of one hundred thousand years, and few believe the Americas to be the original home for the human species.

Fifty miles south of Cuervo is Fort Sumner State Monument. It is a reminder of even a sadder story of the chronicle of US Indian policy. After Kit Carson had beaten the Navajos in 1864, some eight thousand Navajos were taken as prisoners to Bosque Redondo, where fires and drought had destroyed all trees ages ago. A little later approximately two thousand Apaches were made to follow their cousins. Neither of the Athabascan Indian groups liked the place guarded by soldiers of Fort Sumner. Many of the Athabascans escaped, many died. Only five years later the Navajos got permission to return to their home west of the Continental Divide after difficult and long negotiations.

Billy the Kid, a.k.a. William Bonney, is one of the outlaws of the Wild West. He boasted of having killed as many men as he had lived years. He got himself mixed up with a battle of cattle barons. Even when a truce was made, Billy continued fighting to avenge the deaths of his friends. Eventually, Sheriff Pat Garrett shot him in one of the houses of Fort Sumner in 1874, and Billy is buried in a graveyard nearby. Nowadays, there is an iron fence around the grave to prevent the stealing of the gravestone.

West of Santa Rosa, a really old trail crosses Route 66. In search of the mystic golden city of Quivira, Francisco Vásquez de Coronado camped in Puerto de Luna for four days in the spring of 1541 while his men built a bridge over the Pecos River. The village is still there with a church and a more modern bridge.

Santa Rosa, like Tucumcari, is a Route 66 town. Even the airport is Santa Rosa Route 66 Airport. The road or street through the town used to be US 66. Its name was changed to Will Rogers Drive and recently changed again to Old Route 66 and back again. Santa Rosa, or "holy rose," derives its name from the Catholic parish, St. Rose of Lima, established in 1907. The original chapel lies in ruins on the road to Puerto de Luna. The home of Santa Rosa's founder, Celso Baca, however, is still standing and serves today as the town's mortuary.

The town itself originally rose around Baca's Spanish ranch and many of the present three thousand townspeople are also Spanish speakers. Rudolfo Anaya, the famous writer of *Bless Me Ultima!* grew up in Santa Rosa among the Spanish and English speakers before moving near Albuquerque, another town further west on the Road. The area around Santa Rosa provides the setting for much of his earlier work.

Since 1959, Silver Moon has been standing at the eastern edge of Santa Rosa. It is a very Route 66 place. In addition to the actual cafeteria, half the space is dedicated to selling Route 66 paraphernalia. Their T-shirts boast that they have the "best food from Chicago to L. A." In April 2002 my wife had chicken fajitas, and I had roast beef with brown gravy. I'm not much of a gravy man, but this gravy was truly Grandma's recipe.

From 1926 to 1936, Route 66 had a different alignment than the one it follows today. Most of it is under gravel and dust, but it passed by the Blue Hole, a natural spring that has now been made into a city park for the amusement of locals and tourists alike. As a matter of fact, in the spring of 2002 most of the new Route 66 was also under dust and gravel and filled with holes while Santa Rosa's townsmen were repairing and improving the road and the sewage system for the incoming tourist season.

Halfway through the town on Route 66 stands Joseph's, another famous cafeteria on the Road with lots of Road paraphernalia on the walls and curtains with 66 designs. Interesting historical newspaper clippings are posting announcing things like "Hitler killed," "Roosevelt

Dies," or "Truman announces: War Over." Joseph A. Campos and his wife Carmen started the business in 1956 as La Fiesta Drive-In.

Campos was born in 1913 in Puerto de Luna. During the Great Depression he worked in Civilian Conservation Corps camps to support his family. He enlisted in the army in 1942 and served throughout World War II. After the war Campos, began hauling ice and coal  to Santa Rosa while dreaming of having a business of his own. Finally, he saved enough money to buy his own trucks, and a few years later opened a gas station together with his brother Joaquin. Joseph Campos married Carmen in 1948, and together they raised seven children. The drive-in was opened in 1956, and ten years later it became Santa Rosa's first and only cafeteria-style restaurant. The new interstate highway bypassed Santa Rosa, and the businesses downtown suffered badly. In 1985 La Fiesta was handed down to the next generation, and soon became Joseph's Restaurant. Thanks to the revitalization of Route 66, the business has been able to expand to include a new gift shop, a full service bar, and even a nightclub.

A new addition to Route 66 museums is the Auto Museum, Snack Bar & Gift Shop. James "Bozo" and Anna Cordova and family's Route 66 Auto Museum is a great place for anyone interested in classic Route 66 custom cars and memorabilia of early promoters and travelers of the Road, or just "anything to do with wheels." You shouldn't miss it, and you cannot, because the yellow car at the top of a pole stands out from all the other ads on your way.

Beyond the hill on the western edge of Santa Rosa Route 66 crosses the Pecos, one of the legendary Western rivers. The Texan hero Pecos Bill himself is said to have been born somewhere on the river. It is also one of the four important American rivers that the 66 encounters during its journey. The Mississippi we have already crossed between Illinois and Missouri; the Rio Grande and the Colorado River are still ahead.

West of Santa Rosa we drive almost constantly uphill. One of the steep-est hillsides of the Old Road lies a short distance after Palma. The rise on the mile-long stretch is no less than seventy yards. Far in the west we glimpse Cerro Pedernal, in English Pedernal Peak. It rises to a height of more than 7,500 feet. The uphill on the 66 and I-40 goes on. Clines Corners lies more than a mile above sea level. Roy Cline gave Clines Corners its name. He set up a gas station here in 1934. One road ran from Clines Corners south to Alamogordo and El Paso and another road north to Highway 66 and toward Santa Fe. The original 66 head-ed north even earlier, west of Santa Rosa, and followed the traditional trails to Santa Fe via Las Vegas.

On this alignment of Route 66 between Santa Rosa and Las Vegas, there is nothing much to stop for. The scenery is still magnificent, but you can see that from your car. Route 66 crosses the Pecos River again just south of Dilia, a small service town for the surrounding country-side. A few miles north the gate of Bob Gerhardt's Spring Valley Ranch may catch your eye.

First, the old Santa Fe Trail and then Route 66 bypassed Las Vegas on the western side, but both dropped into town to rest before the last stretch. The small village of Romeroville grew to the crossroads. At one time the 66 signs pointed from there to Las Vegas, although today there is hardly anything in the city to tell about the existence of the Old Road. It is true that a shortcut through Clines Corners to Albuquerque was constructed in 1937, and both Santa Fe and Las Vegas lay a good distance north of the Road during its heyday.

The lush pastures of Las Vegas fed horses and cattle on the head-waters of the Pecos and still do. The Spaniards founded the town in 1835 on the low meadows by the Galinas River near the Santa Fe Trail. The trail made the town flourish, and, when a railroad also came to town, the prosperity continued. The historical significance of the city and the sturdiness of its buildings are revealed by the fact that no few-er than nine hundred of the buildings are included in the National Register of Historical Places. General Stephen Kearny declared New Mexico part of the United States in the Central Square of Las Vegas in 1846. In 1880 Doc Holliday shot a man on the city's Central Street. In 1900 Theodore Roosevelt announced himself as a presidential candi-date in Las Vegas. The monument to the Rough Riders and the city's museum are reminders of the share Roosevelt and his men had in the Spanish-American War. In reality, the offensive of Roosevelt's men at San Juan Hill in Cuba has been exaggerated: actually, a black infantry regiment took the hill.

The mountain range of the Sangre de Christo west of Las Vegas rises in places to altitudes way beyond ten thousand feet. The early Spaniards, possibly Coronado himself, gave the mountains their name. They saw the range for the first time as the setting sun was turning them the color of blood, and therefore the range is still called Blood of Christ.

From Romeroville, the old Santa Fe Trail and the present I-25 wander in the southern slopes of the Sangre de Christos in search of suitable passes through both the Pecos Indian Pueblo and the old Spanish village Glorieta, then across the Continental Divide and to the small Santa Fe River and the third oldest European settlement in the United States. Santa Fe was founded in 1608 on a tributary of the Rio Grande. Several Indian towns in the region are of course much, much older. Even on the site of Santa Fe, an Indian Pueblo existed before the Spaniards.

Pecos Pueblo probably dates back to the twelfth century. The place is worth the visit. Even in a short time, you get a good overall image of the life of the ancient and not-so-ancient Pueblo Indians. The visitors' center's presentation film is the best in the field. By 1450, Pecos Pueblo had grown into a five-story fortress with wide expanses of corn, bean, and chili pepper fields. Even a cautious estimate would number its population at that time as high as two thousand people—maybe even more. The coming of the Spaniards touched off the slow dying of the Pueblo. The Indians helped the Spaniards build two missionary stations. The first was destroyed during the great Pueblo rebellion of 1680. The other was finished in 1717, but today it is in ruins.

There is nothing left of the old Highway around here and no sign to remind us where it went. With their gas stations and village stores, the villages of Rowe, Pecos, and Glorieta are small centers of population in the middle of pine forests. We hear Spanish as often as English. All passable roads from the villages lead sooner or later to the new Highway I-25. It is the only road west and northwest through Glorieta Pass toward the most enchanting town in the land of enchantment.

The Oldest Towns of the Old West

Ernest Wallace was a long-time professor of history at Texas Tech University in Lubbock. With anthropologist E. Adamson Hoebel from the University of Minnesota, whom he never met, he nevertheless co-authored one of the first ethno-history approaches to Native American history, *Lords of the South Plains*, about the Comanches. Wallace always asked his PhD students at their orals if one was east of Santa Fe, how would you enter the city. The answer, of course, is from the southwest, given the surrounding mountains.

La Villa Real de la Santa Fe de San Francisco de Assisi, that is, the royal town of the sacred faith of St. Francis of Assisi, is the head and the heart of the Southwest. New and old. El Paso in Texas may be older, Albuquerque in New Mexico and Phoenix in Arizona may have grown bigger, but nothing has been able to deprive Santa Fe of its historical position or even its present significance. *Inside Guides: American Southwest* explains: "Santa Fe is 'in' now, but fads come and go, and if it becomes too faddish, the faddists will tire of it and leave, and voila! There's old Santa Fe, timeless and mellow, calmly waiting."

Before the railroads were built, all Southwest traffic ran through Santa Fe. It was the western terminus of US merchants. Spaniards and Mexicans came from the south, Indians from everywhere, but they all entered the town from the southwest. Due to the mountains, the Santa Fe railroad actually never entered the town proper, remember. With modern techniques, you may have to alter your answer to Professor Wallace a little, but not really much. Although coming from the east, as the Comanches, Route 66 enters the old town heading sort of south by southeast, curves northward, and continues out of town toward the southwest.

Santa Fe is still the capital of New Mexico and has been for four hundred years. In terms of age, no other state capital in the United States comes even close. The capitol building of New Mexico is built in accordance with the pattern of the Zia Indian sun symbol. The building does not have a dome or a tower. The Spanish-type tower of the nearby Bataan Memorial administrative building by the Old 66 dates to a time after World War II.

The tower commemorates a horrific episode. In the spring of 1942, after the Japanese attack on Pearl Harbor, American and Philippine forces in the Philippines withdrew to the Bataan area. Americans began a big delaying action on April 4. After a month of fighting, the defending troops, or what was left of them, had to surrender on nearby Corregidor Island. On April 9 the Japanese started what came to

be known as the Bataan Death March; American and Philippine prisoners from the Bataan area and Corregidor were forced to walk north some fifty-five miles, then put on a train, and at the end walk another eight miles to reach the prison camp. Of some seventy thousand POWs, almost ten thousand died during the march.

According to some sources, in World War II New Mexico lost more soldiers in relation to its population than any other state, many of them apparently in Bataan. The tower was built in their memory.

Canyon Road runs east of the capitol building. It is an old Indian road from the northern mountains, later a part of the Santa Fe Trail and once of Highway 66. Around World War I, artists began to move to Santa Fe and many of them started to live on Canyon Road. It became the town's still vital artistic district.

The old palace of the Spanish and Mexican governors of New Mexico is now a museum on the edge of the Plaza, Santa Fe's central square. The palace museum hosts a variety of artifacts, and Indians have traditionally sold their products to tourists in the patio of the Governors Palace. The building itself is historically of immeasurable value, as it is one of the oldest buildings built by Europeans in all of North America. Unfortunately, an important part of the building was destroyed in June 1993 when a young speedster drove his parents' car head on into the palace wall. The boy's parents were traveling in Europe, and the boy, too young to have a driver's license, had decided to borrow their car. In a TV news interview the poor kid bragged about "making New Mexican history." As far as is known, alcohol was not involved. A couple of years later the Governors Palace had been restored to the way it once was, and Indians have returned to sell their products in the yard. There is no reminder of the adolescent's "historical deed." His name is probably preserved only in police files.

New Mexico is one of the most Catholic states within the United States, and Catholic churches govern downtown Santa Fe. A statue of Archbishop Jean Baptiste Lamy stands in front of the St. Francis Cathedral. The bishop's life is fictionalized in *Death Comes for the Archbishop*, a novel by Willa Cather describing the work of Father Latour in the Southwest. Lamy, or Latour, initiated the construction of the cathedral in 1869 and wanted to make it resemble churches in France, his home country. The 165-foot towers planned by the bishop were never erected, however.

A couple of blocks from the cathedral stands the Loretto Chapel, built by Loretto nuns in 1878 in the image of the Sainte-Chapelle in Paris. It is the oldest Gothic building west of the Mississippi. Its beautiful handmade freestanding spiral staircase leads to the choir loft. Even modern architects and engineers marvel at the structure. The story has it that the staircase was built by an unknown carpenter passing through town; it has been suggested that his hometown might have been Nazareth.

The oldest house by people of European descent in the United States is in Santa Fe. North America's oldest church bell has also been brought there from Spain. The bell is located at the San Miguel Mission. Tlaxcalan Indians brought from Mexico built the mission beginning in 1610 under the supervision of Franciscan Fathers, but local Pueblo Indians destroyed it during their great rebellion of 1680. After the Spaniards returned around the year 1710, they rebuilt San Miguel on the same spot. A small part of the original church foundations, built a hundred years earlier, can be seen in front of the altar and under the church.

In Santa Fe Route 66 is truly a tourist road. From Canyon Road on to the west and south it manages to go by practically all of the above mentioned sights and a few more. It passes by the oldest church and turns south right at the corner to leave the cathedral behind and to pass the famous La Fonda Hotel, another great piece of architecture by Mary Jane Colter, designer of Hopi House at the Grand Canyon. Step inside and stay overnight, or if in a hurry, at least have a meal in the hotel's magnificent garden restaurant Plazuela.

Those interested in museums need not be disappointed in Santa Fe. A large part of the city is like a living museum, but the Museum of Arts is right on the Plaza and the Indian Art School Museum less than a block away. Further up the hill there's an international museum of folk art with a fine affiliated Indian museum. The Wheelwright Museum also specializes in Indian art.

While Santa Fe is an important city, there are no new skyscrapers to be seen. All city houses represent the old Spanish style or the still older Pueblo style. Many are an interplay of these two. Even Texaco gas stations appear to be encased with adobe to make them blend better into the street scene. Santa Fe doesn't even have a proper airfield. If you want to fly to the city, you have to land in Albuquerque and continue from there over land. As the only barriers here are the sky and the earth, according to Tom Snyder, large airplanes would only interfere with the sky.

Many are the movies made of Santa Fe, and some are mentioned above. One not yet mentioned is *lights of old santa fe* (using only small letters throughout its poster) with "Roy Rogers, king of the cowboys" and "Trigger, the smartest horse in the movies." Another film is the 1940 *Santa Fe Trail*, directed originally by a Hungarian, Michael Curtiz, with Errol Flynn and Ronald Reagan as the main characters. In the film the party never reaches Santa Fe, but what makes it more interesting is that it discusses slavery in pre-Civil War America. Considering the time the movie was made, Flynn and Reagan might as well argue about Nazism. In the film, eventually, they decided not to intervene. Was the real meaning also not to intervene in World War II, already started in Europe?

Santa Fe was founded on the site of an old Indian Pueblo, and central New Mexico has always been, and partly still is, Pueblo Indian country. The most famous Indian town in the area is probably Taos Pueblo north of Santa Fe. Two of its tallest buildings, each five stories high, have stood beside Taos Creek for a millennium or longer. The Taos inhabitants claim their houses to be the oldest still inhabited multistory buildings in the world and compete for the honor of being North America's oldest town with Acoma Pueblo and the old Hopi town of Oraibi.

Remains of habitations much older than even Taos can be seen near Santa Fe. At Bandalier National Monument in Frijoles Canyon are sites of old cave dwellings and also ruins of younger Pueblo-type dwellings built on open space. The Puye cave dwellings and buildings of Puye Pueblo are located less than twenty miles from Santa Fe. White researchers have named the builders of the oldest constructions Anasazi. This is the name given to a number of ancient cultures obviously very different from each other, from different ages and different geographical locations in the Southwest. The area is rich with ruins of mighty buildings, villages and towns, and a treasure house of pieces of ceramics. When whites asked the Navajos ruling the area who had made the ruined buildings, they answered, "Anasazi," meaning "the ancient enemies of our ancestors."

For a long time white people believed that the Anasazi were dead and long since vanished from the face of the earth. It took a while before anybody wanted to believe the claims of Pueblo Indians that they were the offspring of the Anasazi. Even the ads for Route 66 invited travelers to marvel at the remnants of the lost ancient "high cultures" and to meet the region's present Indians, who obviously had nothing to do with the Anasazis who had built those ruins.

Modern scientific opinion supports the Pueblo claims and considers the Anasazi the ancestors of the Hopi, Zuni, and other Pueblo Indians. In addition to the Zunis and Acoma, there are officially seventeen living Pueblo villages in New Mexico. When Spaniards first came to the Southwest, there were at least fifty and probably even more of these villages or small towns. The Pueblo Indians got even their name from the Spaniards: the Spanish word *pueblo* means both village and people, and Spaniards gave that name to the farming Indians living permanently in town communities, as opposed to the more transient Navajo, Apache, and Comanche Indians. Thus, the word *pueblo* still denotes a certain Indian people as well as their dwellings.

Northern Rio Grande Valley

North of Santa Fe lie the Pueblos of Nambe and San Juan, and the one closest to Santa Fe is called Tesuque. Pojoaque has a relatively large mall and a tourist shop to tempt visitors to leave their money with the Indians. Tobacco in particular is cheaper in the Indian reservation shops than elsewhere, due to tax regulations. Most of the Pueblos are also involved in the casino business and make a lot of money at the expense of gambling-crazed Anglos.

Jemez Pueblo lies west of Santa Fe. N. Scott Momaday, to date the only American Indian writer to receive the Pulitzer Prize, has his home there. Momaday spent a part of his childhood in Jemez, where his parents worked as teachers. The Southwest and the Pueblos are strongly present in his prize-winning novel *House Made of Dawn*, a name

for the Southwest often used by Navajos and sometimes also by Hopis and Pueblo Indians. The best of Momaday and, in my opinion, the best Indian book of all time is *The Way to Rainy Mountain*. It is the story of the Kiowa Indians' migration from the Northern Plains around the Devil's Tower, Wyoming, to Oklahoma. If you have never read an "Indian book," you still should read this one. The more Indian books you've read, the more you'll enjoy Momaday's.

The area surrounding Santa Fe is also rich with the history and activities of Europeans and Euro-Americans. Chimayo blankets are the common heritage of Indians and white people. The weavers of the blankets are unknown and are likely to stay that way. There is no way to state with certainty which blankets have been made by Indians, which by Hispanos, and which by Anglos, although Anglo-made blankets are probably in a very small minority. The central design of all these blankets is nevertheless the abstract thunderbird, the emblem of all Chimayo blankets.

There is a story that sometime around the year 1810 the village priest of Chimayo saw a fire on a hillside. He found a crucifix where the fire had been and decided to take it to his superiors. The crucifix disappeared three times during the trip and always reappeared in the hole where it had been. At this point everybody understood that the crucifix wanted to stay where it belonged. A small chapel for family use was built on the site. It turned out that the sand from the hole had a healing effect, the number of visitors increased, and the present chapel, or rather adobe church, was built in 1816.

Santuario de Chimayo is still there. The crucifix now hangs on the altar wall. Next to the altar gable, in a side room the size of a closet, there's the hole containing the healing sand. An entire room at the side of the chapel is filled with crutches and other aids left behind by healed believers no longer in need of them.

The town of San Fernando de Taos began around the year 1615 a couple of miles south of Taos Pueblo. Its isolation was interrupted only once a year, when Indians coming from the north brought hides and furs and Rio Grande Indians from the south brought grain and ceramics to the Taos market. As the years went by, Spanish, Mexican, and American fur trappers joined them.

Although Christopher "Kit" Carson, Charles Bent, and many other Americans resided more or less permanently in Taos, the almost bloodless occupation of New Mexico by the United States in 1846 did not proceed peacefully in Taos. Mexicans in Taos did not like the new occupants. The Indians trusted the Catholic priests in the area, and the priests helped persuade the inhabitants of Taos Pueblo to participate in a rebellion in January 1847. Bent, the man chosen as New Mexico's first US governor, was killed, and the rebellion was not suppressed until the US Army arrived from Santa Fe to fight the rebels. Taos Pueblo was conquered, and six Indians were hanged for murders.

During the American Civil War, Kit Carson and his friends wanted to keep Taos and New Mexico part of the United States, although many supporters of the Confederacy lived in the territory. To make their point, Carson and his friends cut the tallest pine they could find, tied the Star-Spangled Banner to the treetop, and brought the tree to the middle of Taos Square. They kept constant guard to prevent possible supporters of the South from tearing the flag down. The United States flag is still flying from the pole in Taos Square. The police station where the young heroes of *Easy Rider* were locked up for a night stands on the edge of the square.

In the beginning of the century, Ernest Blumenschein and Bert Phillips moved to Taos, and other artists soon followed them there. Georgia O'Keeffe, D. H. Lawrence and many others discovered Taos. They are in part responsible for the fact that present-day Taos is a genuine artist town and a highly popular tourist attraction. The town was also among the first to make use of Highway 66, although the road lies far south of it. Anybody traveling anywhere from Taos almost had to drive through Santa Fe and continue from there on the 66.

Important events in world history took place in New Mexico and the Highway 66 area when the nuclear research plant in Los Alamos succeeded in producing the first atom bomb in the summer of 1945. The mountains of northern New Mexico were chosen primarily as the project's location because they were so remote and safe from possible enemy spies and attacks. Los Alamos itself was chosen because the area had uranium deposits needed as raw material for the bomb. A third reason was of course the American Indians; if the project should fail or there was a catastrophe, only Indians would suffer the consequences. Hardly anybody else lived in the area at the time.

After the war, Los Alamos became one more tourist attraction advertised on Route 66. The factory manufacturing nuclear weapons later moved away, and the only research in Los Alamos today is involved with peaceful uses of nuclear power. This at least is the official story. A number of laboratories and research fields are located inside the mountain in the area where nobody is allowed to trespass, and a very wide and good road leads to the foot of the mountain.

Route 66 was never a wide road. Nevertheless, it not only served to make the Southwest familiar; it also largely created the tourist industry that still flourishes in the region. Fred Harvey, Lorenzo Hubbell, and especially Mary Jane Colter created the image of the Southwest. With the railroad and beyond it, Route 66 made the Indian pueblos and Anasazi ruins famous, and created a market for Indian products from roasted piñon nuts to Chimayo blankets. Although the Road ran directly from Santa Rosa to Albuquerque in 1937, tourists still visited Santa Fe. Today, most travelers coming to Albuquerque also visit Santa Fe, and if they have enough time they see Taos, Los Alamos, and Chimayo, too.

Paul Horgan was a historian and a novelist of the American Southwest. He died in 1995 at the age of ninety-one after winning both a Pulitzer and a Bancroft Price in 1955 for a two volume historical epic, *Great River: Rio Grande in North American History*. He describes early travelers on the river as follows: "They saw much along the way. There were long-abandoned towns here and there, and from the ruins the travelers could learn something about the vanished inhabitants. Wanderers sometimes came to the pueblo world from down south on the river where, they said, there once flourished life in river caves that was long since gone. The river went more or less straight south, as you left the pueblo cities." This would almost be an apt description of travelers on Route 66 between Santa Fe and Albuquerque, where the Road rides within the proximity of the river.

Southbound, between Santa Fe and Albuquerque, the Old Road lies under the new Interstate Highway 25. The new road is a good and wide one running downhill in the middle of wide landscapes. Only seldom does it deviate so much from the Old Road that sections of the old concrete foundation can be detected in the shade of the thorny bushes. This is an area governed by ghosts of both natural and cultural history, an area where the annual attacks of wind and rain erode the landscape and where the adobe gradually surrenders before gravity. Each spring, weeds and mesquite make their way into asphalt and concrete. When winter comes they retreat, but the following year they proceed a little farther on top of the asphalt. Year by year, piece by piece, they eat away the surface of the road and finally cleave it all.

Native American villages and towns are situated on rivers; most of the Pueblos are located on the Rio Grande and its tributaries. A couple of Pueblos lie on the Old Route 66 and new I-25 between Santa Fe and Albuquerque. The old Santo Domingo trading post is a bit more than a mile from the highway. Less than twenty miles west of Santa Fe lies Zia Pueblo, whose dwellers have given New Mexico its sun symbol. Other Pueblos on the Road or not far from it include San Felipe, Sandia, Santa Ana, and Cochiti. San Felipe owns Casino Hollywood, and Santa Ana the Star Casino. Sandia operates a casino, too, so you have plenty of chances to lose your money, or maybe even win some, on Indian land along the Old 66 or the new I-25 here.

A great effort by local Pueblos is the modern Santo Domingo Traditions Indian Market, right on the west side of the Road. It is a large shopping center built with style: plenty of parking in the middle, a playground for children, galleries, little shops, many genuine articles by America's Native population. Visit early though, as most things, including the restaurants, close around five or so.

Across the Rio Grande, just a mile west off the I-25 and Old Route 66 is Coronado State Monument named after the Spanish explorer and exploiter, who with three hundred European soldiers and some eight hundred Indian allies ravished the area in 1540. He found no golden city here but the Tiwa Pueblo of Kuaua. During the Great Depression in the 1930s, federal Work Program Administration workers excavated the pueblo and also reconstructed new walls over the reburied original ruins.

City of the Duke

Once past Algodones, you can drive a longer stretch on the Old Road closer to the Rio Grande. From there, the present State Road 313 (Donald Duck's license plate number) runs through Sandia Pueblo, changes to 47 in Albuquerque, and finally becomes Fourth Street. In the very heart of the city Fourth Street turns into a pedestrian area, and you have to get out of your car to see the tall buildings and fountains of the business district. This is the heart of the city, the Civic Plaza.

If you've been too busy to see Santa Fe or were foolish enough to miss it, you may approach Albuquerque from the east, most of the distance on the new I-40. West of Clines Corners, Moriarty is the first locality worth mentioning. Moriarty is named for an Indianapolis rancher who came to New Mexico to treat his rheumatism. One of Moriarty's Route 66 landmarks was the Long Horn Ranch, founded as a café by a tenderfoot from the East—a policeman. According to the billboard, it was a place "where the West stops to rest."

When I-40 was constructed, the West had no time to rest; instead, it hurried past Moriarty. The tables, chairs, and motel beds at the Long Horn Ranch became vacant. Eventually, nothing was left but some ruins and empty space where the ranch used to be. Moriarty, however, still is a Route 66 town. Both in Moriarty and in the next town, Edgewood, many businesses use the magic Route 66 symbol in their advertisement: another Route 66 Antiques, a Route 66 printing shop, and in Tijeras, a Route 66 Automotive & Repair, and a Route 66 Junk.

Along a shortcut a little east of Albuquerque, the road climbs to almost seven thousand feet above sea level, the second highest spot along the journey. From there it descends into Tijeras Valley, which houses the city of the Conquistadors, named in 1705 for the Portuguese Duke of Albuquerque, then also the Viceroy of Mexico.

Tiwa-speaking American Indians had already lived in the area for ages and near the present Old Town of Albuquerque at least since the 1350s. Hernando de Alvarado, one of Coronado's subordinates, was probably the first European to see the place in 1540. After 1610, a few Spanish farms and ranches were established in the Old Town area. All of them, however, were destroyed during the Pueblo Revolt of 1680. It was not until the beginning of the eighteenth century that Spaniards returned. With the railroad in the 1880s, a "New Albuquerque" began a few miles east. With Route 66, during the 1930s and 1940s artists and shop owners discovered Old Town and eventually developed the area into a great tourist attraction.

The plaza in the Old Town center and San Felipe de Neri Church are still where they were in 1706. A number of restaurants, souvenir shops, and other tourist attractions compete for customers around them. Albuquerque Museum lies one block east, and almost opposite it there's the Natural History Museum of New Mexico. The southern edge of the area is lined by Central Avenue, i.e. Route 66. Some twenty blocks from Old Town lies the Civic Plaza and south of it the Crossroads Mall area with its benches, park avenues, flowers, and trees. The mall reaches all the way to Central Avenue, i.e. Route 66. Twenty or so blocks further east lies the campus of the University of New Mexico. It is the cultural center of Albuquerque with concerts, art galleries, museums, and theaters. The architecture varies from Pueblo adobe houses to post-modern monstrosities of glass and steel. The southern edge of the campus is lined by—you guessed it right—Central Avenue, or Route 66.

The Historic 66 runs along Central Avenue all through eastern Albuquerque. Here Lindy's Café has served excellent chili since 1929. The De Anza Motel is the place to spend the night. The best chocolate malts are to be found at the 66 Diner. According to Tom Snyder, even the meat loaf "comes from the recipe of a woman who loved to cook and knew how to do so." I tested Tom Snyder's claim in February 2001; he was right.

Albuquerque's Central Avenue is no doubt the best-preserved urban section of the old Historic Highway. If you want to familiarize yourself with the 66 but have limited time, fly to Albuquerque and walk seven miles east from the river. The roadside boasts one building after another from the heydays of Route 66. There are of course empty spaces in-between, but the atmosphere of the Old Road quickly returns. If you're too tired to walk, rent a car or take a city bus. The bus number, of course, is 66.

The very center of "new" Albuquerque is also where the Old Route 66 and the Very Old Route 66 meet. There is a small clock tower at the intersection of Central Avenue and Fourth Street: Central being the shortcut from Santa Rosa, Fourth Street the original alignment from Santa Fe. Across the street from the clock tower is the Route 66 Smoke Shop. If you still ignore the Surgeon General's warnings, you might want to try their special mix in your pipe.

Albuquerque is a good headquarters for people acquainting themselves with New Mexico, although the city itself is not as interesting, colorful, and easy to possess as its northern neighbor Santa Fe. Albuquerque has about five times as many inhabitants, that is, some 550,000, one fourth of the state's population. In 1946 there were only 35,000 inhabitants. The growth of the city had already begun by then, due to the development of atomic energy and the straightening of the road.

If you are interested in ancient Indian art, the Petroglyph National Monument, a few miles northwest of Route 66, is definitely worth seeing, including interesting inscriptions in stone from times before white vandalism. Besides, the view of the Duke's town is great from the hills.

Pueblo Highway

After downtown Albuquerque, Route 66 crosses the Rio Grande, the legendary river running first from north to south, splitting New Mexico in two, then winding southeast and forming the border between the United States and old Mexico. It is almost sad that the bridge here is nothing but a dull piece of concrete with no arches or anything really to make drivers notice this important moment. Immediately after the bridge, you have to take a sharp turn left if you want to follow the old trail of Route 66. The Road runs at times so close to the western bank of the river that there's a danger of floods. Reeds grow on both sides of the road and birds wallow on the western side.

Soon we are on Indian land again, legally and literally, as Route 66 cuts through Isleta Pueblo Indian Reservation. It doesn't quite go into the actual Pueblo, but the Pueblo can clearly be seen across the tracks from the Old Road, the Spanish type Roman Catholic St. Augustine Church from 1612 proudly showing. Unlike most other Pueblos, the Isletas did not participate in the great Pueblo Revolt of 1680, and many of them fled with the Spaniards to El Paso. The Indians returned the following year, but the ungrateful Spanish now turned against them and destroyed the Pueblo and took hundreds of prisoners back to El Paso. Some of their descendants still live there in Ysleta del Sur, or the Tigua Pueblo. Some escaped to live with the Hopis. In 1742 after the Spanish re-conquest of New Mexico, priests brought four hundred of them back to begin the modern Isleta Pueblo.

If you want to visit Isleta, there are two access roads from 66 and less than a mile to go—much less when you see the sign "Welcome to Isleta Pueblo." You shouldn't take the sign literally, though, and barge into the narrow streets of the village. What the people and government of Isleta really want you to do is to continue a couple more miles and spend much of your money in their casino or golf course or a convenience store.

After Albuquerque, the new I-40 continues west-southwest, while the Old Road took its time going straight south to Armijo, Pajarito, Isleta, and Peralta. It did not turn west and gradually northwest before Los Lunas, eventually to meet the new highway in Suwanee. The location of the bend, Los Lunas, is a charming village on the Rio Grande. *Luna* is Spanish for moon, and grammatically the plural ought to be *las lunas*. However, this time we're not talking about feminine moons; instead, the name of the village refers to a family that once lived there. The family's name was Luna, and, therefore, the plural has the masculine article *los*.

The old and dignified Lunas family mansion lies to the left immediately after the bend. Built in the 1870s in Southern colonial style architecture by the Santa Fe Railroad for the Luna family in exchange for some of their land, this building is so beautiful that Josefita Manderfield Otero, one of the original owners, has never left the building. Although she passed away in 1912, she has still been seen several times on the second floor of the mansion, now a restaurant, often sitting by the window looking down to the lawn.

After the Luna Mansion Restaurant the village center is behind you, but before the settlement ends you can still fill your stomach at the Route 66 Cafeteria—or, at least, you used to. Los Lunas is in the area where you never consider how hot or mild the chili may be. The question is only: "green or red?" This also applied to the Route 66 Cafeteria. So when the waitress asked me, I thought I was prepared and without a blink said: "Green." She looked at me and said: "I knew it, cause you sure don't look like a communist." I wonder what she would have said had I asked for red chili. Had I become a communist? I doubt that, but next time I'm at Los Lunas I'll ask for red chili just to find out.

After the village of the moons we hit desert. The Old Route 66 and the Santa Fe Company Railroad travel together like brothers across the sands. There are no trees and not much else either—a few wormwood bushes of sage, a few tough shoots of wild pumpkin. The desert sun is hot, and there is no oncoming traffic. Suwanee lies in the distance, mirage-like. A bridge across the railroad and a dirt road. Not there. A pompous ranch gate. A small trading post. We drive on, toward the

rumble and thunder of a new highway. From Correo you can already see it. Good-bye, desert peace. The train we still hear. Then the Old 66 drowns under the new highway.

Willa Cather described the Southwest scenery in her *Death Comes for the Archbishop*: "From the flat red sea of sand rose great rock mesas, generally Gothic in outline, resembling vast cathedrals. They were not crowded together in disorder, but placed in wide spaces, long vistas between. This plain might once have been an enormous city, all the smaller quarters destroyed by time, only the public buildings left."

If you're more interested in the newer alignments of Route 66 you can continue straight west on Albuquerque's Central Avenue and then join I-40 to Correo. This way you can drive faster, and the scenery is still beautiful. You also cross the Rio Puerco and have a chance to see one of the many bridges that have become part of the 66 pilgrimage. This is a proud example, and New Mexico's longest single span of the Parker Truss bridges, named after their developer Charles H. Parker. Built in 1933 and remodeled in 1957, its span widens 250 feet.

No matter which route you take, after Correo everyone must continue on I-40 if they want to drive into Laguna country. The pueblo is named for a lake that once rested just west of the present day pueblo. The richest open pit uranium mine in North America was worked on the Laguna Indian Reservation from 1952 until the early 1980s. Laguna is the only Indian Pueblo you can see from I-40. However, the Old 66 did much better: it passed through Laguna. The road turns west toward the Pueblo and then sharply right between cotton trees. You have to watch carefully from the left window if you don't want to miss Laguna church and the town center as you drive past them. If you missed the sharp right, don't worry. Continue straight ahead, pass the Laguna post office, and take the next one right. That will take you even closer to the Laguna church.

This white Catholic Mission San Jose de Laguna is worth stopping for. The altar is a colorful Mexican type, but both walls are decorated with Pueblo symbols. Before the church was built, a Laguna delegation traveled to Santa Fe to ask Governor Pedro Rodriguez Cubero to send a priest to the pueblo. Cubero told the Indians to first build a church, and only then he would send a priest for them. After many years of toil and sweat, the church was finally finished in 1699.

The section after and including Laguna, just a few miles long, is one of the most beautifully preserved stretches of the Old Road. It winds gently among the trees with the mesas in the background. We have to be careful about playing children and pedestrian traffic as a rule. We are on reservation land. Only visitors at best, often invaders and conquerors. Laguna itself was born as a result of several moves and conquests. It is one of the youngest New Mexico pueblos. The oldest houses date to the beginning of the nineteenth century. Further up the Road, there exists an even newer village called New Laguna with many houses built in nice rows by the Bureau of Indian Affairs.

After Laguna, Route 66 runs in the middle of real Indian country. In principle, of course, it has been doing just that ever since Chicago, and particularly since Oklahoma, but the driver who does not realize he's on Indian land now has got to be blind. Unfortunately, even blind people get driver's licenses in these parts of the world.

There is enough of barren terrain. This is the home of aridity, and the lean years of harvest of the 1930s have moved here from Oklahoma. At times and places the drought is so intense that trees compete for dogs. Paraje is a name among the others, still within the reservation lands. There's a small trading post in Budville, another in Cubero, accompanied by a saloon and diner dedicated to the 66. The village of Cubero lies a few miles north with many houses in ruins.

The Whiting Brothers Motel in San Fidel has not received guests for a long time. It's unlikely that any of the four brothers are alive anymore. Originally, the brothers had a lumber business and a gas station in Saint John, Arizona, in the late 1910s. They moved their operation to Route 66 and expanded their business east and west along the highway. Finally, their chain consisted of service stations, small cafés, and motels from Oklahoma to California. Usually, each unit operated as an independent business whose manager or owner paid a commission to the brothers for the right to use the trade name and for the services of the Whitings, the most important being the acquisition of gasoline.

In the heart of New Mexico the sea seems as distant as it could possibly be. And yet Ernest Hemingway finished his *Old Man and the Sea* in Cubero. Perhaps he wanted to go away from the sea when he had enough material for the novel. Living on the seaside might have given him so much new material that he would not have been able to finish his book. This situation is familiar to every researcher. A time comes when you have to stop collecting material and write the report. Otherwise the collecting will go on forever and the report never gets done. Thank goodness for deadlines.

After the Indian reservations of Isleta, Canyoncito, and Laguna, I-40 and US-66 touch the northern edge of the Ácoma Reservation. Ácoma Pueblo itself is somewhere south of the road, not visible from it, but worth the side trip. The center, Sky City, lies high upon a mesa with its houses of two and three stories and its Spanish-style church. The dwellers are mostly Catholic, but the interior of the San Estéban del Rey Mission church, completed in 1640, has a dirt floor and no benches. With the Santa Fe cathedral, this church has a key position in Cather's *Death Comes for the Archbishop*.

According to its inhabitants, Ácoma has nestled on its hilltop forever. This may have a taste of exaggeration, but there's no denying that Ácoma's Sky City is one of the oldest, if not the oldest, among American towns. It used to be difficult to reach, because there was only a steep and narrow path leading to the hilltop. Today, a passable road will take you there, but tourists are taken to Sky City in buses. They have to leave their own cars in the parking lot of the visitors' center, museum, and shop down the Mesa. If you are more interested in big winnings and gaming than in American Indians, there is no need climbing to the Sky City. Ácoma's Sky City casino is right by the interstate. If you are interested in both American Indians and the Old Road, the tribe operates the Ácoma Route 66 Interpretive Center also just off I-40.

The Spaniards thought they never would have been able to conquer

Ácoma had the Indians not welcomed them. The Spaniards returned the friendliness with plundering. Apparently, some of the Spaniards caught a couple of turkeys walking around, bred by the Indians mostly for the feathers, and put them in their pots. The Indians were infuriated by such an act and killed the cooks. The Spaniards retaliated by destroying almost the entire pueblo, hacking off men's and women's hands or feet, and taking some of them into slavery in Mexico. The children were given to the priests to raise. Ácoma has been a scene of Indian resistance more recently. Sometime in the 1950s, a couple of Ácoma Indians killed a state patrolman on Highway 66 as a protest against white oppression. The hapless patrolman had seemly wanted to give the men a speeding ticket.

If Ácoma is one of the oldest Indian towns, the Navajo Ramah Reservation west of it is one of the youngest reservations. It is outside traditional Navajo country and was created when the Navajo Nation purchased the land to add to their main reservation. At the northern edge of Ramah towers the steep-edged cliff of El Morro, looming over the surrounding plateau like a landmark. By the foot of the cliff in a cool sheltered place, the melting snow and the rain have created a pond of water. It is an important place, inviting to travelers, men, and animals alike. Many waterside plants here are rare in this area. Mosquitoes, also rarely seen around these parts, have flown their way here as well.

Anasazi people inhabited El Morro and maybe even their predecessors lived here. Ruins of two pueblos are still on top. One of them boasts almost nine hundred rooms, and 1,500 people may have lived in them in the fourteenth century. The buildings were inhabited for only a hundred years, maybe less. Maybe they were originally built only for use whenever a particularly hot summer or drought forced the people to stay longer in the shade of El Morro before moving to their real homes—maybe to Ácoma in the east or to Zuni villages in the west.

The Anasazis made their signs in the rock of El Morro. People traveling from Ácoma to Zuni Pueblo and back added more petroglyphs. To the Zunis, the rock is still "A'ts'ina," a place with rock paintings. Antonio de Espejo is the first Spanish conqueror who reached the place on March 11, 1583. If he inscribed something in the rock, his sign has disappeared. However, Espejo wrote the oldest report on "a pond by a large rock" known to us. While colonizing New Mexico, Governor Juan de Oñate inscribed the oldest European name in El Morro on

April 16, 1605. This writing can still be read, the same as the many later Spanish inscriptions. We can also read how Diego de Vargas, who reconquered New Mexico in 1692, conquered the area at his own expense for the Holy Faith and the Royal Crown.

To Spaniards El Morro was no more than a tall cliff or a big rock. With Anglo conquest, it became Inscription Rock. The rock also has American inscriptions and drawings. James H. Simpson, a lieutenant of army cartographers, and his companion, cartographer Richard Kern, not only left their signs on the rock but also copied the drawings of earlier visitors into their notebooks during a couple of days in September 1849. Other California-bound travelers stopped at the rock in the same year; one band robbed Zuni Pueblo. Even Lieutenant Beale's camels visited El Morro in 1857.

Railroad builders originally planned to lay their tracks in the shadow of El Morro, but eventually they built the railroad twenty-five miles further north. Highway 66 later strengthened this development. Thus, El Morro remained far from the main route, and only the local route came close to it. Writing on the rock was prohibited in 1902, and the old petroglyphs were protected. The area was made a national monument.

Both Oñate and Vargas were traveling to Zuni country via El Morro. It was in Zuniland that Coronado had met Pueblo Indians for the first time in 1540. The first Pueblo Coronado probably stumbled on was Hawikuh. Today, there are nothing but ruins left of the buildings that originally stood three-to-four stories high, and people walk there on a second-story level on earth and rock rubble. If the Zuni let people visit Hawikuh, that is. They do not always.

Hawikuh is in ruins, and the central Zuni Pueblo has changed shape drastically during the past 350 years. In place of the former concentrated urban Pueblo center with buildings of several stories, a village of low houses now lies on the northern side of the Zuni River. A Spanish-style church is here, too. It's true that this church also went to ruin once, and the roof even fell in at the beginning of the nineteenth century. The church has been restored lately, however. The altar is like any Catholic church altar, with maybe a tinge of local color, but on the northern and southern walls are pictures portraying katsinas, the mediating spirits of the traditional Pueblo religion, related to various seasons.

Across the Continental Divide

If American Indians were overlooked in the past, they became important for the tourist industry after World War II. According to Tom Teague, New Mexico motel owner Ralph Jones explained in 1947: "My friends, just because you live here among them all, do not lose sight of the fact that there are literally thousands of travelers who have never seen an Indian. Indians have tremendous pulling power. And don't forget the value of the cowboy, either."

Route 66 runs north of Ácoma and the Zuni Indian centers, mostly north of the new I-40. Around Grants the Highway crosses a lava field, and south of the town lies El Malpais National Monument. The soil there is really as "bad" as the Spanish name suggests. The signs of violent volcanic activity are clear. The wide network of caves bears the cold name of ice caves. The temperature inside the caverns is constantly below freezing. There is no avoiding Indians here either. The most important Malpais vistas can only be admired by wandering some twelve miles along an old Pueblo trading trail.

Grants itself started out as a railroad town because there was water there to cool the steam engines. Later, oil was also found in the area, and the pipes of oil refineries create the town's northwest skyline. Grants has earned agricultural fame as the center of an important carrot area. The "largest truck stop in the world" is located on the western edge of Grants. It includes not only a gas station and a café but also a shopping center, a post office, and much more inside the same building. In real honesty, however, the actual largest truck stop may be in Walcott, Iowa.

The new mining boom began in the 1950s when a Navajo named Paddy Martinez found uranium near the town. Unfortunately, the safety measures involving that substance were not very strict, and knowledge about it was lacking. This indifference has made the local inhabitants, particularly the Indians, suffer from the ill-effects of radioactive radiation. The New Mexico Museum of Mining still exists, and some tailings nearby are on Indian lands. But what choice did Navajo Chief Manuelito have but to make peace with Kit Carson in Grants in 1864? His people were starving and being massacred. The alternative was worse, but the peace was not that good either. It sealed the Navajo defeat and made them travel "the Long Walk" to Bosque Redondo.

Grants is truly a town of the Old Road. Route 66 runs right through it. Many of the hotels and cafeterias and even the laundry advertise themselves with the name of the Old Highway. The weary traveler has no difficulty finding a decent bed by the road. For food, try the Spanish type family joint of El Cafecito providing "authentic New Mexico cuisine." For many Europeans, American coffee is not very tasty, but both in 1999 and 2002 my wife was pleased with Cafecito's coffee. The major thing here is not to forget the dessert, and, I repeat, do not forget the dessert. El Cafecito's Fritta Frutta is something you've never tasted before but want to taste ever after. Your choice of filling includes peach, cherry, and apple.

Next morning, if you want to make the long side trip on a bumpy dirt road, you can visit Chaco Culture National Historic Park, a main center of the ancient Anasazis during the period AD 850 to the 1200s. For anyone interested in ancient Indian cultures, this is a must. It also is a UNESCO World Heritage Site. If you are interested in even older history than the Anasazis, or actually of any humans, visit the Dinosaur Museum.

Westbound on Route 66 and soon after the small town of Thoreau, Route 66 and I-40 cross the Continental Divide. Here it lies "only" 7,264 feet above sea level. An *Indian Village* right at the Great Divide attracts tourists. Beautiful scenery opens up to the north. Unfortunately, less beautiful scenery may be right in front of you: This is the only place where I have ever met Navajos begging for money with nothing to sell or give in return.

While the highways steer clear of Indian centers as a rule, in Gallup they created one. People go so far as to call this town, founded as a railroad station in 1881, an "Indian capital of the United States." American Indians are an essential part of the street scene. The Zuni Reservation is to the south. The large Navajo Reservation with its capital Window Rock is to the north. Rittenhouse's traveler's guide gave the name of the town as Shiprock, but the real Shiprock, named after a ship-shaped rock, stands on the northern border of the Navajo Reservation in the northwest corner of New Mexico. Window Rock lies in the immediate vicinity of Route 66 and Gallup. The name is provided by a nearby rock with a large hole, a window, created by erosion. A little farther west is the Hubbell trading post at Ganado, and a little farther north from there, the beautiful Canyon de Chelly, the Navajos' "stone canyon."

Roads numbered with one or more sixes cross in Gallup. Road 36 came from Apache Creek, the Zuni Reservation, and Wanderwagen in the south. "The Devil's Road," the 666, headed north from here running through the Navajo Reservation to Shiprock and via Colorado to Monticello, Utah. Now they have changed the numbers, but the sixes are still there. The roads from south are 602 and 610, but 666 is now 491. Road 264 still runs to Window Rock, Ganado, and Tuba City diagonally across Navajo country from southeast to northwest and through the Hopi Reservation. Joining forces with 118, Route 66 runs from east to west right through Gallup beside the railroad tracks and continues to enliven the town. A number of shops, amusement centers, hotels, bars, and pawnshops attract the townspeople, tourists, Indians, truck drivers, and railroad men. At the pawnshops, Indian jewelry is cheaper than anywhere else. Indians frequently bring their works here with no intention of ever redeeming them. Most of the money they obviously spend in the amusement centers on the Road. People have also called Gallup the capital of drunken Indians.

The real landmark in Gallup is the El Rancho Hotel, founded in 1937. It has obvious connections to the world of cinema. Humphrey Bogart, Rita Hayworth, Spencer Tracy, Katherine Hepburn, and Ronald Reagan all spent nights here. A second-story balcony circles the magnificent lobby of the hotel, its walls decorated with the pictures of the movie stars who have stayed there. None of the important or famous stars are missing. Even the hotel rooms are named after Hollywood actors. In 1996 we stayed in the W. C. Fields room and tried to recall all the movies that corpulent and—if you can deduce that from a black-and-white movie—red-nosed gentleman appeared in. The room was big, with plenty of cupboards and ample room for luggage. The combined toilet and bathroom was a small one, and the first-story view of the backyard left much to hope for. The room cost fifty dollars a night. El Rancho's more modern motel across the street would have cost forty dollars. Of course the sales tax, rarely announced as part of prices in North America, was added to the price in both cases. The next time we spent a night in a second-story room named after an actress. The direct view of Route 66 was much better. No change in price by 2002. Ten years later, however, the price had more than doubled.

Some of the money the tourists have brought to El Rancho is attached to the mirror on the back wall of the bar. An old Finnish ten-mark bill is there, as well as notes from Germany, the United Kingdom, and Holland. Erroll Flynn once rode his horse straight into the hotel bar. They did not serve the horse, however, nor did they serve Flynn until the horse had been ousted. The bar is like a Wild West saloon with wooden roof beams and a large stage, but a jukebox and a TV-set represent more modern technology. A painting of relatively high quality portrays a beautiful buxom woman doing her hair. She must have consoled lonely wanderers, regardless of whether their vehicle was a donkey, a horse, or a car.

In the El Rancho saloon, good manners are preserved. Once we ate there on Sunday afternoon. Having spent days in Chaco Canyon and the dusty roads, we fancied a beer with our meal. The elderly lady serving us looked down upon us with eyes of surprise and high morals. "Whaddya mean kids? Today is Sunday," she said. We apologized and settled for coffee and a coke.

According to a story R. E. Griffith, the brother of D. W. Griffith, the famous pioneer of movie directors, planned El Rancho. However, there's a small *but*: D. W. Griffith did not have a brother named Raymond E. Griffith. It's possible that the man in question was a silent movie actor who later took up writing manuscripts and producing. He was known in Hollywood as a great liar, and it may well be that he had nothing to do with El Rancho. Maybe someone else planned the hotel, or the individual who planned it was not called Griffith, least of all one with the initials R. E. The present owner of El Rancho, Armand Ortega, nevertheless advertises his hotel as planned by D. W. Griffith's brother. Ortega himself is a fourth-generation Indian trader.

Aside from El Rancho, Gallup tourist attractions include the Grand Hotel and the Drake Hotel. The old El Morro Theater also remains, a block away from the Old Road. The whole town gains some dignity from the old courthouse and town hall on top of the town hill, gazing down the valley like guardians and keeping a keen eye on the traffic on Route 66. The only mosque on Route 66 raises its minaret tower at the eastern end of town.

From Gallup the Road goes on to Manuelito and Lupton—the first named after a Navajo chief, the second after a railroad officer. Between the two towns, the road crosses the border into the Navajo Reservation and Arizona. There used to be a handsome arch here with a big 66 sign on top. One side of the arch welcomed travelers to New Mexico and the other bid them farewell. The arch was so cinematic that John Ford was compelled to include it in his interpretation of *The Grapes of Wrath*. Unfortunately, the arch was later demolished, and now only cold signs tell us that we are crossing the state line.

8

The Arid Zone

On the Edge of the Largest Indian Reservation

After New Mexico follows Arizona. Once again John Steinbeck's *The Grapes of Wrath* gives a proper description of Route 66 in the new state: "They crawled up the slopes, and the low twisted trees covered the slopes. Holbrook, Joseph City, Winslow. And then the tall trees began, and the cars spouted steam and labored up the slopes. And there was Flagstaff, and that was the top of it all. Down from Flagstaff over the great plateaux, and the road disappeared in the distance ahead. The water grew scarce, water was to be bought, five cents, ten cents, fifteen cents a gallon." Tom Teague's *Searching for 66* is equally accurate for the eastern part of Arizona: "Vegetation gave way completely, revealing the most beautiful badlands in America. Red, violet, green and gray layers of clay were laid down here by an ocean several epochs ago. Desert winds of succeeding eons sculpted canyons, buttes and mesas." It feels as if the best vistas are to be found in Arizona. I know many who second that.

The Old US-66 splits northern Arizona from borderline to borderline, in many places following the railroad tracks for long stretches. In the eastern part of the state Route 66 runs relatively close to the new interstate highway, often as its frontage road. In the middle it runs right under it, but in the west it deviates from the new highway between Winona and Flagstaff. Further west, when I-40 takes a shortcut between Seligman and Kingman and makes a bend between Kingman and Topock, the Old Road goes totally on its separate way. In places the Old 66 is impassable, the asphalt cracked and the cracks overgrown with grass like the desert. Sometimes the Old Road is only a branch to a trading post that refuses to capitulate to post-modern triviality and its small stories. It still likes to live the tall tale of the West.

Both the old and the new road run in the middle of Indian lands. Apaches live in the south, Navajos in the middle and north, Hopis also in the north, Hualapai and Havasupai canyon Indians in the northwest, and Yavapais in the southwest. Ruined Anasazi and Sinagua villages are everywhere.

Roughly speaking, the area is hot in the summer and cold in the winter. For long stretches, Route 66 runs more than 6,500 feet above sea level, and a lot of snow can cover the road in winter. At least when it remembers to fall. In the winter of 1996 the skiing season was the briefest on record—only two weeks and even they were not in succession. The next winter there were such snowstorms that the roads were blocked in many places for days on end. The record of 1996 was passed to history, however, by 2002. That winter there was no skiing season at all, as the snow decided to travel only in the sky and left the earth cold. The year of 2012 began with a snowstorm, but hot weather also came early. Summer rains usually come in July, if they remember to come at all. That the summer rains may not come is one reason why snow in the winter and the water into which it turns are important to the area's vegetation. Rain dances are no laughing matter around here; they are solemn prayer.

Arizona may not be an easy place to live. Johnny Cash put it beautifully and bluntly in his title song for the Jicarilla Apache Tribe production of the film *Gunfight:* "The country is not pretty, when you're hungry." Arizona's name is believed to stem from a word meaning "small springs" in the tongue of the Pima Indians living in the southern parts of the state. Maybe Spaniards coming from Mexico learned the location of springs from the Pimas, and eventually the positive-sounding name came to refer to a wide area north of the springs. According to fake etymologists, Arizona means the dry western zone of the old New Mexico; the name is supposed to come from the words *arid* and *zone.*

Arizona may not be an easy place to live, but the landscapes truly are magnificent, at least, when you have your belly full of Navajo Tacos, Hopi Tacos, or Hualapai Tacos, i.e. fry bread filled with salad, meat, cheese, and beans. Or Southwest Quesadillas, Fajitas Quesadillas, Hualapai Quesadillas, or even Don Juan Quesadillas, all served in these parts in large portions. Route 66 continues from the New Mexico desert through the Petrified Forest and Painted Desert into one of the world's largest pine forest areas. The Grand Canyon is near, tall

mountains loom in every direction, and eventually the Road descends to the bank of the Colorado River. Originally, Route 66 ran through Arizona for 376 miles. The longest remaining unbroken stretch of the Road is in Arizona: 160 miles between Seligman and Topock.

The town on the eastern New Mexico border is Lupton, after G. W. Lupton, who originally worked for the Santa Fe Railroad Company as a switchman in Winslow and, finally, as the company's director in San Francisco. The railroad, particularly the Atchison, Topeka, and Santa Fe, still has an important position in the Southwest, first and foremost in the Arizona area through which US-66 and the new I-40 run. The Atlantic & Pacific Company also has its own history, albeit largely the same as that of the ATSF. Nowadays, BNSF locomotives pull the trains, as the Burlington Northern and Santa Fe companies have joined forces. Most of the new engines are light orange in color.

The first thing on the Arizona side of the border is the Painted Cliffs Welcome Center, a nice little stop to use the restrooms, take a breath, and collect material about sights in the Grand Canyon State. Franciscan priests Silvestre Vélez de Escalante and Francisco Atanasio Domínguez also stopped around here on November 16, 1776, when they were returning from the Hopi village of Oraibi. Their trip had been in vain, as they had not managed to convert the Hopis to Christianity. They had to stop and camp by the Painted Cliffs because of a snowstorm. The Hopis had saved them from starving to death, however, and from Painted Cliff they had only a day's journey to the familiar Zuni Pueblo.

Coming into Arizona, Route 66 crosses not only the state line but also the boundary of the United States' geographically largest Indian reservation. The change between Manuelito and Lupton is clear, although no signs point out the boundary here either. Manuelito is a small and quiet village. So is Lupton—in principle.

However, the number of roadside advertisements is much greater inside the Navajo Reservation. It feels as if each and every member of this Indian people, numbering almost three hundred thousand, wanted to put up a billboard advertising his jewelry shop, rug shop, or simply himself to tempt tourists or simply to hide the beautiful landscape.

First, there's Fort Yellowhorse, the old fort of chief Yellow Horse. It's a log house adjacent to a cliff, surrounded by fences of pales. More accurately, it used to have fences. Time has taken its toll here, too. But not to worry. Half a mile away is the new Yellowhorse Trading Post, a house larger than the old one and right next to the cliff. On the edge of the cliff are a number of animal figures that depict what life may have been like on this stony terrain before the arrival of white people, before the trading post, and before Route 66. The shop sells anything that you can link stereotypically to Indians, and maybe some handmade Navajo art that is of real value.

In Lupton, the Road takes a sharp turn to the left and goes under the new highway to its south side. Now we have left the Yellowhorse Trading Post, but ahead is the Ortega trading house, a mixture of Indian traditions combining a wigwam and an igloo, a store owned by the traditional Southwest merchant family almost in the middle of the desert. The ice-cream ad by the door is adequate.

After Ortega one sees hardly anything but billboards by the road and empty names on the map. Sometimes not even those are there. Whenever the number of billboards intensifies, you can be sure that a trading post lies just ahead. We pass the Navajo Lupton district chapter hall. Fort Courage must have been named to emphasize the courage of the US Army. Houck and Cedar Point. The sandy road takes a bend through—what was the place? But from Sanders, anyway, road 191 runs south to Apache country and finally all the way to Aqua Prieta, Mexico. From Chambers, road 191 also runs north to Ute country and, finally, all the way to Moab and Price in Utah. After Sanders the highways leave the Navajo Reservation, but they barely touch the western corner of the southern hook's northern border. Even the name of the locality is Navajo, if you want to call this place a locality. It is a mere dot on the map.

Tepees and Wigwams

After the Navajo Reservation we reach the Petrified Forest National Park and its Painted Desert gate. The Painted Desert itself is an extremely beautiful chain of multi-colored landforms following the highway on the northern side of the Little Colorado River, approximately from Houck to the Grand Canyon. Most of the area lies within the Navajo Reservation, and only a small corner of it is national park. It is true that northeast of Winslow is a tiny Painted Desert Park, maintained by Navajo County. Many hues of red, yellow, and even blue tint the sand and stone. They are all raw material for Navajo sand paintings.

The Petrified Forest National Park was founded in 1906, and ever since the opening of Route 66 it was one of the most intriguing tourist attractions on the Road. The park's natural beauty and many wonders lie along thirty miles of road that leads to sites on both sides of the new highway. A Fred Harvey Trading Post is still at the park's gate, and another Harvey shop is on the southern end of the park road about a mile from the gate by the Giant Logs.

The Long Logs, the Giant Logs, the Crystal Forest, and the Rainbow Forest are all petrified trees. Originally, they grew in soil with plenty of water, but when the water disappeared and evaporated they petrified into hard crystal. Surprisingly, *The Rough Guide* series of traveler's guides, mostly meant for young people and nature lovers, shows no interest in the petrified trees. The series considers them nothing but dark and boring trunks lying on the ground. It is true that the luster of these trees lying on the ground does not reach the level of polished bits of petrified wood, but their colors and shapes are nevertheless marvelous, if the petrifaction alone is not marvel enough. It is as if the pattern of trees, complete with annual growth rings, had been chiseled in stone. Especially in the old days people used to ship petrified lumber from the area by the truckload, but now such lumber is protected. Plenty of it is available for tourists, however, in the National Park shops, not to mention the tourist traps encircling the southern edge of the park, or practically any gas station or souvenir shop within a fifty-mile radius. The petrified lumber is used in jewelry in the manner of semi-precious stones, and when it's polished it has amazing hues and beauty.

Neither does *The Rough Guide* praise the Agate House of the Petrified Forest, built entirely from petrified wood. In this case I share the sentiment of the guide. No doubt the ancient Indians as well as the Indians dwelling in or around the Petrified Forest used petrified wood as their construction material. However, the restoration of the Agate House appears more than a little non-Indian.

There are, however, plenty of Indian culture remnants in the national park. Notable among the park's many Indian petroglyphs is Newspaper Rock—not exactly like a modern newspaper, but during the centuries passing Anasazis have scraped scores of messages into it with their stone knives. More Indian inscriptions can be seen by the ruins of Puerco Pueblo. The houses of the Pueblo do not resemble the Agate House very much, although they are only some five miles apart.

The Tepees are also related to Indians, although this is more due to the misconceptions of the white name-givers than any Indians who ever dwelled in this area. The Petrified Forest tepees are cone-shaped mounds of eroded rock. Their foundation is ferrous oxide. A white strip of sandstone runs across the hem of every tepee and the very top of its cone is clay. Iron content defines the darkness of the red color.

Beyond Chambers the Old 66 has been impassable for a long time. The new highway is the only road to drive. The same is true after the Petrified Forest, unless you haven't driven through the National Park and approached Holbrook from the southeast across the Little Colorado River along Road 180. Coming from the northeast, you have to drive down I-40. You may at times glimpse a stretch of the Old Road somewhere to the left, but there is no way to get there before Adamana, and even then only back east and into a blind alley.

In Adamana, named after sheep rancher Adam Hanna, there is nothing to see apart from Indian tepees, the white man's only image of an Indian dwelling. These tepees are made of concrete and plasterboard, and they are in the Petrified Forest Indian Center. Here you can buy everything that has been linked to Indians at any time and has nothing to do with Indians. On the other hand, the trading post also has an excellent collection of genuine Indian jewelry, Navajo art, and Hopi katsinas. The ratio between price and quality is better than in most similar shops.

The next town is Holbrook, the center of eastern Arizona. Holbrook was founded in 1882 as a station for the Atlantic & Pacific Railroad, which opened the same year. One of Fred Harvey's first cafés was here, in a dining car on a short dead-end track. Long before that, dinosaurs traveled in the area, according to the dinosaur museum just east of town.

Holbrook is very much a Route 66 town, so much so that the *Holbrook Tribune-News*, which has been serving the area since 1909, proudly displays the shield sign of Route 66 beside its masthead. It is possible that the White Motor Court maintained here in the 1920s and 1930s was the first real camping ground in the United States. Holbrook was an important tourist center on Highway 66 especially after World War II, and it has partly held its position ever since. No wonder. The Petrified Forest is nearby. To the north lie Navajo and Hopi country and all their wonders. In the south are many lakes and the pine-covered Mogollon Rim, nowadays also boasting the Apache White Mountain ski resort and casino.

Holbrook itself is packed with Indians up to the street names. Route 66 approaches the town along Navajo Boulevard and then turns right along Hopi Drive. The Powwow Trading Post with its neon lights is like a remnant from the past. The Algonqian term "powwow" originally meant a negotiation or some other event. Today, it refers to almost any meeting or party of Indians.

How about the Joe & Aggie Café? Is the coffeepot still warm? The sandwiches could be better, considering the price. Or how about Ted Julien's Roadrunner, the Holbrook 66 shop? Nostalgic signs and badges from days gone by. T-shirts, sweaters, Indian jewelry, Coca-Cola junk, katsinas, brass things, Route 66 stuff. Some of it unusual. Step right in: looking around costs nothing.

Ted Julien is one of those old-time gentlemen who have the basic values of life figured out. He has never had the time to visit Finland, although he visited Europe in the service of the US Army. Like others of his age group, he remembers the "key" things about my northern homeland: Finland paid her debts and fought the Soviet Communists hard in the Winter War. The talk goes on, and there's a torrent of questions. The talk is friendly and amicable. It costs nothing, either. Ted Julien also advertises his daughters Angie and Grace on his business card. One side of the card portrays a roadrunner posing in front of an Arizona U.S. 66 road sign. On the other side, the 66 animal next to the road sign is the legendary jackalope.

I have been a constant visitor at the Roadrunner since 1996 and so has my brother. In April 2002 he and I had a rendezvous in Flagstaff, he coming from Denver and I arriving from the east. When I stopped at Ted Julien's and asked whether my brother had gone by recently, Julien raises his hand high in the air to show the height of my brother before saying "yes." He is not the only one who claims to remember us because we are tall. My brother is 196 cm, or six-foot-four, I am merely 187, or six-foot-one.

"Nothing much has changed here," said Julien in 2002. It was getting to be mid-April. Outside, it was windy and seventy-seven degrees. But opposite his Roadrunner shop at the corner of Navajo Boulevard and Hopi Drive, across that little kind of a plaza, there was a new mural of Holbrook before the Route 66 era. It was done by Liz Nichols in early 2002 and depicts a train and two mail riders on a Holbrook street.

If you have never lived in an Indian tent, don't worry; you can still do it in Holbrook—almost, anyway. All rooms at the Wigwam Village are like that. The motel consists of individual cabins shaped like a tepee, not a wigwam, in an area where the Indians have never lived in cone-shaped tepees any more than in round-roofed wigwams. Does it matter: one Indian dwelling or the other? To white people they are the same. But does anybody ever ask the Indians' opinion?

Of course, it all began with an ice-cream cone. Sometime in the 1930s, someone had built an ice-cream stand in the shape of a cone in Long Beach, California. Frank Redford saw it and built a cone-shaped café and gas station in Horse Cave, Kentucky, in 1933. Tourists visiting the nearby Mammoth Cave could hardly believe their eyes when they saw "Indian tepees" in Kentucky woods. The next thing you know, there were cone-shaped lodgings in the area. Redford got a patent for his tepee model and started to sell his houses to other roadside motel owners. For some inexplicable reason, the product was named "wigwam." Within fifteen years, the Wigwam Village motel chain had seven motels in six states.

Holbrook's Wigwam Motel opened on June 1, 1950. The first owner, Chester E. Lewis, built a tepee village according to Redford's plan. The interior also represented the "genuine" Wild West, complete with Navajo blankets and the rest. When the tourist stream dwindled, the motel became dilapidated and closed down in 1974, but after enthusiasm revived for Route 66, the motel was restored and reopened in 1988. Apart from the motel office, all of the buildings are "Indian tents." Each "wigwam" has a bathroom and air conditioning, and some of them have double beds. They are like any other motel room in this part of the country—except for their shape. The other wigwam villages have vanished altogether. Only two others remain: one in Cave City, Kentucky, and another in Rialto, California, right on Route 66.

Navajo Highway, and a Bit of Hopi, Too

The railroad and the highway introduced isolated southwestern Indians to the rest of the world and made them part of the United States. Both Navajos and Hopis were employed to advertise the Road right from the beginning of the 66. The highway made it possible for inhabitants of Chicago and the Midwest to get acquainted with real Indians in New Mexico and Arizona. Many of them used the Road for this purpose—and still do. And why not? The landscapes in the Indian country are breathtakingly beautiful, the Navajos and the Hopis are friendly without exception, and the representatives of both nations are very good at selling to tourists even Indian merchandise made in Hong Kong or Taiwan—at a good price, too.

Route 66 relics west of Holbrook are almost all destroyed. The trading post dedicated to the memory of Apache Chief Geronimo tries hard to survive, who knows for how long? We left Apache County soon after Adamana, and the remains of the Old Road lie unused in Navajo County all the way west to Winslow. County lines in Arizona are drawn exactly the way only a white man afraid of Indians is able to do. Even the rather narrow Navajo County stretching from north to south includes a part of the Hopi Reservation, a part of the Navajo Reservation, and a part of White Mountain or Fort Apache Reservation. Most of the county's inhabitants are probably white people from the towns of Winslow, Holbrook, Show Low, and Snowflake. If, for example, the Navajo Reservation with its population of over a quarter of a million people were all in one county, it could easily happen that an Indian would be elected as a representative for the state legislature. Nothing prevents the Indians from trying as it is, and every once in a while one of Arizona's counties gets an American Indian to the Phoenix capitol, be it Navajo, Apache, Papago, or someone else.

North of Winslow lie the ancient ruins of Homol'ovi Indian Village. The southern border of the Navajo Reservation is about ten miles away and the southern border of the Hopi Reservation is some thirty-five miles as the crow flies, but this is a sacred place of the Hopis, whose clans lived here before white people or possibly even Navajos came to the area. Now it is a state park where Hopis have certain privileges.

The studio of David Johns, perhaps the most famous contemporary Southwest Navajo artist, is in Winslow, where the artist and his family also live. Johns is known for his abstract paintings reflecting the southwestern atmosphere and American Indians. His most famous and well-known work is inside a dome in an office building in Phoenix.

Albert Wareing, a chief executive of a construction company, was interested in European architecture and art, and he wanted to build something of the kind as the new headquarters of his company. One possibility was a big dome filled with paintings following the example of the Sistine Chapel in the Vatican. Wareing even traveled to Europe to find a painter. Once, he thought he had found one, but it did not quite work out.

Lovena Ohl was a well-known gallerist and expert on Native American art in Scottsdale before her death in the early 1990s. She came across Albert Wareing, who told her of his problem. Ohl then suggested that he use a local artist instead and even promised to find him one: David Johns.

Johns took on the task with enthusiasm but also with worry. He had never done anything similar. He told us that when he went up to the ceiling the first day, he felt so dizzy that he had to come down immediately. Back down again, he pulled himself together, made some sketches, climbed the ladder again, and started painting. In the following couple of years, he filled the dome and the upper walls with southwestern figures and symbolism. The Navajo Yeibicheis, the Comanche leader Quanah Parker, the Apache leader Geronimo, the thunder clouds of the Pueblos, and various members of southwestern Indian Nations eventually populated the surface.

In the dome, as in all his works, David Johns looks for a harmony both in colors and in modes. In his paintings, symbolism of the Navajos, Hopis, Comanches, and Apaches reflects the magnificent and mysterious charm of the American Southwest. Northern Arizona University in Flagstaff has made Johns an honorary PhD, and his works have been exhibited in galleries not only in the United States but also in France, Germany, Switzerland, and Finland.

In Johns's paintings, Navajo, Hopi, Apache, and Comanche symbols together recreate the wonderful world of the Southwest. Unfortunately, the lives of real Indians have not always been as harmonious. Before the arrival of whites, many Indian nations, tribes, and clans fought for supremacy on the plains and mesas of northern Arizona. At times the struggle for control of the land and, more than that, of the water was bloody. Then followed the wars against the Spaniards, Mexicans, and U.S. settlers. Tom Teague explains that the Natives "know what 'equality of conditions' means. For them, it means they can't be different anymore. Witness the Navajo-Hopi Relocation dispute along Route 66 in Arizona." This is true: the situation is not much easier today. The disputes between the Navajos and the Hopis frequently involve violence, although fortunately nobody has been killed in the past few years.

According to historical evidence, Hopis settled the area first and ruled over a much larger area than their present reservation. The Apaches and Navajos came to the Southwest perhaps not long before Europeans, possibly as late as the sixteenth century. The Navajos adopted many practical skills and spiritual knowledge from the Hopis, including parts of their myth of creation. Their long-term coexistence has confused matters to the extent that many Navajos even consider the ancient Pueblo Indians, the Anasazis, and the Hohokam, their ancestors.

Toward the end of the previous century, the authority of the United States in northern Arizona stabilized, and Navajos and Hopis alike were ushered to their reservations. The US Congress founded the Navajo Reservation with a specific new act in 1868. President Chester A. Arthur gave the executive order for a Hopi Reservation west of Navajo country in 1882. The area of the Hopis dwindled to a quarter of their established area during the Spanish and Mexican reign. Navajos constantly visited this area, and many made their homes there. The growth of Navajo population and their need for land resulted gradually in the growth of the Navajo Reservation, until it almost encircled the Hopi Reservation in the 1930s. Navajo visits into Hopi country continued, and many Navajo Indians lived there permanently, in spite of Hopi protests. In 1962 a court declared that a part of the Hopi land belonged to the Navajos who had lived there for a long time, and a large part of the reservation was made into an area common to Navajos and Hopis, the so-called joint use area.

Disputes and marriages between Navajos and Hopis continued. Finally, Congress decided to separate the disputing parties and to divide the land. The Navajos living in Hopi country were in principle supposed to leave, and the Hopis were correspondingly supposed to leave that part of the JUA that was going to become Navajo Reservation land. Most of the Hopis and Navajos involved refused to go anywhere. Many of them were forced to move, and their houses were burned. The Hopi Reservation shrank by half. Fighting and demonstrations on the new borders as well as in Winslow and Flagstaff began then and continue today.

Treaties allowed the Hopis to visit their sacred places, which were now inside the Navajo Reservation. However, Navajos frequently prevented the visits. Hopis also have the right to gather the eagle feathers they need for their religious ceremonies in the traditional eagle area, now inside the Navajo Reservation. During the feather-gathering season, however, Navajo police often stop gatherers, claiming that Hopis need a special permit from the Navajo administration. The answer of the Hopis is that they already have the permit from the US government. It does not make things any easier that a part of the Hopis think that they got the permit to gather the feathers from the Creator, and therefore permits from the United States or the Navajos are unnecessary. However, the Navajo police stop the gatherers.

A few thousand Navajos continue to live in Hopi country despite the division, particularly in the northern part of the Hopi Reservation where few Hopis live. The Hopi tribal council has attempted to reach an agreement for long-term land leasing with them. There has been talk about a ninety-nine-year lease, and a few Navajos have already agreed. Some Hopis feel that even ninety-nine seconds are too much. Furthermore, both parties have their white supporters, of course, serving to complicate matters even more. Many Indians even feel that if the local white inhabitants and the officials of Arizona and the US government would stop hassling with the land dispute between the Navajos and the Hopis, the situation would improve sooner and easier. At the moment, it seems that it will never improve. Therefore, it is possible to witness Indian warfare on the northern side of the Old 66 even in this day and age.

Here, Navajos are scattered far and wide, mainly as ranchers. The population centers are Ganado and the smaller Leupp, Dilkon, and Jeddito, the last one now encircled by the Hopi Reservation. There are roads from all of them south to the Old 66, or the Interstate Highway 40 of today. Hopi villages, or rather small towns, are grouped along Road 264 on the tops and bases of three table mountains, i.e. mesas. Most of the Hopis are farmers, although they also breed cattle. The Hopi village farthest to the west, Moenkopi, lies outside the reservation, but it, too, is surrounded by the Navajo Reservation. Across the road is the Navajo town Tuba City, named after a former Hopi chief. In the store you can tell the men apart by their hats. Navajos, breeding cattle and sheep, use cowboy hats as a rule; Hopis prefer baseball caps. The rule is not without exception, however. Even some Hopis are good rodeo riders.

There are also constant marriages between Hopis and Navajos. In everyday intercourse the relations can be very friendly. The representatives of both peoples are equally dependent on the will of the US government and especially Congress, as well as the public opinion among the local white population. The principal source of income for both tribes has been the Peabody coal mine on Black Mesa. Whatever differences there have been between their cultures, many of them have leveled out with time. Both tribes work hard on many issues together. Hostility raises its ugly head only when the interests of one or the other are at play, or it will manifest itself—as in Finland, England, and most other countries—when people are at football games or basketball games, or when they are drunk.

Maybe it is true in a more general sense that we look for enemies from those who are like us. Hopis and Navajos, Turkey and Greece, Swedes and Finns, Texans and Okies. But has Texas ever conquered Oklahoma as Sweden conquered Finland, Turkey conquered Greece, and Navajos occupied the Hopiland?

Route 66 travels on.

Joseph City lies between Holbrook and Winslow. It got its name from the Mormons (named after their prophet Joseph Smith) who founded the town in 1867 as an agricultural center. Attempts to change the area into a verdant valley through artificial irrigation did not succeed, however, and Joseph City led a meager life. It became a railroad station town and eventually a service town for the highway. Nowadays, the town's pride is the big Cholla power plant, turning coal and oil into electricity for the needs of Phoenix, the capital of Arizona.

A couple of miles west of downtown Joseph City stands the Jack Rabbit Trading Post, one of the true monuments of the Road in the Southwest. Decorated with statues and pictures of jackrabbits, this tourist business has operated on the southern side of the new highway since 1949. James Taylor founded it and leased it to Glenn Blansett, the grandfather of the present owner back in 1961. Blansett bought the place in 1967, when Interstate 40 was opened to traffic. Phil Blansett bought the place from his father a couple of years later. In 1995 he decided to retire and sold the post to his daughter Cindy and her husband, Tony Jaquez, the current proprietors.

Originally, the Jack Rabbit, like the Meramec Caverns, was one of the most industrious advertisers on the Road. You could see the silhouette of a jackrabbit in the outskirts of both Chicago and Los Angeles, hundreds of miles from the trading post. Clifford Haby, a sixty-something-year-old man from Texas, reminisces that as a youngster he used to tell his mother and sister how many miles were left to the Jack Rabbit, until the others noticed the small roadside signs that had only the jackrabbit silhouette and the distance in miles. Today, Jack Rabbit signs are few.

Still, the Jack Rabbit is an impressive place, today maybe even more so than before, for its position among the legends of the Old Road. "If you haven't visited the Jack Rabbit, you haven't visited the Southwest," as the claim goes. A large painting of the jackrabbit silhouette across the road from the trading post confirms, "Here it is." You can celebrate your arrival with a glass of the trading post's own cherry cider. It is probably the best drink in the world—at least it tastes like pure bliss beneath the Arizona sun.

The trading post is a typical Southwest and Navajo store offering the traditional merchandise, tourist junk, and Indian trinkets no Indians would ever mistake for their own. Old Road souvenirs at the Jack Rabbit, however, are the cheapest along the Road. With the Route 66 revival, one of the side rooms of the trading post has become a small museum exhibiting pictures of the Road, road signs, and a full-size cardboard James Dean. A guest book records few Finnish names, but in early May 2002 it was fun to find two familiar ones. My former pub-

lisher and his significant other, a colleague of my wife, had been there just a few days earlier. We did not run into them on this trip, but some of our Navajo friends did.

From Holbrook, Route 66 runs mainly under the new highway, following the northern bank of the Little Colorado River. Just before they finally cross the river, the old and the new highway separate. The Southwest Indian Center is at the corner. It's a typical tourist trap and a shop of Indian trinkets. From it, a line of rotting telephone poles leads you eastward into the solitude of the desert on a stretch of 66 replaced by the new I-40 in 1958. The Old Road doesn't take you far, however, before you reach a dead end.

Leading to the west, Historic Route 66— now State Route 87—and the new interstate cross the Little Colorado River side-by-side. The river here is not big, but at least you can see it from the bridge. Soon after the crossing we come to Winslow, 4,855 feet above sea level. The new highway curves around it like a longbow arched to the north. The Old 66 dives into the heart of the town. On the town's western edge it goes on even after intersecting the new highway, only to end at a Road-Closed sign and vanish in the sand.

Winslow was founded in 1881 at the end of the wagon trail leading to the Atlantic & Pacific Railroad. Today, the town is a small but interesting stop along Route 66. Earlier in its history, however, Winslow was much busier. Traffic on Route 66 was so heavy that it became the first divided highway in the state running west along Third Street and east along Second as it still does today. Twelve passenger trains stopped in Winslow every day on their route between Los Angeles and New York, and as many as eight Trans-World Airlines flights a day landed at Winslow. Now, the region surrounding the town lives mainly on farming and is served by two Amtrak trains daily and practically no passenger air service.

Fred Harvey's Spanish-style hotel, La Posada, still stands in Winslow. Built in 1930, it is the masterpiece of architect Mary Jane Colter, who designed many of the Harvey buildings. With the company's decline, La Posada closed in 1959. The Santa Fe Railway Company bought it and converted it into offices. Much of the original interior and art has been destroyed or sold away. At one point the building was facing demolition. For years a popular movement tried to preserve it as a part of the Southwest and Route 66 tradition. These efforts finally succeeded in 1997 when Allan Affeldt and Frank Randall purchased La Posada. Affeldt negotiated for three years with the Santa Fe Railway before all legal and financial obstacles were finally overcome. Daniel Lutzick joined Affeldt and Randall as the general manager of the building. Restoration is underway with the help of the Arizona State Parks Heritage Fund, the Arizona Department of Transportation Enhancement Grant program, and several Route 66 aficionados and preservation organizations. Planning has resurrected Colter's guiding fantasy of the Pajaros family, Spanish *hacendados* who came to the area in the early nineteenth century and gradually built La Posada and an empire around it, until the 1929 market crash forced the last Pajaro to sell everything to the Santa Fe Railway.

Today, La Posada warrants a stop, even if you don't want to stay overnight. If you do, the rooms are quite moderately priced. They vary in shape and size, but each is dedicated to a former celebrity. In this, La Posada almost repeats El Rancho of Gallup, except that here every celebrity is not necessarily a movie star. Rooms are named for Clark Gable and Cary Cooper, but also for Charles Lindbergh and his wife, Anne Morrow. You can even book the Howard Hughes hideaway. A self-guided tour explores the great public spaces of this marvelous house.

In La Posada's Turquoise Room Restaurant, the Don Juan Quesadillas are the best quesadillas on Route 66 with plenty of cheese inside and served with a nice portion of fresh salad. The lemonade, although more than two dollars a glass, is worth every cent. My wife claims it tastes like a margarita without tequila.

And, of course, the gift shop is filled with all kinds of stuff: Indian things, china, souvenirs, Route 66 memorabilia, and books. If you happen to run into a big dog lying on the floor of the shop, don't worry. This is a friendly canine.

Winslow remains an important stop on the railroad and on Route 66. Burlington Northern Santa Fe Railway still has their Arizona Headquarters in the east wing of La Posada. The Winslow depot and Amtrak station is practically an addition to the great hotel. The main entrance to La Posada originally was from the tracks and not from the Old Trails Highway, which later became Route 66.

Winslow is immortalized in the Eagles song "Take It Easy." Winslow has even designated "the corner" to match the lyrics: "Standin' on a corner / In Winslow, Arizona / And such a fine sight to see / It's a girl, my lord, in a flatbed Ford, / Slowin' down to take a look at me." Everything is there: the guy with his guitar at the corner of Second Street and Kinsley Avenue and a mural by John Pugh showing the girl and her car almost as a reflection in windows from the street. In her eyes there is interest but no promise. If your collection of Route 66 memorabilia is still incomplete, you can supplement it across the street from the corner. Roadworks Gifts and Souvenirs on the second floor carries hundreds of Route 66 items, a large selection of Santa Fe Railroad gifts, and plenty of "Standin' on a Corner" stuff.

A number of restaurants and other service-trade businesses in Winslow swear by the name of the Old Road, or rather by its number. Falcon Restaurant, serving travelers for some fifty years between the streets going east and west, has gained some reputation among travelers of the Road. As a family restaurant, it is a tidy place, but the breakfast is nothing worth writing home about. Jeff Durfee, a Minnesota resident who shared the breakfast with us, stated that it was possibly the most miserable restaurant breakfast he had ever had. However, the waiter of the Falcon seemed to be an anamoly for people around these parts.

We lucked out, however, at Sue's Place along the street going west. Sue's Place is not as old a house as the Falcon, but its interior is more like a traditional diner: a long counter with bar stools and a row of tables by the windows. It also has a separate room looking more like a restaurant. The lunch was cheap, good, and generous and the service as friendly as it can only be in the United States.

John Lorenzo Hubbell, "Glass Eye" or "Four Eyes" to the Navajos, as he wore spectacles, was one of the most important southwestern merchants of the late nineteenth century. His home and largest trading post, nowadays a national monument called Hubbell Trading Post, lies northeast of Winslow, but Hubbell also had a store and a big warehouse in the town proper to make a better use of the railroad. His name can still be seen on the wall of the house on 66 going east, although the letters are fading fast. Even today you can buy quality art inside the building, now operated by the Arizona Indian Artists Cooperative. Since you buy directly from the artists, the prices are lower than from most other sources.

Winslow's Store for Men has disappeared. Once the store had perhaps more billboards on Route 66 than Jack Rabbit or Meramec Caverns. You could read the "Men" ads as far as Paris or Guam, wherever the US Army was stationed. The store offered the latest in men's clothing, designed to attract beautiful women. Maybe the beautiful women later got bored with the clothes, as the store went bankrupt when the Old Highway was closed, and it has never returned.

West of Winslow, you soon pass from Navajo County into Coconino County. Route 66 approaches the southern border of the Navajo Reservation once again, although the road does not quite cross it. The landscape remains empty and flat. The snowy San Francisco Peaks appear closer than before, but the pine forests are yet to appear.

Space and its wonders stop our earthly wandering. Meteor City is a small trading place on the Old Road and south of the new I-40. It has an intersection of its own from the new highway, and that is maybe the only reason for its survival here in the middle of nowhere. Despite its grandiose name, Meteor City is only one building. It is a strange cupola shaped like half a ball, like a meteor that has come out of the sky, hit the ground, and embedded itself half into it. Inside, the building is like any other large store in the area. There is only a very limited supply of foodstuffs but plenty of local textiles and ceramics, and, naturally, all kinds of tourist junk that has nothing to do with the Southwest, Indians, meteors, or Route 66. You can get a free postcard as long as you promise to mail one to a trading post from your hometown.

The road to the crater is still somewhat further west and also has an intersection of its own from I-40. Meteor Crater is one of the oldest Route 66 attractions and definitely the biggest of them all. The diameter of the hole is almost three miles and the depth is no less than 570 feet. It was created by a meteor strike some fifty thousand years ago. Meteor Crater is such an exceptional thing that it has naturally given birth to a multitude of legends and myths. Some Navajos claim that their ancestors came to the earth on the meteor, creating the crater a long time before the Hopis and other heirs of the Anasazis. Therefore, they have an older claim and right to the area than the Pueblo Indians. The Navajos who came here later merely joined their tribesmen who had come here on the meteor. Unlike most other Indians, Navajos and Apaches and a group of tribes from northwestern Canada belong to the so-called Athabascan or Dené peoples, whose ethnic features are remarkably different from other Indians. The Navajos call themselves *Diné*, and their language actually lacks the sound for *v*. According to the European view, the Denés came to North America across the Bering Strait much later than other Indians. The wildest story of them all has it that a second group of Navajos also came to earth on a meteor that landed somewhere in Siberia. A part of the people traveled east and to North America and became the Navajo and the Apache peoples and the Canadian Dené. Another part traveled west and reached the edge of Europe, eventually to become—Finns!

White people officially learned about the Meteor Crater sometime in the 1870s, although nobody at the time knew it was created by a meteor. People thought the hole was a result of a volcano eruption. There are craters like that in the area, after all—Sunset Crater, for example, some twenty miles north of Flagstaff. In 1902 Daniel Moreau Barringer, Jr., a mining engineer from Philadelphia, acquired rights to the Meteor Crater and surrounding area. He found remains of small meteors in the vicinity of the crater, as well as traces of the rare minerals the meteors had carried. Barringer spent the next quarter of a century looking for the remains of the big meteor from the bottom of the large crater. Initially, he excavated the middle of the hole under the assumption that the meteor had hit the ground vertically. Later, Barringer realized that the meteor could have hit the ground at an angle and started excavating the edges of the crater. The excavations consumed time and money, however. Having spent no less than six hundred thousand dollars on them, Barringer had to give up the search in 1929. It was not until much later that other people found the remains of the gigantic meteor from the very edge of the crater that Barringer had searched only cursorily due to his lack of funds.

Barringer had a small store, a restaurant, and a lookout tower with a view across the crater. The current owners have established a visitors' center there. They allow tourists to go right to the edge of the crater, and, with a special license for a special fee, to visit the crater bottom. The visitors' center has a good presentation of the crater's creation and of meteorite research in general, but if you are not particularly keen on astronomy, you may want to reflect upon whether it is worth paying ten dollars or more to see a hole in the ground—a big hole, yes, but nevertheless only a hole.

Two of Everything

Arizona is Wild West. Like Michael Wallis wrote in his *Route 66: The Mother Road*: "Few tourists realize that so much violence has taken place at this once busy highway refuge. The ghosts of Apache and Navajo warriors, slain pioneers who never reached their destinations, a foolish young cowboy named John Shaw, and a gaggle of brightly painted whores wait for their next incarnation."

Past Meteor Crater are two of everything. First Two Guns, then Twin Arrows, the former named after weapons used by white men, the latter after weapons used by Indians. Both of them are full of stories told by local inhabitants as well as ruined dwellings and the perpetual wind. If you have really keen ears and plenty of luck, you may hear the song of the jackalope, a quiet "whee-up, oee-up" under the full moon. Do not confuse it with the howling of the coyotes, though. That, anybody can hear.

Two Guns still has a service station and a camping site for trailers, but it seems closed. The tracks of the Old Road, becoming more invisible year by year, finally disappear into and under the brush. What is left is something reminiscent of asphalt and a paling yellow lane line. You get the best view of the old village when approaching it from the west on I-40 and taking exit 230.

A cavalry scout patrol was traveling a military road here in 1874 and came across the burning remains of a wagon caravan. Indians had attacked the settlers. At least that is the story. The pioneers had been killed, their domestic animals stolen or chased away, and the wagons set afire. The soldiers dug the bones of the pioneers out of the ashes and laid them in a common grave by the roadside. They arranged a search for hostile Apaches but never found them.

Despite their ethnic kinship, Apaches and Navajos often fought each other. Apaches stole Navajo ponies, women, clothes, and food.

In 1878 Navajos finally found out how the Apaches had been able to escape the cavalry at Two Guns. A Navajo scout was riding through tall grass and by accident came to a spot where a deep cleft led into an underground cave. Apaches were in the cave. The Navajos sealed up all possible openings to the cave, gathered sagebrush and set it on fire so that the smoke drifted into the cave. Inside, the Apaches did all they could to put out the fires. They even slaughtered their horses and tried to quench the flames with animal blood. Meanwhile, the Navajos increased the fire and sent volleys of bullets into the cave. Only a few of the Apaches had enough strength left to sing their death song, the one the jackalopes still repeat, and then there was nothing but silent smoke. The name of the place is still the Apache Death Cave.

Two Guns got its name from white men's pistols. According to a story, the first permanent dweller in the area called himself Two Gun Miller and claimed he was an Apache. He killed his neighbor in a fight, but the court considered it self-defense. Some friends of the victim wrote the words "killed by Indian Miller" on the tombstone. This angered Miller, and he wrecked the stone. Two Gun was sent to jail for a time for the desecration of the grave. When he got out he returned home and soon started again to carry two guns at his sides.

In 1905 two young cowboys called John Shaw and Bill Smith rode to Winslow town, sings the incessant wind. At the Second Street saloon the pair saw six hundred silver dollars on a dice table operated by Frank Ketchum. Soon the guns were out of their holsters, and the two friends rode into the night with the money. A posse had a hard time finding Shaw and Smith. Some of the chasers took a train all the way to Flagstaff after them. There was a tip-off the following evening, saying that the two desperados had been seen near the Canyon Diablo station. The sheriff and his deputies got there quickly. They fired more than twenty shots into a storehouse. The bullets killed Shaw and stunned Smith. The former was buried near the Apache Death Cave, the latter was taken to Winslow to be patched up by the local physician. In the meantime the cowboys and tramps in the saloon remembered that before the robbery Smith and Shaw had put money on the counter to buy themselves drinks. Then they had made their heist and never got to have their drinks in the thick of their escape. The men thought that, villain that he was, Shaw had earned his drink nevertheless. So the whole bunch took off to deliver the drink. They dug up Shaw's body and poured a shot of whiskey down his throat in the pale light of the dawning sun.

Goods carts, stagecoaches, and all kinds of horse-drawn vehicles would stop at Two Guns. One of the saloons was named The Last Drink, possibly in Shaw's memory. There were many other saloons along "Hell Street." Whorehouses, too, of course. B. S. Mary, the madam of one of them, was such a formidable sight that even all the local animals got a crush on her. The yearning can still be heard in the song of the jackalopes.

When Federal Highway 66 came to Two Guns and people traveled on rubber wheels, the going in the Wild West had already quieted down. Otherwise, the American Automobile Association would hardly have endorsed the town as a good place to stop for a rest. A number of "Indian pueblos" appeared there to delight the tourists. Some travelers found their way to the Apache Death Cave, but the unmarked graves of the pioneers and John Shaw remained hidden under the sagebrush. Then haste entered the scene, and so did the new Interstate 40. There was no longer any need to stop at Two Guns. The restaurants disappeared, and the inns became ruins. In 1971, an underground gas tank exploded and destroyed the rest of the remaining buildings. The once proud Mountain Lion store is no more than a heap of rubble. The fading name no longer scares even a regular rabbit, let alone one with horns.

Not far northwest of Two Guns is the long and at places deep rift in the earth's crust known as Canyon Diablo, Devil's Canyon, difficult to cross on foot, on horseback, in a car, or on a train. The railroad bridge and the canyon itself are worth seeing. Unfortunately, the road leading to the canyon is in such bad shape you almost need a four-wheel-drive to make it.

But the travel goes on and so does Route 66. You will have to find your way westward on the new highway, toward two huge arrows sticking from the ground some fifteen miles away, as if a giant Indian had once shot them there. The story has it that fighting between whites and Indians took place here, too. The Indian archers were such marksmen that each arrow they shot killed one settler. However, one of the pioneers was a Finn so tough that it took two arrows to kill him. Hence the name Twin Arrows.

In 1996 the service station and the eight-chair diner were for sale, and the place was closed for the time being. The menu had faded in the scorching Arizona sun until you could barely read "Rattlesnake Hip Roast," "Sagebrush Coffee," and "Fried Jackrabbit Ears." We could not make out the prices. Of course, I had visited Twin Arrows before. Once, my wife and I saw a jackrabbit escape into the bush. I believe he was still in possession of both his ears, but the antlers we did not see.

By the summer of 1998, Twin Arrows Trading Post was open once more, although the service station was still closed. Route 66 root beer and T-shirts were the best sales items. I saw this as a sign of an improving economy here in the remote corners of the desert. But in April 2002, plywood again covered the windows. Despite the ads on I-40 still promising that Twin Arrows was now open and luring drivers to "check and see," no one was selling either gas or root beer. Even one of the arrows had started to deteriorate. All the people were gone; only the jackrabbits remained. We still did not see any with antlers.

Threat from the North

Winona is a small village east of Flagstaff. The crushed red stone from Winona's quarry is used to pave the roads in the area. You can find the red paving on both the Old 66 and the new I-40. Aside from the crushed stone there is not much to say about the village, although Bobby Troup's song pleads: "Don't forget Winona." Well, maybe the old and abandoned road bridge in the hollow of the river is worth remembering. Or the Leupp intersection on top of the hill. Leupp road that takes you onto the Navajo Reservation is the shortest route from Flagstaff to the Hopi mesas. Indians often sit by the crossroads selling roasted piñon nuts.

Just before Winona the old and the new highway go their separate ways. The new I-40 takes a bend to the southwest and skirts Flagstaff on the south. The Old Road continues for a while west-southwest and then winds through a beautiful stand of pines to Flagstaff as the town's Main Street. The name used to be Santa Fe Avenue, but in the early 1990s the name was changed officially to Route 66.

Another road comes to Flagstaff from the north: Highway 89 from Cameron, Tuba City, Kayenta, and Colorado, or Page, Utah, and Salt Lake City. Just before the city center the eastern and northern roads join each other firmly and proceed together to the south and the heart of Flagstaff. Relations between the two roads have not always been so congruent. The clash of their interests is obvious. The road coming from the east is the old route across the nation, the military road, the cart trail, the Prairie Road, Route 66. The competitor from the north and northeast once tried to supplant the elder road with the vigor of youth and the power of uranium. As in his *Quest for the Golden Circle*, Arthur Gómez quotes Robert L. Beers, Chairman of the Durango Chamber of Commerce, once claiming that "when the road through the Navajo Indian Reservation is completed and the Four Corners cutoff is built, a tremendous flow of traffic that previously traveled US 66 will be funneled into our city."

In the post-World War II atmosphere, roads were being opened and constructed primarily for the needs of the Cold War. Congress passed the act that created the interstate system for defense considerations, thus making all interstate highways military roads, in a sense. The aim was also to construct roads to all places that had energy resources or some mineral of military importance. In the Southwest this mostly meant oil, coal, and uranium: oil and gas in the Farmington region of northwestern New Mexico; coal in the Black Mesa, Hopi, and Navajo country; and uranium in both southeastern Utah and the Navajo Reservation.

A decent road across the Navajo Reservation had been in the planning stage for a long time and was on the wish list of many a chamber of commerce. In 1947 a group of economy-oriented men founded the Navajo Trail Association and proposed to the Bureau of Indian Affairs (BIA) the construction of a road through the largest reservation. According to the proposition, the road was to run from Shiprock, New Mexico, to Tuba City, Arizona, from where it would later go south to join the older Route 66 in Flagstaff. Furthermore, if a good road could be constructed from Shiprock to Durango and from Durango to Denver, it would spell a whole new major route between the east and the west. It would shorten the distance between Denver and Phoenix by a couple of hundred miles and provide tourists with easy access to the magical Four Corners, where the borders of Arizona, Utah, Colorado, and New Mexico meet, forming four ninety-degree angles. Especially, the Farmington oil producers demanded the road in their area. While US 66 facilitated cheap transport from the oil fields of West Texas and Oklahoma, only a narrow cart road led to the production area in the San Juan Valley. The building of an oil pipe from the Four Corners area to California began. The construction of a road from Farmington through Pueblo country to Albuquerque along the present Highway 550 started in 1950.

When a uranium refinery was built near Tuba City, the Navajo Trail began to come true. The new road ran from the Monument Valley uranium mines to the border of New Mexico and Arizona. Roads built by the BIA were also improved to create a link from Monument Valley to Tuba City. Initially, these roads were not tourist routes. They were gravel roads meant for large, ore-hauling trucks, and their only role was to get chunks of uranium rock from Monument Valley to the refineries in Durango and Tuba City. The threat to Route 66 was distinct, however. Businessmen of Flagstaff and the area east of it feared that the new northern road would lure traffic there, away from the Old Road. Whereas the 66 made a U-shaped curve south from Chicago, the new road could mean a straighter route across the nation from Chicago through Omaha and Denver to Los Angeles and Phoenix. After a road like that, would three thousand cars, the standard number in 1950, still drive each day through Winslow and Holbrook? Thank goodness the Grand Canyon prevented a road from Tuba City to Las Vegas in Nevada.

Edward Ellsworth, an Arizona congressman elected from the Flagstaff area, stressed the importance of Route 66 in terms of defense. If the West Coast were attacked, Route 66 would be the major evacuation route for the people of Los Angeles and Southern California. In Ellsworth's opinion it was more important to improve the already existing 66 than to waste money in constructing a road to the sparsely populated Hopi and Navajo lands. Such strong opposition did halt the opening of the northern highway. The Four Corners area roads were covered with asphalt by the end of the 1950s, but the Navajo Trail did not materialize. With time, the mines produced less. Tourism became a source of income more important than mining. Navajos themselves wanted a better road into their area and hoped it would bring tourists to Monument Valley in their territory.

The road was finally constructed with the help of Indian policy. Stewart Lee Udall, a young Arizona congressman, claimed that the Navajos and the Hopis could never develop in their economy unless a good road ran into their area. President John F. Kennedy appointed Udall as his Secretary of the Interior and put aside a record sum of seventy million dollars in his first budget for the improvement of Indian reservation infrastructures. Both white and Indian residents of the Four Corners were left to wait for the economic benefits the highway would bring with it.

Around the same time the days of the Old Route 66 began to seem numbered due to the interstate highway program and after the mid-1960s, there was not much opposition in the Holbrook-Winslow area to the opening of the Navajo Trail. After all, the area was to get Interstate 40. Soon the same interstate system created the shortest link between Kansas City and Los Angeles on highways I-70 and I-15. For a time there was more traffic on the Navajo Trail than the Old 66, but as it consisted—and does—of several parts and crossroads, it never got a reputation like Route 66. Few Arizona residents today are even aware of what Navajo Trail means. It is an extremely beautiful trail through the barren and magnificent landscapes of North America, but in mythology it will never threaten the position of Route 66.

In the Shade of the Pine Tree Forest

"If the father of Flagstaff was the railroad, the mother must have been the lumber industry," writes Platt Cline in his *They Came to the Mountain: The Story of Flagstaff's Beginning*. Flagstaff began, indeed, with the railroad and grew with it. It is still a railroad town. The Burlington Northern Santa Fe cars whistle through downtown Flagstaff at about half-hour intervals. Passenger traffic has dwindled to two Amtrak trains a day. Early morning, when most people still sleep, around 5:00 a.m. one of them takes passengers east, and they will reach St. Louis in the afternoon. The other, departing before nine p.m., takes people to Los Angeles by the next morning. Unless the trains are late. And both of them always are.

Flagstaff with its more than sixty thousand inhabitants is one of Arizona's major urban centers, along with Phoenix and Tucson. It is the unofficial capital of northern Arizona and the center of the area in every way. Flagstaff hosts Northern Arizona University, with more Native American students than probably any other university in the United States. The Northern Arizona Museum and Research Center, founded in 1928, is an important supporter of cultural heritage.

Lowell Observatory on the western edge of the town is still an important astronomical research center. Dr. Percival Lowell founded the observatory on top of Mars Hill in 1894. It was the highest point he could find close to a railroad station. The history of the observatory has its share of both amusing and valuable scientific observations. It was here that Lowell imagined he saw canals filled with water in Mars. He thought Mars had inhabitants who irrigated their dry planet with polar glacier melting waters, brought to the cultivation areas with the help of an immense canal network. Edgar Rice Burroughs introduced some of Lowell's observations in his Mars novels.

Clyde Tombaugh, who died in January 1996 at the age of ninety, began his career as an astronomer at Lowell Observatory. In 1928 Tombaugh sent Lowell Observatory some drawings he had made of Mars and Jupiter, having observed the planets with his homemade telescope. The observatory hired Tombaugh as an assistant whose job was to observe photographs taken in the direction of Neptune and Uranus. The astronomers had detected some disturbances in the orbits of these planets, which led them to suspect that there was still an undiscovered planet orbiting our sun. Eventually, they found what they considered the ninth planet of our solar system in February 1930 and named it Pluto. This is also how Mickey Mouse's dog got his name. Only after the discovery of Pluto did Clyde Tombaugh start to study astronomy in earnest at the university. Later, he served as a teacher of astronomy and physics at the universities of Arizona and New Mexico State.

The second largest solid forest of Ponderosa pines in the world spreads itself around Flagstaff. The largest of such forests lies in Siberia. Flagstaff even got its name from the pine trees. According to the foundation story, a group of settlers from Boston came to the area in 1876, tempted by the rich soil and mineral deposits. Their disappointment was so great that the settlers soon moved elsewhere. They stayed long enough, however, to celebrate the hundredth anniversary of the United States by hoisting the Star-Spangled Banner atop a tall pine. The pine became a milepost on the California wagon road, the ancestor of Route 66 and the present I-40. The original pine tree long gone, a new pine now grows in the same spot with a little monument beside it. Another pine flagstaff stands right in the town center in front of the chamber of commerce building on Route 66, right next to the railroad and across the street from the railroad station.

As any town of real importance, Flagstaff started out with the railroad. It was constructed through the town to take advantage of a spring that provided the water to cool the steam engines. Town's Well is still there on a pine-growing hill bank, the headwater of the small brook running toward the railroad a hundred yards away.

Flagstaff almost became a cinema center as well. A long time before Route 66 went anywhere, a young film director and a film producer took a train trip through the area, carrying a great manuscript for a hit movie in their pocket. They could see in their mind's eye how real cowboys and Indians would fill the screen in the authentic environment. Nobody at Long Island Studios in New York in 1911 could tell a cactus from a flower pot, and there was no way they could produce suitable riding scenes. Flagstaff, surrounded by Zane Grey purple sage, would be a splendid place to shoot a successful movie. When the train arrived at Flagstaff, an ice storm met them. This was enough for Jesse Laskey and Cecil B. DeMille. They repeated what the settlers of 1876 had done. DeMille never stepped out of the train even for a walk before they reached Los Angeles. The first full-length motion picture in the world, *Squaw Man*, was filmed in Hollywood in 1914.

Locomotives required firewood or coal to increase the pressure in the boilers. Flagstaff had plenty of lumber. It was also good material for train cars, furniture, and—you name it. Small lumber companies began to appear by the railroad, and the trains transported the timber and lumber elsewhere. Three sawmills operated in Flagstaff after World War II. The smallest of them belonged to the Babbitt Brothers Trading Company. The family set up the company in the 1890s mainly to trade in cattle, but later they extended their operation to cover other fields as well. The same family is still powerful in Flagstaff. You run across the name Babbitt everywhere. Babbitt Lumberyard, Babbitt Grocery, Babbitt this, and Babbitt that. There's Babbitt's Sport Center on Leroux Street between Aspen and Birch, and there's Babbitt's Clothing, Flyfishing & Gifts on Aspen between San Francisco and Leroux. Bruce Babbitt was President Bill Clinton's Secretary of the Interior.

Flagstaff started out as a railroad town. Soon, it also became a highway town. Route 66 arrives from the northeast and turns south on the northern side of the town center. The right side of the highway is lined with motels: the Americana, the Pony Soldier, the Motel 66, and the Whispering Winds, just to name a few. The railroad runs to the left of the highway: the Atchison, Topeka & Santa Fe, now the Burlington Northern & Santa Fe. A few restaurants and stores are squeezed between the motels. The same is also true of the Museum Club. In spite of the name it is not a museum, but rather the mecca of country music. The locals have nicknamed it the Zoo.

Dean Eldredge began stuffing animals in 1918. His great dream came true in 1931, when he founded the museum to house his collections of stuffed animals, rifles, and Indian artifacts north of downtown Flagstaff. The log house, advertised as the largest of its kind in Arizona, was built around five trees so that they became part of the building's internal framework. The frame of the main entrance is still the original Ponderosa pine stump with two branches. Dean Eldredge's museum sold Hopi ceramics, Navajo rugs and silver jewelry, and woven baskets.

When Prohibition was over, a Flagstaff saddle smith called Doc Williams turned the museum into a nightclub. Some of the stuffed animals still perch, however, on branches of the trees around the dance floor. The owners changed as the years went by, but the drinks flowed and the music played. In the 1960s and 1970s Don Scott changed the music powerfully in the direction of country music. Willie Nelson, Waylon Jennings, Barbara Mandrell, and Asleep at the Wheel all played at the Museum Club. Some of them still do once in a while. At times the going at the Club got so tough that the nickname Zoo seemed well deserved. Saturday night fights were not uncommon. It was a place where university students, townies, and farmers met—not always on peaceful terms. Catherine Feher-Elston of Flagstaff recalls that the going was so wild that the place began to lose customers, when "decent folks" could not summon the nerve to go there. However, "decent folks" are usually the people with the money.

An important landmark of Route 66 and a piece of the history of honky-tonk, the Museum Club is listed in the catalogue of historic places, and various magazines have chosen it "one of the best ten roadhouses," "the readers' choice for a dance place," or "bar of the month." In recent years, the owners have taken measures to make the place more peaceful for "decent folks." They also clean up. There are no more broken glasses on the floor, and the staff includes security men to keep order. Stacie and Martin Zanzucchi, the owners, also ensure customer safety with Operation Safe Trip, launched in 1985. Safe Trip is a collaboration with the Friendly Cab Company, and the Museum Club pays for your taxi ride. Just call 774-4444, hop in the cab, and say, "Take me to the zoo." When you are ready to leave, someone behind the bar will call you a cab to see you home safely.

Thanks to international interest in Route 66, the Museum Club has become a must for 66 travelers. German is often spoken there and, occasionally, Japanese. In April 2002 a wild bunch of Finns were having a birthday party at the Zoo. My brother, a semiprofessional country and rock 'n roll musician, sang "Get Your Kicks" and became a hit with the Navajo, Comanche, and other local girls, who lined up to ask him for a dance.

Right next to the Museum Club is the Crown Railroad Café. It used to be connected to the Crown Motel, which is now a Howard Johnson. The original restaurant on Route 66 was built in the mid-1960s. It saw some rough times in the late 1980s but was restored and renovated by the present owners John and Christine Cavolo, who purchased the place in 1996. In 2000 they opened another Crown Railroad Café west of downtown. Both restaurants are filled with railroad symbols that also dot their menu. An extra treat in both places is the German-made 1:22.5 scale electric trains that travel around the rooms high up on the walls.

Other restaurants on the right, or west, side of Route 66 include the Adobe Grill, owned by Rose Nackard Malone and Paul Malone. Diners enjoy specialties, including roast beef, seafood, soup, and salad, beside a handsome fireplace in the main hall. Smokers may light up in the bar. West of the Road, Alpine Pizza serves pizza, pasta, and other foods in a rugged Western atmosphere.

Here in the West, you will probably need Western clothing. You will have seen stores specializing in Western clothes along the 66 ever since Illinois—places with names like Circle A, Circle H, or Circle K. A popular method of branding cattle in the Wild West—and the present West—is to brand a circle around the first letter of the owner's family name. By Flagstaff you are approaching the end of the alphabet, and so the Western store here is the Circle Q on the right side of Route 66. Remember, the railroad is on the left side. The Circle Q has stood right next to the Road for more than five decades. It used to have a large billboard advertising its business across the street, but in the late 1990s the city ordinance prohibited billboards on the rail side of Route 66. During the past few years, the Circle Q has significantly increased the use of the number 66 in its advertising and interior design. It has also had to give in to the expenditure pressures of the era. No longer is all its merchandise labeled "Made in USA." The service is as friendly as ever. They claim to be happy to serve each one—and you are pleased to find it out.

San Francisco Street

As you enter Flagstaff from the northeast, Babbitt Ford is the first business in the nuclear center, before the road begins the descent into the valley with Mars Hill at the other end. Flagstaff lies in this hollow. The railroad still runs on the left side of the Road, and the only buildings on that side are the railroad station and opposite it, across Beaver Street, the Chamber of Commerce with its flagstaff.

San Francisco Street runs from the railroad station's eastern gable southwest toward the university and northeast toward the mountain peaks that gave the street its name. Those San Francisco Peaks reach majestically towards the sky west of Flagstaff, higher than any other place in Arizona. They got their name from early conquistadors or maybe from latecomers, who thought they could see the west coast and the lights of San Francisco from the mountains. Flagstaff is more than a mile and a quarter above sea level, and Humphrey's Peak ascends to 12,643 feet, often reaching the clouds.

The first two blocks of San Francisco Street north of Route 66 are the heart of Flagstaff. Beaver Street, two blocks west, officially divides the town into an eastern and a western part, while Route 66 divides it into a northern and a southern part. Nevertheless, San Francisco is the real Main Street, or the second Main Street after Route 66. Right at the corner of Route 66 was a saloon with a beer bar and billiards, and across the road was an ice-cream and coffee parlor for a couple of years. The bad economy of the millennium has hit Flagstaff so hard, however, that many businesses have had to close, those two included, although there is a Flagstaff Coffee Company almost at the corner on 66. Photo Outfitters on San Francisco Street, Flagstaff's only really professional photographer's studio, was closing in 2002. Sadly also the landmark McGaugh's Newsstand is gone. It was so much more than a simple newspaper kiosk. It carried a multitude of books on local literature and natural wonders, several books about the Road, and a striking selection of newspapers. The Barnes & Noble on Milton, which is Route 66 after the railroad bridge, cannot replace McGaugh's.

At the corner of Aspen and San Francisco stands the old Babbitt Supermarket building. A shop sells sportswear and camping wear downstairs. Then there's Phyllis Hogan's Winter Sun, a drugstore selling herbs, medicinal plants, Indian jewelry, and handiwork. Together with local Indians and folk healers, Winter Sun gathers and makes traditional medicines to alleviate practically any ailment. Hogan's big herbarium used to be upstairs but has now found more spacious facilities.

The Monte Vista Hotel is an old Flagstaff landmark on the other side of Aspen Avenue only a block from the railroad station. It was built in the early 1920s mainly for train passengers coming to town. Today, the Amtrak train stopping at the station is usually so long that it cuts the car traffic at the San Francisco Street crossing. The Monte Vista was once one of the largest buildings in Flagstaff and the pride of the town. Now there are new and even more impressive hotels outside the nuclear center, but the Monte Vista can still be regarded as the most central hotel in town. It may have a little too much patina in places, and many things may appear frazzled, but the hotel's old-time atmosphere is unmistakable.

Route 66 joined the railroad in bringing guests to the Monte Vista. Many lumber deals were made at the hotel and many famous people visited it. Among other rooms, I have spent a night in the tiny Alan Ladd Room and lived for a couple of days in the Clark Gable Suite. It was a one-room "suite," but with plenty of windows looking out onto both Aspen Avenue and San Francisco Street. The best room is probably the one dedicated to Carole Lombard. The bar and the saloon downstairs have seen better days. On a nearby corner was a shop selling souvenirs and things related to the Road. They probably had the best selection of Route 66 T-shirts found in the Southwest, but by April 2002 the place had closed and the space was for rent. The relatively small Monte Vista restaurant, owned and run separately from the hotel, had become a Thai restaurant. I have nothing against Thai food, but the old place offered the best oatmeal on Route 66, perhaps better than anywhere else in North America—aside from your mother's.

Past the Monte Vista Hotel is Flagstaff's old post office building, a historic preservation target, operating nowadays as an office building. On the other side of Birch Avenue is one of Flagstaff's old public buildings, the courthouse with its handsome towers, clearly of the same era as the Monte Vista Hotel.

If you turn south onto San Francisco Street from Route 66, you first cross the railroad yard. The railroad station and a lumberyard are to the right. The Du Beau Hotel lies right behind the station. This old hotel, built in 1929, is also one of the landmarks of old Flagstaff and is included on the National Register of Historic Places. Now a hostel, it once hosted Los Angeles movie stars and Chicago gangsters. The neon sign on top of a contraption looking something like an oil tower can be seen far and wide over the roofs of the low buildings in downtown Flagstaff.

Opposite the railroad station, the Route 66 roadside is lined with souvenir and jewelry shops. Here the street-side scenery has changed rapidly since the beginning of a new millennium. Much of the old western charm has been replaced by yuppie shops and design boutiques, probably due to more and more of their clientele moving in from Southern California to spend their retirement or prime in the cool shadows of Flagstaff's pine forests.

If you would like to go to the mountains for the weekend or to camp in the pine forest, look inside Peace Surplus at the corner of Beaver Street. They sell all kinds of backpacks, camping gear, freeze-dried food, rope, canoes, skis, shoes, and Finnish Suunto compasses. The name of the store is probably a comment to the stores selling army surplus gear.

The Weatherford Hotel lies on Leroux Street a block away from Route 66. This building is another of Flagstaff's old landmarks included on the National Register of Historic Places. The ground floor of the hotel also boasts one of the town's most popular bars, Charly's Pub. If the music and energy of the Museum Club are not enough, the going is sure to get better at Charly's.

Route 66 continues west from the station past administrative blocks. The city hall lies to the right, and behind it towers the massive, castle-like town library. Route 66 curves to the left soon after the city hall and goes under the railroad.

When the name of Santa Fe Avenue changed to Route 66 in 1992 and the town hosted the second international Route 66 festival, the shield-shaped sign of the Double-Six did not yet appear in too many store windows. By 1996 hardly a window in downtown Flagstaff lacked the Double-Six, and the town's Chamber of Commerce was enthusiastically marketing the Old Road again. By 2002 some of the 66 signs had vanished, unfortunately, because of the recession. Santa Fe Avenue is also back on the maps as Historic US 66.

After the railroad underpass is a stretch on the right where several dilapidated office buildings and the famous Flamingo Hotel used to stand. A story has it that the hotel was haunted by someone who was shot there. Is that why they had to tear it down? Anyway, a new Rodeway Inn is there today, and little farther on is the Barnes & Noble in an almost castle-like building.

The large university campus lies to the left, and in front of it Route 66 turns right, becoming West Route 66, rises onto the hill, and gradually leaves Flagstaff behind. Still in town there's the Athletic Club on the right, and further on the right the Flagstaff Tabernacle. On the left, a camping site advertises Western traditions. The next thing is either a stretch of the new highway or an overgrown path where the Old Road used to run.

The Golden Circle

Flagstaff is a great town for tourists with its old southwestern or western streets and scenery. It is a sophisticated university town with many European features, but with much of the frontier roughness remaining. It is also an excellent base from which to visit tourist attractions in the area. The town is located on the southwestern edge of the area that Stewart L. Udall, then the Secretary of the Interior, described in 1961 as the Golden Circle. "The boundary of this remarkable region," he said, "is a golden circle, encompassing the greatest concentration of scenic wonders to be found in the country, if not the world." Besides Flagstaff, the circle's other important towns are Gallup and Durango. Both "Flag" and Gallup lie on Route 66. As the 66 is the oldest passable route into the circle, Flagstaff has remained as its most important center.

Walnut Canyon lies only a few miles east of Flagstaff. The Walnut Canyon road starts from the same intersection as the road to Winona. The canyon is full of ancient ruins of houses built by the Sinagua Indians, whose name comes from the Spanish words *sin aqua*, "without water," and it refers to the Spaniards' astonishment at how little water the Sinaguas had to survive with.

North of Flagstaff lies Sunset Crater, a volcanic cinder cone. The volcano's eruption has left widespread lava as well as fertile soil that nurtured ancient Indians' crops. Several ruins of Anasazi villages or lone dwellings are nearby. The largest of them is Wupatki, which has lent its name to a national monument. Wupatki includes the ruins of a rather large two-story building and a ceremonial field in front of it. A little distance away there is another trampled area, which archaeologists and historians believe to have been a ball court. The Anasazi acquired rubber balls in trade from Indians in present Mexico and may have acquired the game that way as well. This is likely the northernmost pre-Columbian ball court in the Americas.

When the Wupatki soil was exhausted, perhaps as a result of drought, the people moved elsewhere. North and northeast of Wupatki lies the famous Navajo trading post Cameron, then Tuba City and the Hopi mesas. Many people among the Hopis can still trace their ancestry to people of some of the Wupatki area villages. Even farther northeast, inside the Navajo Nation, is the Navajo National Monument, the site of more Anasazi ruins.

Far to the north, a long drive from Flagstaff, by the shore of Lake Powell on the Utah border lies Page, the only town on the Navajo Reservation where you can buy alcohol. Well, not exactly. Perhaps to allow for the sale of liquor, the reservation boundary has been drawn with a notch to exclude Page. On the Utah side of the state line, you can find beautiful scenery: Hovenweep Anasazi village ruins, the wondrous stone arches called Natural Bridges, the verdant valley of Zion Canyon and the long tunnel leading to it, and Bryce Canyon, where erosion has created every stone shape you could ever have imagined and some that are beyond imaginable. According to the Mormon settler Ebenezer Bryce, it would be "a hell of a place to lose a cow."

In his *Route 66 Traveler's Guide,* Tom Snyder recommends four additional side trips. One of them runs from Las Vegas, Nevada, to Zion National Park, then to Arizona and the North Rim of the Grand Canyon. From there you can continue across the Colorado River over the Navajo Bridge and south to Flagstaff via Wupatki and Sunset Crater. You can get back to Las Vegas by driving on the 66 to Kingman and from there north over Hoover Dam to Nevada. The route recommended by Snyder is well worth the recommendation.

The mountains the Spaniards called San Francisco Peaks tower west and northwest from Flagstaff. They form the western boundary of the Navajo's traditional country and are sacred to them. They are also sacred to Hopis, as the Hopi katsina spirits live on the San Francisco Peaks. Some people in fact call them Kachina Peaks. The name Kachina even appears on some maps. Navajos, however, are less than keen on using the Hopi name for the mountains. To white people, the most interesting things about the San Francisco Peaks are probably the good camping and skiing opportunities. Flagstaff's ski resort, the Snowbowl, is situated there.

Just six miles west of Flagstaff, Interstate 40 and Route 66 under it cross the Arizona Divide at 7,335 feet above sea level. Much of the route here takes you to the slopes of pine-covered mountains. Properly, the road is called Brannigan Park Road/Old Highway 66. With no special natural landmarks but the pine trees, this is another extremely beautiful stretch of the Old Road.   .

The red cliffs of Oak Creek Canyon lie south of Flagstaff. To get there you must descend three quarters of a mile from the pine forest along only a few miles of road. The landscape is breathtaking, but you need to keep your eyes on the winding road.

Down in the valley lies Sedona, a real mecca for tourists and maybe even too full of them. It is difficult to find the real thing among all the tourist paraphernalia, and you may also well ask how genuine the town's Southwest atmosphere is. But there actually are two Sedonas. The road from Oak Creek Canyon takes you to the shopping street, usually filled with tourists, shops, exhibitions, and the like. Over the little hill on the southwest lies the real center of the town with fire station and police headquarters and the town hall. This Sedona is a peaceful, sleepy little town, almost the opposite of tourist Sedona.

A little further off lies the old mining town of Jerome. It was already abandoned once as its minerals were exhausted, but recently it has been revived as an artists' colony and a tourist destination. And not far from it is Tuzigoot, another site of Sinagua occupation worth visiting because of the ruins and because of a fine little museum.

To the south, right on the Golden Circle, are Montezuma Castle and Montezuma Well, both remnants of the Anasazi culture. Their name refers to the last Aztec leader. That is because the first white men who came here would not believe that the ancestors of the local Indians could have built such fine apartment buildings. Instead, they imagined that Aztecs from Mexico had built these houses, now in ruins.

Montezuma Castle is a magnificent cliff dwelling in the middle of the canyon wall. Montezuma Well, a natural pond of water, lies at the end of a dirt road in a desolate nook of Arizona where you would hardly expect to meet European civilization. Nevertheless, nearby, in the tiny community of Rimrock, is the Primo Deli and Café, open Tuesday to Sunday, 11:00 a.m. to 8.00 p.m., at least, and with an ample selection of sandwiches, treats for coffee lovers, and homemade Italian pasta and bread. The service is good, and the couple who own the place are friendly.

You can continue farther south to Phoenix, the capitol city of the arid zone. And here it is really arid. Even in Phoenix you're not out of touch with the Old Road. At Sky Harbor, Phoenix's international airport, in terminal four, the Roadhouse Café is decorated with Route 66 memorabilia. The Roadhouse souvenirs include a Jack Rabbit sign, an image of the Twin Arrows, Route 66 license plates, and a big map of the Route from Springfield to Los Angeles.

At the Edge of the Grand Canyon

Flagstaff has always been the gate to the South Rim of the Grand Canyon, the largest and greatest among the natural wonders of the Golden Circle. Even Albert Einstein said about it: "One cannot help but be in awe when he contemplates the mysteries of eternity, of life, of the marvelous structure of reality."

The South Rim is easier to reach and therefore more popular than the North Rim, although Flagstaff is a good jumping-off point for the North Rim as well. When my wife and I first visited the South Rim on a bus from Flagstaff in December 1974, we were naturally eager to see the first impressive cliffs. All we saw through the bus windows, however, was the handsome pine forest. After an hour's drive the bus stopped. The driver told us that this was the Grand Canyon, but still we saw nothing but pine forest and a cluster of buildings. We followed other passengers into the largest of the buildings (the Bright Angel Lodge by Mary Jane Colter) and through it. And yes indeed, there was the Grand Canyon, dropping for a mile or so, the North Rim visible dimly some three miles away. You only had to look down.

To get to the other side, you would have to drive a couple of hundred miles or walk or ride a burro down to the bottom of the canyon and up the opposite slope. This cannot be done without spending a night at the bottom. You would need to carry plenty of water. Since that first time I have returned often and twice visited the North Rim. The landscape is equally impressive every time, the North Rim possibly even more so than the South. The landscape before you depends on the time of year and the time of day. It is never the same. It never takes more than fifteen minutes to grasp it all, and yet you would not get bored if you looked at it for the rest of your life, and still you would never learn to know it all.

The Grand Canyon is one of the oldest and most popular national parks in the United States. It has been one of the Route 66 attractions since the beginning. Harvey's store and restaurant still operate on both rims of the canyon. Apart from the Fred Harvey Company, the Grand Canyon divides the rest of the world. On the northern side of this great boundary, the animals and plants are different from those on the southern side. The canyon is too deep and too wide for most animals to cross. Even the wind is not strong enough to carry seeds from one rim to the other, not to mention insects. On the nine thousand hectares area of the North Rim forested with nothing but Ponderosa pine, lives the white-tailed Kaibab squirrel with pointed ears. On the southern slope, the tuft-eared Abert's squirrel leaps from one bull pine to the next. The northern chipmunk has gotten its name from Utah, the southern from the Gila, river and desert. The porcupines wandering on the northern side of the canyon have "golden hair," while those in the south are ordinary Arizona porcupines. The northern field mice are the Rockies species, the southern the Mogollon slopes species. And so on.

Most tourists prefer the more accessible South Rim. Flagstaff provides many transport options. The most direct route to the canyon, however, is a railroad line built in 1901, departing from Flagstaff's western neighbor Williams, Arizona. The trains stopped running for a while, but now the engines are once more puffing to the South Rim through the pine forest to delight the tourists and take their money. This piece of track is so famous that even Thomas the Tank Engine, the fictional steam locomotive from children's literature and TV, has made this run a few times.

Williams is an old Wild West town west of Flagstaff on Route 66. It took its name from nearby Bill Williams Mountain, really only a hill, a mere 9,264 feet above sea level. Bill Williams was a fur trapper and a mountain man, who came here for the first time in 1826 and spent the winter in the area, hunting and trapping. Ute Indians killed him in Colorado in 1849. The heyday of the town of Williams was the first half of the century before Flagstaff became the more important tourist center. The Old Road still has many friends in Williams, however, whose life it vitalized longer than any other locality along its route. In

October 1984, Williams became the last town where the new interstate highway replaced the Old 66.

Approaching from the east, Route 66 curves nicely down to Williams in a little valley. In town, the highway divides much as in Winslow: Railroad Avenue takes you west and Route 66, the original highway, takes you east. Streets here have many names. The westbound is Bill Williams Avenue, Grand Canyon Avenue, and Railroad Avenue. The eastbound is Route 66. All streets are worth traveling. You see plenty of Route 66 signs here. The visitor information center on Railroad Avenue just opposite the railroad station has a corner dedicated to the Old Road with memorabilia and a place to write your memories of your travels on the famous road. Many have, some in Japanese. Between the two streets, just before they rejoin and steer you out of the town, is a tiny park overseen by the statue of Bill Williams himself.

Dinosaurs and Peaches

In western Arizona the trails of the Old 66 and the new I-40 differ significantly. The town of Ash Fork is an old stagecoach trail station and naturally an old railroad station as well. Its mines have now dwindled to five stone quarries. The town was founded under ash trees on Ash Creek in 1882. The original townsite burned in the 1890s, and the town moved to the present site on the other side of the railroad tracks at the elevation of 5,144 feet. So we have clearly come down from the mountains. Look for De Soto's Beauty and Barber Shop as an excellent reminder of days gone by. The historic marker in Centennial Park tells the story of white men's travels before Route 66.

Five miles west of Ash Fork the new highway continues south and the old one turns closer to the edge of the Grand Canyon. With little oncoming traffic, the road running from the pine forests to the plateau begins the longest remaining unbroken stretch of the Old Route 66.

Strange rock formations appear on the left side of the road. These walls and circles are certainly manmade. The sign by the gate tells you that you have reached mile 154: Eclectic Rock. A couple of miles farther, the road crosses the railroad. An old bridge there is closed, but indicates some remnants of the original 66, now covered with dirt, grass, and tumbleweed. You can still see traces of the Old Road's double yellow centerline.

We soon approach yet another railroad town, founded in 1886 and named for the Seligman brothers, a pair of New York bankers and stockholders of the Atlantic & Pacific Railroad Company. Seligman is a veritable bastion of Route 66 and its tradition. Here are the headquarters of the Arizona Route 66 Association. Many people consider Seligman the birthplace of Historic 66. The Delgadillo family of Seligman has long had an important role in the activities of the association.

Angel Delgadillo's father worked as a locomotive engineer on the Santa Fe Railroad, but in 1922 a major strike stopped the trains, and the father started working as a barber. He founded his own barbershop and a pool hall in 1924 on the future route of the 66. Angel Delgadillo was born in a house by the roadside in 1927. He carried on the tradition and barbershop of his father. When the new I-40 deprived Seligman of tourists and travelers, Angel and his wife, Vilma, rose to the barricades and got others to join them. Thus, an Arizona barber joined ranks with Jack Cuthbert, the barber from Oklahoma. Who says that the importance of barbers vanished with the invention of the razor?

It is largely due to the Delgadillos that the road between Seligman and Kingman was named Historic Route 66. Similar signs have later appeared on other stretches of the remaining or preserved sections of the Old Road. Angel and Vilma Delgadillo's souvenir shop has become a more important livelihood than the barbershop, but the barber's chair is still there for visitors to see. Foreign notes of money on the wall tell you that the place is internationally recognized as a must stop for every Route 66 traveler. After all, if Angel Delgadillo is the "Mayor of Route 66," this must be the town hall.

If you don't meet the mayor himself, he's probably away helping a film crew or otherwise promoting Route 66. Vilma Delgadillo and her sister Dina Rampelotto Matus often run the curio shop. The parents of the sisters came to the area from Austria via Mexico. Dina still spoke English with a slight Mexican accent, but did I also detect a slight German inflection? In April 2012 she passed away at the age of seventy-eight, a great loss to her family and all of the Route 66 society.

Across the small alley, right opposite the barbershop and, of course, also on 66, Angel's brother Juan Delgadillo ran his own Snow Cap Drive-In café and gas station until his death in 2004 at the age of eighty-eight. The Snow Cap is still there with a small and curious Route 66 garden in its yard. Many pots are filled with plastic flowers, each pot marked with the number 66. An odd squirrel eats a snake atop a plate of burgers, and the company car is decorated with flowers, paintings, and, of course, Route 66 signs. Juan Delgadillo must have loved good ice cream, too, as a Ted Drews sticker adorns the company car, now driven by Juan's wife Mary and their two sons Robert and John.

A stone's throw from Angel Delgadillo's barber shop to the west on the Road is the Copper Cart Restaurant, also one of Seligman's legendary Route 66 sites, and Pope's General Store, a great 66 store, beside it. It's a place worth visiting, but beware: do not touch the Edsel parked in front of the store! The last guy who did is buried on the other side of the sidewalk, his boots still showing. A conversation with the driver and the travelers of the Edsel is also in vain. I will let you find out why.

From Seligman, the Historic 66 runs along the northeastern edge of the Juniper Mountains closer to the Grand Canyon and the Colorado River bend. The railroad goes in the same direction, making its way between the mountains only a mile or so south of the Road. Chino, Audley, and Pica are old stations or train stops. Nobody on the Road knows anything about them. There's the first advertisement of the Grand Canyon caverns. In Vaca an old, rusted oil tank lies in the middle of the desert. The pine forests are thinning out. Prairie dogs run across the road. Finally, the road begins a slight downhill grade. You can already see houses and the long-awaited sign. Turn left! The whole place is for sale, though. Can the hotel really be open?

But don't use the hotel unless you want to spend a night there, or have a meal, or stop at the restroom. Turn left and continue to the old attraction of Route 66, the Grand Canyon Caverns. It is the largest dry body of caverns in the United States, although it is an old sea bottom. The only connection to the Grand Canyon itself is the fact that the latter is relatively close, only some thirty miles north of the caverns.

The caverns are worth stopping for, despite the commercialism embodied in the restaurant, the shop full of memorabilia, and so on. The caverns are totally different from those at Meramec. Meramec had water. These caverns are dry. At best they go three quarters of a mile underground. Mummified remains of trapped animals include an unlucky mountain lion that fell into a hole more than a hundred years ago and could not find a way out. Nothing is left of the poor beast but the bones and some skin wrinkled around them.

Like the Meramec, the Grand Canyon Caverns are private property. It is not a family business, however, and, therefore, the guides are not as young as those in Missouri. We were lucky to be guided by the sixty-three-year-old Bryan. He did not take his job too seriously, but he told us everything necessary. During his time in the US army, Bryan had visited Europe but had never gone as far as Finland. When you go to the caverns, look for Bryan to guide you. He has a beaver tattoo on his arm. And how do you recognize the Grand Canyon Caverns? Follow the signs to a place where you see a large green dinosaur. It is the same kind of Route 66 pet as the jackrabbit in Joseph City. No dinosaurs inhabit in the caverns, but Bryan might show you a giant sloth.

But we have no time to get slothful; we have to continue our journey. We have spent too much of it in Arizona already. But it can't be helped. The desert is beautiful.

Peach Springs. The name alone makes your mouth water. And they do cultivate peaches and apricots. The town lies on the southern edge of the Hualapai (or Walapai) Indian Reservation, and it is the Hualapai Tribal Nation's service and administrative center. Only sandy roads and stony paths lead from there to the edges of the Grand Canyon, including Road 18 to Hualapai Top, the end of the road. Most of the Hualapai and Havasupai Indians live on the bottoms of canyons. The blue-green Havasu Falls can be reached only on foot or on mule-back from Hualapai Top. That is, if the Havasupais allow it and vacant lodgings are available at Supai on the canyon bottom.

Peach Springs is a welcome sight for anyone looking for human settlement. Many miles in the recent past we have seen nothing but empty spaces. Don't be lured to turn onto the health center road, however, even if you see plenty of government houses there. Continue another mile down the hill and pass the sign that says Peach Springs.

On the left side of Route 66 stands the Hualapai Lodge. It has beautiful artwork on the walls, good food, and nice accommodations at reasonable prices. This also is the home of Hualapai River Runners who can offer you a thrilling trip splashing through nine sets of rapids on the Colorado River in the Grand Canyon. From here you can also take a trip to Grand Canyon West, the newest development in the Hualapai economy. If you have seen the South Rim and the North Rim, the West Rim may offer you still a different view. Since 2007 you can also have a view from above on a glass bottomed observation bridge

Past the Hualapai Lodge on Route 66 another two hundred yards or so are some old buildings on the right. There you can obtain permits for sightseeing, hiking, camping, fishing, and even hunting on the reservation. The permits are issued by the Hualapai Wildlife and

Outdoor Recreation Department. The department is housed in a very distinctive stone building.

The Spanish Priest, Fr. Francisco Garcés, who named the springs in 1775 after St. Basil, entered Peach Springs into European annals. In the 1820s the trail from the Rio Grande to California was blazed through the Hualapai lands and brought the local Indians really into contact with Europeans. When Lieutenant Edward Beale's camel patrol passed Peach Springs on September 17, 1858, many Hualapais were already working in mines for the newcomers. Beale called the place Indian Springs. Mormons had preceded him there, however, and planted the first peach trees. For a while, Peach Springs was the westernmost terminus of the Santa Fe Railroad until the company was permitted to continue the railroad all the way to the West Coast. Before that, the ATSF really ran from nowhere to nowhere. The railroad also made Peach Springs the main village of the Hualapais. Advertisements from 1883 mentioned ten saloons near the station. The Shell gas station from the 1920s on Route 66 is likely to be one of the oldest, if not the very oldest, gas station still in operation in the United States—or in the world.

The next stop on both the Road and the railroad is Truxton. It was probably named by Lieutenant Beale for his mother Emily Truxton Beale and his grandfather, Commodore Thomas Truxton. The army had a small garrison there in the 1870s. In 1883 it became a watering spot for the railroad. The actual town was founded in October 1951, when Donald Dilts opened the Truxton Café and service station. Its long-time owner Mildred Barker died August 7, 2012, and the café may be closed, but I hear that the Frontier Motel attached to it is still open.

Originally, the US government planned in the late 1920s to dam the Colorado River north of Truxton, which would have become the headquarters of the dam's construction and the finished dam's maintenance center. The plan brought many businessmen and tourists to the town on Route 66. Eventually, they built the dam at Boulder City instead and later named it after President Herbert Hoover. Truxton is once more a minor tourist curiosity.

From Springs to Oasis

We have been driving downhill since Seligman, and in the Crozier Canyon the downhill continues. In Valentine we return to the Hualapai

Reservation, or an outlying piece of it surrounding the town. The reservation boasted an Indian boarding school from 1917 to 1937 and after World War II until 1969. The school building is still intact—well, maybe a broken window and a bit of graffiti. According to some information, there was a small Hualapai school there right at the beginning of the twentieth century. The US Indian agent also acted as the local postmaster, and the official name of the area was Truxton Canyon. The school was discontinued, however, along with the post office. When the post office was reopened in 1910, the rules stated that a new name was necessary. The name came from Robert G. Valentine, the Commissioner of Indian Affairs at the time.

Hackberry also has a spring, probably the one Lieutenant Beale called Gardiner. Miners were digging nearby sometime in the 1870s and gave the spring its present name, possibly because there was a large hackberry tree growing there. The Old 66 visitors' center in Hackberry is possibly the most curious on the Old Road: a really original house, a herbarium, and a desert garden right next to Route 66. It was founded by Bob Waldmire but sold in 1998 to John and Kerry Pritchard, as Waldmire had decided to move back to Illinois.

Although he came from the home of the Cozy Dogs, Bob Waldmire was a vegetarian and had been for a long time. In fact, he did not use any animal products, not even clothing or shoes made of animal leather. His most significant deviation from that respect for nature was the fact that he owned a car and had owned several over the years. Bob Waldmire even lived in a car for years, be it a Volkswagen minibus or a Chevrolet "school bus," now both at the Illinois Route 66 Hall of Fame in Pontiac. Such dwellings were easy to move where he wanted or where the road took them, mostly one direction or the other on Route 66. In 2006, the Volkswagen became the character Fillmore in the motion picture *Cars*.

Finally, the Road became Waldmire's career and life. He began to sketch scenes of the Road. Some five years later he had finished a sixteen-page pictorial map of Route 66. The map is full of small and large details and plenty of text. Since its publication in 1992, the map has sold more than ten thousand copies. In the summer of 1996 it was hard to find, and by 2002 it had become a true collector's item. Maybe a new edition of the map will be available by the time you read this. Aside from the map, many drawings by Bob Waldmire have made their way into postcards. All self-respecting Route 66 shops sell them. Tom Teague's book *Searching for 66* also has a number of Waldmire drawings.

Bob Waldmire wanted to found an international bio-regional Old 66 visitors' center in Hackberry. The center would sell not only Waldmire's own work but also nature products like Funk's Grove maple sirup and Cabin Creek pecans. The "peace library" of Ed Waldmire, Bob's father, sat at one corner of the visitors' center. A cactus garden and a nature path were outside. A warning sign stated that the desert begins here, and there will be no more water ahead, this despite a creek running some distance to the left of the Road.

According to a leaflet you could acquire from the visitors' center, written by Waldmire, the land ahead "lies within a broad, gently-sloping bajada—an alluvial plain of sediments washed down from surrounding hills. Perched on the edge of the Mohave Desert at an altitude of 3,600 feet, the region receives an average annual precipitation of 10 inches. Although the desert may appear lifeless & drab at a glance, closer observation will reveal an abundance of life & activity. During summer months, many creatures become nocturnal in their habits."

The Pritchards have yet to become as legendary as the Waldmires, but much of Bob Waldmire's dream is kept alive in Hackberry. The front of the place looks the same, although cleaner. Since the new owners are not constantly on the move, you are more likely to find the center open. The desert hasn't quite yet begun.

At Hackberry, just past the visitors' center, Route 66 begins a long and gentle curve. It is no less than seven miles long, the longest unbroken curve on any US highway. Just after the curve and before we reach Kingman is the small Valle Vista, undoubtedly the youngest settlement on Highway 66. It was founded in 1972 next to a golf course. The fiscal crisis that began in 2008 has hit Valle Vista hard. Some 10 percent of the people there have lost their housing. It is almost as though the grapes of wrath had finally arrived to this Arizona desert on their move west from Oklahoma. From Valle Vista's Outpost Gas service station (if it's still there) you can drive straight into Kingman. To the left, runs the familiar railroad, and the sharp peaks of the Cerbat Mountains loom far to the right. There is no way of telling that the mighty Colorado runs behind them. The pine forests are far behind us.

Even the dwarfed junipers have starved. This is the true desert. Kingman is one of its oases.

Kingman is a small center of western Arizona. It was founded in 1882 and named after locomotive engineer Lewis Kingman. The old and the new highway cross each other here. The new one arrives proudly from the east on four lanes, preening itself, its chest curved up like a bow. The old one descends from the north humbly next to the railroad tracks. Humbly, yes, but not defeated. It is still an important artery for the inhabitants of northwestern Arizona, be they Indians or Europeans. In Kingman it only stops to get a drink of water and makes its way into the desert and over the mountains. This is something the new highway is too afraid to do. It makes a long curve south like a coward to avoid the difficult mountain passes.

In Kingman, the Historic 66 runs along Andy Devine Boulevard. Andy Devine was a cowboy movie star. He was born in Flagstaff but grew up mainly in Kingman, where his father ran the historic Beale Hotel, now unfortunately abandoned. The hotel was of course named after Navy Lieutenant Edward F. Beale. Greta Garbo stayed at the hotel once. Charles and Ann Morrow Lindbergh also stopped there on July 8, 1928, while establishing a forty-eight-hour airmail route between New York and Los Angeles. The romantic couple of the hotel, however, is Carole Lombard and Clark Gable. They were wed on March 19, 1939, in the nearby courthouse, or maybe, as others claim, in the local Methodist church.

On Andy Devine Boulevard a large advertisement greets travelers. It tells us that Kingman is a Route 66 town. And, indeed, even its motto is "The Heart of Historic Route 66." Almost opposite the sign is Mr. D'z Diner, one of the legendary places on the Road. The diner's sign is spelled wrong, as someone has replaced the possessive ending "s" with a "z." Last we visited Mr. D'z, the place was really busy, as many customers had rushed in to get lunch at the same time. The young staff at the diner did not know which way to turn—nor did the older generation. Some half a dozen people came to take our orders. We were just about to leave when the lunch finally arrived. Nor were we the only ones to suffer such a fate that day. The specialty of the diner, the local root beer, tasted cloyingly sweet in our mouths.

Kingman, with the neighboring Oatman, is the set for a 1984 movie

Roadhouse 66. Starring Willem Dafoe and Judge Reinhold and directed by John Mark Robinson, much of the movie is spent on an automobile race from Kingman to Oatman and back with great sceneries of the desert.

A museum worth visiting is the Mohave Museum of History and Arts on Beale Street, practically at the corner of Andy Devine. Founded in 1960, the place is not too big, but it has a nice collection of dioramas and murals that depict the settlement story of northwestern Arizona. A block away is the local Route 66 museum, also worthy of a visit. By the Kingman railroad station rests the last Santa Fe steam locomotive to make the Los Angeles to Chicago run.

Deserts and Donkeys

You can continue from Kingman straight west and through Union Gap to the Colorado River and Davis Dam, or northwest to Hoover Dam and from there across the Colorado River to Las Vegas. The Old 66 turns south before the new Highway I-40 and travels the western edge of the Canyon. The red, green, and yellow trains of the Burlington Northern & Santa Fe puff along on the eastern edge. Finally, you have to turn to face the mountains, although the downhill does still continue for a time. The new highway cuts the old one and proceeds now more directly southward than Route 66. It does not turn toward the river until after Yucca. The Old Road rolls down the most desolate of all deserts. The signs tell us that here the Historic Route 66 is also a National Back Country Byway. The donkey on the next sign may refer to the drivers who choose this route.

The Old Road goes downhill in the desert. A sign warns us about a flood at Meadow Creek. For someone looking at the landscape, the sign appears not only unnecessary but silly as well. After a while the warning signs appear again and the rolling downhill continues. But the rolling is caused by the network of creeks and washes cutting the Road at times. Most of the time they are dry, nothing but shallow depressions in the desert ground. Sometimes the rain or the melting snow can fill them, however, with a fast, fierce, and gushing current strong enough to wash away any car crossing the riverbed.

Things here change slow if at all. Just replace the "they" with "we" or "us," and John Steinbeck's description of the Joad family crossing this area in *Grapes of Wrath* could be from your travel log:

The sun drained the dry rocky country and ahead were jagged broken peaks, the western wall of Arizona. And now they were in flight from the sun and the drought. They drove all night, and came to the mountains in the night. And they crawled the jagged ramparts in the night, and their dim lights flickered on the pale stone walls of the road. They passed the summit in the dark and came slowly down in the late night, through the shattered stone debris of Oatman; and when the daylight came they saw the Colorado River below them.

The landscapes on this scenic byway are truly beautiful, as the emptiness of the desert appears grand, at least to a Finn who grew up in the middle of forest. Little, if any, traffic mars the view. The road begins to ascend toward the sharp peaks of the mountains ahead. Here Route 66 is narrower and more winding than anywhere else. This stretch of the Road is not recommended for trucks, buses, or trailers—or drivers who tend to lose their nerve. A steep canyon drops down on the right edge of the road with no bank, not always even a safety fence to break a fall. No complaints about the landscape, though. It is best to keep watching the road, however, and keep both hands on the wheel.

Sitgreaves Pass is 3,652 feet above sea level. It is named for Captain Lorenzo Sitgreaves, who led an expedition west from Santa Fe through Zuni Pueblo and finally to San Diego, California, in 1851. Despite claims that the members of the Sitgreaves Expedition were the first white men to see Sitgreaves Pass as well as the Wupatki ruins and the Great Falls of the Little Colorado River, Sitgreaves may not ever really have gone through the pass that bears his name. The Little Colorado River falls and the Wupatki ruins were also known at least to the Spaniards and possibly a few American fur trappers before Sitgreaves Expedition. Richard Kern, who traveled with Sitgreaves, was still the first man to make sketches of both places on paper that has lasted until our time.

Sitgreaves Pass is Mojave and Hualapai country. Indians attacked a pioneer caravan in this pass in 1862, one of the extremely few times outside Hollywood that this kind of confrontation really happened. The pass ends on Gold Hill Grade, which may be the steepest hill on Route 66. First it curves gently downward, and then it turns equally gently and fools the driver into thinking that the same will continue all the way down. But the hillside gets steeper and the bends sharper, and the cliffs on both sides of the road get steeper as well, either rising or falling. When the capacity of cars was still weak, many locals backed their cars up the hill to reach the top. The hill got its name from the gold dug from its sides. Some digging still goes on. Barbed wire stops people from leaving the road. No-trespassing signs are frequent. We can also see something like precipitation tanks farther from the Road. Something secret still goes on at Gold Hill Grade within this breathtakingly beautiful Black Mountain landscape.

Below the hill lies Oatman. At one time it was the last stop in Arizona before the crossing of the Colorado River into California. It also used to be the most gold-rich town in Arizona; it was founded as a mining town in 1906. When the older Vivian mine began to peter out, a new find was made at Tom Reed's mine. The gold lasted until the 1930s. The fatal blow for Oatman came in 1942 when Congress declared that gold mining was no longer essential to the war effort. So, who knows? Maybe some gold still remains. Modern miners do not use burros, but the offspring of the burros left behind by the old miners still stalk Oatman streets among the tourists, half-tame, an amusement, and a pain. Route 66 made Oatman a boom town. Clark Gable and Carole Lombard spent part of their honeymoon hiding here. The town's boom period ended in 1953, when the 66 changed its route to run through Yucca and skirt the steep hill. The new I-40 also uses that route.

Hollywood rediscovered Oatman, when a few scenes of *How the West Was Won* were filmed in town. Some of the sets built for the movie are still standing as fronts of houses. This enhances the town's Wild West image and appeals to tourists. And Oatman definitely is a tourist town, drawing more than five hundred thousand visitors each year. The Main Street is lined with saloons and shops. John and Bonnie Nowak's grocery store sells carrots to feed the burros. The saloon feeds those on two legs. The food is very good here, too: the helpings are generous and the prices are reasonable. The interior design is straight from a low-budget Western. The figures leaning on the counter wear cowboy hats and six-shooters at their sides. Stan sits in his corner wearing a derby and bangs the piano keys to pioneer songs.

The origin of the town's name is hidden under the gold dust of Western romance. According to one story, a band of Yavapais or Tonto Apaches abducted twelve-year-old Olive Oatman near the Gila River bend and sold her to Mojave Indians. Six years later Henry Grinnell managed to recover Olive near present day Oatman. Some claim that Olive survived her Indian captivity well, later married a white man, and led a normal life until she was sixty-five years old. Others claim that Olive was so distraught she had to be put in a mental institution where she soon died, possibly by her own hand. According to another version of the story, Oatman was named after John Oatman, a child of Olive and some Mojave man; and John Oatman lived near the present town. There are yet others who claim that the town got the name from John Oatman, but he bore no relation to Olive, who did not have sex with a single Indian during her captivity. Everybody, of course, is free to believe what they will. I think that Oatman was named after some miner's donkey. A beast that devoured the oats the miner was packing. Originally, the place was called Vivian after the Vivian Mining Company. But who then was Vivian?

The Old 66 descends gradually from Oatman toward the Colorado River. Between the river and the Old Road lies the Fort Mohave Indian Reservation, established in 1865. It stretches across the Colorado and into three states: Arizona, Nevada, and California. In 1936 a great flood washed out Mojave homes in Arizona. To replace those homes, a new village was built in 1947 outside Needles on the California side on land bought by the tribe and later declared part of the reservation.

Route 66 follows the Colorado River for a while and finally meets it at Topock. Lieutenant Amiel W. Whipple, who noticed three peaks rising prominently from a range of rocky hills, originally called the place Needles. For a while there even was a post office called Needles, Arizona. When the California Needles was established, the Arizona town changed its post office name to Powell. Other names for the town have included Red Rock and Red Crossing. In 1891 a new settlement was organized with the name of Mellon after the legendary Colorado steamboat captain Jack Mellon. The post office of that name lasted from 1903 to 1906, before closing because of diminishing population. Eventually, the settlement grew and in 1915 was once again ready for a post office. Residents wanted it to be called Needles, but as a post office of that name existed already on the California side, they had to settle for Topock, a name the railroad was using for its stop there.

You can smell the water of the Colorado River a long way from the bank. Here and there you catch a glimpse of the river promising something better, something cooler to those who cross the hot desert. In early June 1996 the temperature at Topock was 118 degrees Fahrenheit, almost 48 degrees on the Celsius scale. The tape that circled the windshield of our Ford Taurus melted deep into the paint of the car here, if it had not done so before. When we stopped to get more gas, everything in the car melted, including us.

Old Topock is still 498 feet above sea level, but almost on the level with the Colorado River surface. Topock's tiny neighbor Golden Shores has grown with the older town. Because of the river, the shores themselves are an oasis in the desert where you can swim and enjoy water sports. The real holiday and recreation resort lies further south, however. Lake Havasu City is part of the crazy dream of the Arizona businessman Robert P. McCulloch. He cut through a small neck of land with bulldozers and created a new island in Lake Havasu, the reservoir created by Parker Dam. For a bridge to his island, he bought the London Bridge in 1968 and had it shipped from England. The children's song, "London Bridge Is Falling Down," however, refers to an even older bridge replaced in 1831 by the one McCulloch bought. McCulloch, some say, was under the impression that he was buying the Tower Bridge, the pride of London supported by the two towers. In any case, London Bridge was taken apart, packed into crates and shipped to Arizona. There it was reassembled as the drawing card of Lake Havasu City. Holiday apartments and hotels were constructed in the vicinity and the holiday resort by the Colorado River boomed. I doubt that we would have driven to Lake Havasu City in 118-degree heat had the London Bridge not been there.

Lake Havasu City itself is a typical example of town planning, or unplanning, in the United States, something that Americans, apparently, are happy with, but a European cannot but wonder. Despite its many swimming places and amusement centers, most of the beach is empty, desolate, and difficult to walk, sometimes impassable. There is no use looking for European-style beach boulevards; maybe the people here cannot even dream about such things. Everybody uses cars to drive from one spot to another. Delightful spots here and there do not mitigate the whole, which cannot be praised in any language.

The lake was no gift to the Chemehuevi Indians on its shores. When the reservoir was created in 1939, it flooded more than 20 percent of their land. The Hoover Dam had already ended the annual flooding of the river that sustained Chemehuevi agriculture. The future did not look good. In 1951, however, Chemehuevis received compensation for their losses, and twenty years later, the tribe reorganized itself. Since then, they have built a resort on the California side. Motor boats take you there across the river. The Chemehuevis also have a casino. Maybe that is paradise enough to some people.

9

Through Purgatory to Paradise

By the River

Somewhere far north, where the journey began, it rained. It was cold. Fields lay on both sides of the Road, and woods as well. Then the trees disappeared, and nothing but the open prairie lay ahead. And to the sides. And behind. For a long time 66 was truly the prairie road. Then across the Staked Plains and up the hills through large stands of pine around Flagstaff, and then we thought we had seen the last of forests. We expected no fecund vegetation before the artificial gardens of Los Angeles. How wrong we were. Suddenly, the jungle strikes while we are still in Arizona. It literally jumps at us. The old fire station in Topock is already left behind. Now and then we can glimpse the Colorado River and its golden shore to the right, and then green is all around. Route 66 dives into a tunnel of vegetation. You could hardly call this a forest, but enough vegetation is here to tower above the roof of our car. In places the jungle must really make a tunnel of the narrow road.

The wooden railroad bridge is hidden by reeds. Then the new I-40, and all excitement is gone. All you can see from the new highway is desert and the handsome arches of the old bridge.

The name of the town of Topock is a distorted version of a Mojave word meaning "bridge" or "fording place." The Old 66 bridge has retired from its original job. The US pension system does not provide a sufficient income, and therefore the old bridge has taken a new job. It carries pipes across the river. Cars cross the Colorado on a new bridge.

On the other side lies the fabled California, the home of black Amazons in the fairy tales of the ancient Spanish plunderers. Nothing changes on the other side, however. The heat is still over 100 degrees. As the day grows older, we must be approaching 120°F. Michael Wallis in his *Route 66:The Mother Road* is quite blunt: "July. Needles, California. Say no more. Fill the tub with ice, drool over pictures of the North Pole, close the blinds, sleep naked without even a sheet. Try anything to get cool. None of it will help. It's hot enough outside to make a rattlesnake sweat. Each day starts like an egg hitting a hot skillet greased with butter. The desert sun is hard at work before travelers can recover from the rude bleeps of automated wake-up calls—at desolate motels in a no-man's land between the old highway and the interstate."

In *The Grapes of Wrath*, the Joad family arrives in California "tired to the bone." The new state does not cheer them up very much. In the movie, John Ford has made them despise the sight. "Is this why we traveled such a long way?" You can hardly blame the Okies in search of a better life. Once we leave the river behind, nothing but desert stretches ahead with little vegetation.

Route 66 leaves I-40 to follow the river north for a while. Then it crosses the new Highway I-40 and runs for a moment on its left side. Highway 95 from the faraway Blythe on the highway between Los Angeles and Phoenix comes from the south to join it. Twelve miles from the bridge lies Needles, a town by the river. But as John Steinbeck wrote, "The river is a stranger in this place." The Colorado runs strong between the reeds. On the other side of the river, made vague by the mists twirling above the water, loom the jagged peaks of the Arizona Black Mountains. They reach for the vast expanse of the sky like needles. That is how this California town got its name. It has fewer than five thousand inhabitants.

In Needles the Old 66 is proudly called Broadway. The morning is quiet, the day is quiet, and in the afternoon the heat of the sun makes everything even more quiet. People look for shade beneath a few palm trees and by the stores. Small motels, small shops, small people; the 66-Motel, the Palms Motel, the Old Trails Inn. The Hungry Bear will quench your hunger. The golden bear is California's emblem.

Needles is the last center of population before the endlessness of the Mojave Desert. When the Joad family was unenthusiastic about the landscape in California, Tom reminded them that there was still a desert to cross. Only after this ordeal of purgatory can you hope to reach the paradise of the California Valley.

John Steinbeck describes in chapter twelve of *The Grapes of Wrath*: "Up from Needles and over a burned range, and there's the desert. And 66 goes over the terrible desert, where the distance shimmers and the black centre mountains hang unbearably in the distance. At last there's Barstow, and more desert until at last the mountains rise up again, the good mountains, and 66 winds through them. Then suddenly a pass, and below the beautiful valley, below orchards and vineyards and little houses, and in the distance a city. And, oh, my God, it's over."

But in chapter eighteen, the travel still continued:

> They looked down on the desert—black cinder mountains in the distance, and the yellow sun reflected on the gray desert. The little starved bushes, sage and greasewood, threw bold shadows on the sand and bits of rock. The glaring sun was straight ahead. Tom held his hand before his eyes to see at all. They passed the crest and coasted down to cool the engine. They coasted down the long sweep to the floor of the desert, and the fan turned over to cool the water in the radiator. In the driver's seat Tom and Al and Pa, and Winfield on Pa's knee, looked into the bright descending sun, and their eyes were stony, and their brown faces were damp with perspiration. The burnt land and the black, cindery hills broke the distance and made it terrible in the reddening light of the setting sun.

Dusty Furnace

The Mojave Desert in southeastern California is an old sea bottom, but the only thing here that reminds of water is thirst. The Mojave is the center link in a chain of big deserts reaching from the Great Basin in Nevada and Utah to Chihuahua in northern Mexico. It is "hot as hell" in all those places in the summer, in some also in the winter. In sharp contrast, the bitter cold of desert winter nights makes some of them feel more like "the Russian hell." Similar to the Grand Canyon or the impassable mountain peaks or great oceans, the chain of the three deserts has also acted as a great divider. The flora and fauna on the eastern side of the desert zone are very different from those on the west. Not for a long time did Europeans dare to cross the Mojave and discover that California was not an island after all.

During World War II the desert proved useful, however. The soldiers of the US army trained for desert warfare in the Mojave. General George Patton's tanks rolled in the sand as if they were in the Sahara. Business flourished in Needles, Amboy, Chambless, Ludlow, and other towns on Route 66. Now Chambless is only an insignificant place of shade in the desert. In Steinbeck's book the Joads drove across the desert at night. It was one way to avoid the scorching sun. The youngest members of the family wondered whether they could see bones of animals or even men who did not have the strength to make the crossing by the roadside in the light of day.

In the 1930s, packing lots of water was still a good idea for both the car and the passengers. Just to be on the safe side, it is not such a bad idea today either. Professor Dave Warren of Santa Fe recalls that when he was a little boy and the family was crossing the Mojave Desert on the 66, his job was to wipe the sweat from the face of his father who was driving. The cars of the 1940s had no air conditioning.

Some thirteen miles west of Needles, Road 95 leaves I-40 for the north and follows the trail of the Old 66 for a while, until it turns north towards the Nevada oasis and gambling den Las Vegas. This joint stretch of the Old 66 and 95 is one of the most dangerous on the Route. We are already well into the desert but not yet hopelessly far from the Colorado River. No houses are around, but hitchhikers appear by the road as if from thin air. Judging by their looks, you would not dare give them a ride. When the Old Road turns west from the 95, yet another hitchhiker stands by the roadside in dust-covered, worn cowboy boots and clothes difficult to tell apart from the sandy surroundings. You can almost sense the smell through the window of the car. Hot vapor rises from the road, the car, and the man. As the sun keeps grilling our car like a baked potato, we feel like giving the man a ride out of sheer compassion, before he fries. Here on the eastern edge of the Mojave Desert, however, showing pity is being sick. It can kill you. There is every reason to heed the warnings of the traveler's guides.

Here in the middle of nowhere, on the east side of Goffs, Alex Cox set the opening scene of the film *Repo Man*. A straight road, a desert, and a speeding car. A billboard, behind it a policeman, a motorcycle, and a short chase. The speeding car pulls over, the policeman wants to look at the trunk. His last mistake. With radiation he's gone, only his boot left standing on the 66 asphalt. The car continues speeding. We shall meet it again in Hollywood.

In 1931, Route 66 was straightened from Needles to Essex. It used to make a northern curve through Goffs, as the railroad still does. Even the cart road preceding them, like Route 66 and the ATSF later, wound there to make use of the lower terrain and sources of water. Only a few houses stand in Goffs. A store by the railroad, although there is no real train station left. The Old Road crosses the railroad, and the journey continues. The heat increases. Hardly any traffic and seemingly even fewer trains. Could it be true? Don't all the trains going through Flagstaff have to cross the Mojave Desert as well?

Wooden telephone poles follow between the road and the railroad. The oldest 66 goes under the newer version and the interstate highway constructed on top of it. To the right is the town of Fenner. This is not only the Old Route 66 but also the National Old Trails Highway. The asphalt has already crumbled badly—or is there any left? When we reach downtown Essex, the road is probably gravel.

Downtown Essex? The post office still stands at the crossroads, a few houses ahead, but the road is closed. One of the traveler's guides urged us to summon our courage and continue along the sand road, neglecting the road closed signs. But how do you go on if there is a bar across the road in front of your car and then the road ends? And what if there really is an unsafe bridge?

We have to turn back to the freeway humming further north. It is not any cooler there. The mountains on both sides loom too distant and none are ahead as yet. We turn south towards Amboy at the next intersection. When the hum of the freeway fades, we feel as though we have left civilization behind us once again and are making our way back to the endlessness of the desert. If jackalopes live here, the coyotes can eat them already roasted.

The names of the towns, if half of them can any longer be called towns instead of old water places, are in alphabetical order from west to east: Amboy, Bristol, Cadiz, Danby, Essex, Fenner, Goffs, Home, Ibex, Java, and Klinefelter. Probably the railroad was built here in that direction, or at least the map was charted so. People have always preferred crossing the Mojave Desert from east to west. So did the Okies, so did the Joad family, so do we. Before Amboy is a long straight stretch of road. Nowadays, Amboy has maybe four inhabitants, maybe fewer. Roy's Café still stands in the town center established there by Roy Crowl in 1938. Maybe a marine from the Twenty-nine Palms Base in the south still goes there, or maybe a tourist group in search of Route 66 nostalgia. Once the owner Buster Burris, Crowl's son-in-law, employed more than a hundred people. Seventeen of his wreckers used to tow away wrecked cars from the roadside. No wonder Burris eventually owned almost all of Amboy.

Later Burris put the town on sale as the new interstate took all the traffic, all the people, and all the car wrecks to the north. For a while Amboy seemed to be dying, and it still was a very quiet place in 1996, although Walt Wilson and Tim White had bought it in the previous year. Since then the town has changed hands several times, and in 2005 it was bought by Albert Okura, who promised to preserve the town for pilgrims on 66. And he did. In 2008 Roy's was open for business once again. It still is, however, a quiet place.

Amboy and Roy's Café are 66 legends. They have also made it into motion pictures. Part of the 1986 movie *The Hitcher* was filmed in Amboy. In Dominic Sena's 1993 movie *Kalifornia*, a novelist and his wife give a ride to a murderer and his not too bright girlfriend. They reach Roy's Café late at night. The novelist's wife sees a wanted ad for the murderer on TV, and the murderer shoots the barkeeper. They drive on to Nevada. In 2006 Amboy made a more positive appearance in *Cars*. This animated film shows a former Route 66 boom town called Radiator Springs, which is loosely based on Amboy.

Near Amboy lies the Amboy Crater, a small extinguished volcano. This heat feels suitable to a volcano. Bagdad and Siberia are now hardly more than names on the map and hardly visible in the terrain. The name Bagdad must refer to the temperature or the American idea of what the temperature is like in the capital of Iraq. Or did Beale's caravan of camels pass through here as well? But what does Siberia refer to? A lonely wanderer's wish concerning the temperature of the place?

Bagdad was once an important railhead of the Santa Fe, a watering place for the steam engines. It had a post office from 1889 to 1923. It had homes, stores, and a Harvey House restaurant. By World War II the boom had ended. Nothing was left but a few houses, a gas station, and the Bagdad Café. It was a lively little place owned by Alice Lawrence. Nevertheless, café and town have faded into the desert or moved farther ahead on the Road. Copper, silver, and gold were once mined here.

Originally, Route 66 in the Mojave was mainly a footpath and plank-covered trail across the desert. The new highway splits Ludlow in a way that makes it impossible to follow the Old Road; it simply is not in its original place. Only a bridge over I-40 and a stretch of its frontage road remains of 66. Nevertheless, an old motel is to the right.

Ludlow is clearly still alive, perhaps the only place deserving the name of a town between Needles and Barstow. The local traffic on the southern side of the new highway uses a road that according to some is the Old 66. In the distance you can see one truck after another pushing on the freeway east and west, as do busy businessmen and tourists in their smaller vehicles.

Suddenly, we reach an oasis and a promise of something better: Newberry Springs, whose springs produce so much water that it is possible to raise fish here. Most of the fish are exported to Japan. Japanese is even spoken at the Sidewinder Café. A few words of German, too, but no Finnish; we were taken to be German again. Luckily, I can correct this misunderstanding swiftly. Sidewinder Café has abandoned its original name. When the German-American film crew was filming *Bagdad Café* there, the café adopted the name of the movie. Andrea Pruett sells food and drinks to weary travelers and locals, some of whom are always dozing at the window tables. It is not difficult to have a chat here.

The 1987 movie has since become a Route 66 cult film. In the original movie, Marianne Sägerbrecht acted the plump German Mrs. Jasmine, CCH Pounder the black barkeeper Brenda, and the old Western movie villain and hero Jack Palance acted the old Western movie villain and hero, artist Rudi Cox. The movie was so popular even in the United States that they made a TV series based on it, although it lasted only one season. Brenda was none other than Whoopie Goldberg and the role of Jasmine Zweibel was given to Jean Stapleton, former wife of Archie Bunker in *All in the Family*.

At the very beginning of the original movie, a German couple have a family row, and the man and woman separate in the middle of the

Mojave Desert. Through a coincidence, the couple's thermos comes to the café before the man. When he arrives, he wants decent coffee, which is hard to come by in the United States. At least all the European coffee connoisseurs claim that American coffee is usually too watery. To top it all, the café's percolator is broken, so the German tourist is told there is no coffee. However, the man pays no attention to what the waitress is saying, grabs the thermos on the counter (his wife's thermos), pours himself a cup of coffee, drinks it happily, and states that at last he got decent coffee in the land of America.

Andrea Pruett smiles benignly when I ask her where the thermos has vanished from the counter. "The movie people took it with them," she says, "but they left the magic. Our coffee is still great." My brother had a cup and confirms this.

From Desert to Civilization

Newberry Springs is only a leap away from Daggett. Although many features of the desert can be seen, the increasing green reveals the presence of water. In Daggett you can already consider that you've made it through the Mojave purgatory. In Daggett the Joads were inspected by California officials. The grandmother of the family was already dead by then, but they kept the fact from the officials. The inspection was cursory, as they were in a hurry to get the grandmother to a hospital. In this way they could bury her in green California. Today, Daggett is mainly a large marine base, or are we already in Barstow? The garrison is easy to spot on the right side of Route 66, mostly on a slope descending to the almost dry bed of the Mojave River.

For a moment we need to drive the new highway. Then we are back to the Old Road, if this ever really was part of the 66. A few S-curves, and then we arrive at the center of Barstow. Turn right along Montera Road, under I-40, and to the Main Street. Barstow is a town on the western edge of the Mojave Desert, and you have returned to civilization, want it or not. Barstow was once a lively base and trading post from which gold miners continued their way towards Death Valley. In 1881 they hit silver near the present town. Four years later a couple of hotels, a church, thirteen saloons, and a small Chinatown were already there. The ghost town of Calico, over ten miles from Barstow, is a popular tourist center where the visitors must have spooked away every ghost that may have dwelled there.

Barstow itself was founded as a railroad station. It got its name from the director of the Santa Fe Railroad Company, William Barstow Strong. The Western America Railroad Museum is there, collecting, preserving, and sharing the history of railroading in the Pacific Southwest. Next door is the Route 66 Mother Road Museum. With Route 66, Barstow became a refuge for Hollywood movie stars looking to escape the limelight during weekends. A few motels and inns remain on Barstow's Main Street: the Barstow Motel, an El Rancho Hotel, and, of course, a Route 66 Motel. Several big hotel chains are also there, even two of some of them.

In *The Grapes of Wrath*, the Joads continued straight west from Barstow like most of the 1930s Okies and other economy refugees. They left the 66 and traveled the edge of the desert to the town of Mojave. From there the road ran through Tehachapi Pass, between the Sierra Nevada and the Coastal Mountains to Bakersfield and the California Valley, a paradise of grapevines. John Steinbeck describes the last stretch: "They popped down the mountain, twisting and looping, losing the valley sometimes, and then finding it again. And the hot breath of the valley came up to them, with hot green smells on it, and with resinous sage and tarweed smells. The crickets crackled along the road."

Route 66 turned southwest after Barstow and started to climb to the San Gabriel Mountains. So does the new Interstate 15 coming from Las Vegas through Barstow. The people more interested in a manmade artificial paradise than the natural paradise of the California Valley will take this road. We continue on the old one.

The landscape past Barstow is infinitely more fruitful. Lenwood, Hodge, Helendale, and Oro Grande look like places where you could live. The Mojave River follows the road, or vice versa, to the right. Detached houses are here and there, with gardens, orange trees, and even some grapevines. Someone has grown weary even here; the ruins of a green motel remind us that the traffic on this road was once livelier. Now by no means is the traffic lively. The Road is in reasonable condition all the same. The private residential community of Silver Lakes and the Mojave Resort tempt particularly pensioners away from the Los Angeles hum, drum, and scum.

Before Victorville the Lost Highway bicycle bar appeared suddenly on the right side of the Old Road, as some 66 fanatics would rather travel the Road on a silent two-wheeled vehicle than a four-wheeled one devouring unleaded gas. Several cement plants and some steel manufacturers are along the road, and then the handsome steel-arched bridge built in 1930 over the Mojave River. Over the hill, and there is Victorville, where the Old Road and the new I-15 meet again. The California Route 66 Museum in Victorville is at the corner of Sixth Street and D Street. The museum was established in 1995, but the building itself once was the Red Rooster Café right on 66. The other museum in town was dedicated to the old Western movie stars Roy Rogers and Dale Evans. The museum had Rogers's parade car with its bullhorns, pistols, and silver dollars. Rogers's horse Trigger and Evans's horse Buttermilk were now stuffed museum exhibits. So was their "wonder dog," Bullet. In 2003 the museum moved to Branson, Missouri, south of Springfield and Route 66. Whether that was a wise move remains to be seen. Currently (August 2012), the museum is closed.

Roy Rogers was born Leonard Slye in Cincinnati, Ohio, in 1911 but moved early on to California to pick fruit and drive a truck and mostly to sing on the radio and in the movies. When Rogers made his last film in 1975, he had appeared in almost a hundred pictures. He licensed his name to be used in a chain with some six hundred restaurants and on many other items. Somebody has estimated that in licensing, only Walt Disney products have surpassed those of Roy Rogers.

From Victorville, the only way up the mountains is the new Interstate 15. Before the summit lies the legendary Old Summit Inn. Then the summit and Cajon Pass at nearly 4,260 feet above sea level. The way down is a wild one, as only about seventy miles remain to the sea. Cajon Pass is one of the few original gateways to California. Twisted Joshua trees line it like sentries on both sides. Indians from the desert, early Spanish plunderers and priests—they all came through this pass. The archetypal mountain man and fur trapper Jedediah Strong Smith and his follower on many fronts, Christopher "Kit" Carson, both traveled to the San Bernardino Valley this way.

The downhill is really impressive. Just a few hours ago we were in empty desert. Then a stretch of four-lane freeway at Barstow and back to a normal two-lane road. But now, three lanes all going the same direction. No, four, five, six or seven. Each lane has a car or several cars ahead of us and behind us, all cruising downhill at more than sixty miles an hour. On the right a small sign flashes by, guiding us away from this traffic hell: Historic Route 66. But how are we going to switch lanes in the middle of this crowd? If someone makes a mistake here, a hundred people will die and another thousand will break a limb. On the Old Road the hill is even steeper, but the driving is less furious. The soft green of the mountains beautifies the landscape and pacifies the heart.

In the past you had to choose at the foot of the hill whether you went left on the earliest road later named City 66 to San Bernardino or took a shortcut right on the edge of the city and turned west to Los Angeles. The same choice must still be made: either left to San Bernardino on I-215 or right on I-15 to I-10 and Los Angeles.

On the Orange Road, West along the Mountainside

San Bernardino County is the largest county in California. It reaches from Death Valley across the entire Mojave Desert and from the Colorado River to the San Bernardino Mountains. This is the county where Route 66 runs the longest stretch on the whole journey, maybe some three hundred miles, maybe even more. The capital of the district lies on its western border. It got its name from the ruined San Bernardino monastery, which brought Spanish priests here in 1810. Mormons founded the town itself, however, forty years later on land purchased from Mexican farmers. When the Mormons left, the railroads came, and San Bernardino became an intersection of several railroad lines.

The tracks still follow the 66 faithfully through a constantly varying area of industry and railroad yards. The road carries little oncoming traffic besides a few trucks and forklifts. Most of the people use the new freeways. Smog coming from Los Angeles hides the smell of the orange blossoms. According to the American Lung Association, San Bernardino County has the most polluted air in the nation.

Citrus is still a multimillion-dollar industry, but as Tom Teague pointed out in his *Searching for 66*, "Along Route 66 urban development has squeezed it out." In the Road's heyday, Teague writes, "groves and packing houses lined the route for thirty miles. Roadside juice stands—shaped like the fruit—aroused, then slaked the thirst of many a traveler. Okies worked the fields, children sorted the produce, and Orientals on treadmills kept the conveyers moving in packing houses."

You can buy orange juice from a store, however. This is yet another achievement of the Old Roadside. America's greatest culinary feasts were all born in the sphere of Route 66: pizza in Chicago (no matter what New Yorkers claim), the hotdog, ice tea and the ice-cream cone in St. Louis, orange juice in California (no matter what Floridians may say), and the McDonald's burger in San Bernardino (and this is something nobody can say nothing about).

From 1939 to 1948 the New England brothers Richard and Maurice McDonald developed the model of their family restaurant in San Bernardino, a model later copied thousands of times. They compressed the selection of their production line into a few items and started the mass production of hamburgers. They could get the customer a hamburger, a drink, and French fries in twenty seconds, directly to the car when needed—fast food, and cheap. Richard McDonald was a brilliant PR man. He designed the golden arches logo—a letter *M,* each half resembling the Gateway Arch in St. Louis—and the uniform red-and-white exterior of the restaurants. In 1952 the brothers had eight drive-in restaurants on the West Coast. At the time, McDonald's prepared about one million hamburgers and 160 tons of French fries. The menu was the same in all the restaurants, the prices were the same everywhere, and they strove to keep the same quality.

Salesman Ray Kroc became curious about why the McDonalds needed so many ice-cream soda machines. He admired the brothers' operation in San Bernardino and persuaded them to expand their hamburger chain across the nation. Art Bender got the first license when he opened his own restaurant in Fresno, California, in 1956. By 1960 the franchise comprised two hundred restaurants. The next year Kroc bought the whole business from the brothers but kept the name McDonald's. The brothers moved back to New England.

The first students from McDonald's Hamburger University in Chicago graduated in 1957. The business has never stopped growing. The limit of one hundred million hamburgers was broken in 1968, the year they introduced the most popular hamburger in the world, the Big Mac. Finland got her first McDonald's at Tampere City Square in 1984. A McDonald's restaurant opened in Beijing in 1992 and the largest of them all, a seven-hundred-seat restaurant in Moscow, a couple of years earlier.

McDonald's is pretty much the same everywhere, although the standard menu sometimes gives way to local specialties. The Arch Deluxe hamburger never appealed to the "adult taste" of Europe, with or without bacon, and in a couple of years it was also withdrawn from the American market. In 1998 a special rye bread and Swiss cheese burger was introduced in Finland as McRuis, the Finnish for McRye. The McRuis is better for your heart than the normal Big Mac. Salads have now joined the menu, and the chain emphasizes local materials in their preparation of the food. This policy is part of their response to criticism that they waste energy and materials and objections to their reliance on commercial beef production in developing countries. Nowadays, the McDonald's *M* is the most famous logo in the world.

Many fast food chains have followed the example. Burger King, founded by Matthew Burns and Keith Cramer in Florida in 1953, has since become McDonald's main competitor. The McDonald's business idea has copies in other food markets as well: Kentucky Fried Chicken, Pizza Hut with pizza slices and pan pizzas, Dunkin' Donuts selling donuts with holes in the middle or without them, Dairy Queen selling ice-cream products in addition to hamburgers, Wendy's, Arby's, Hardee's, Subway for sandwich lovers . . . All of them can be found both on Interstate Highways and the Historic 66. But the traditional diners where the hamburger beef is still roasted in quality grease and where you can choose other things than "minced meat inside wheat bread"— those you are most likely to find on the Old Road.

In San Bernardino the 66 turns west and crosses under the freeway to continue along the edge of the San Bernardino Mountains towards Los Angeles and the sea on a street most often named Foothill Boulevard. A street is what the Historic 66 is around here and has been for a long time. Maybe it was never a link to the outside world around these parts, but merely a local route to Los Angeles, if even that far.

Today, the area from San Bernardino to Los Angeles is an almost unbroken urban zone. Of course, the old towns are still there, and they all have their own style, but they have grown together. San Bernardino, Rialto, Fontana, Bennet, Rancho Cucamonga, Upland, Claremont, San Dimas, Glendora, Azusa, Duarte, Monrovia, Pasadena. Oranges, grapes, stores, supermarkets, apartments. Buses, convertibles, roadworks, gas stations. Steep curves, street changes, and debates about which is, or was, the real 66.

There's the California Theater in San Bernardino, or was it open any more—was it even standing? The Wigwam Motel still stands in Rialto. The tepee-shaped motel cottages stare at the Road going by with blank expressions. We heard rumors that the area is used for carnal pleasures. The Wigwam has pulled itself together, however, and is catering to customers who merely want to spend a night sleeping inside a clean and cozy Indian lodge.

In Rancho Cucamonga a supermarket stands at the site of California's oldest vineyard. The same premises house a Route 66 museum and a visitors' center, albeit a small one, whose artifacts are mainly on display in the windows. The manager of the center is J. Robert (Bob) Lundy, "Dr. Route 66," who apparently wrote his PhD dissertation on the Old Road.

In Upland, a statue by the roadside portrays a pioneer woman and child, the Madonna of the Trails. It is one of twelve such monuments erected by the Daughters of the American Revolution to commemorate the spirit of pioneer women. The original idea during the first decade of the twentieth century was to mark the Santa Fe Trail with female statues. In the late 1920s, however, the National Society of the Daughters of the American Revolution joined the effort, and together with the Old Trails Road Association chose to establish a monument of a woman with two children and a rifle at twelve sites across the country from Washington DC, to Los Angeles, CA. The statue was sculpted by August Leimbach, a German artist who lived for years in the United States, mostly in St. Louis.

In Upland, the Madonna pays homage to the hard trek of Jedediah Smith and his troops, the first people of the United States to cross the Colorado River, the Mojave Desert, and Cajon Pass but also to the travels of the seekers who came later.

Historic Route 66 signs guide us to make sharp turns and to go around blocks. Traveler's guides advise us to make the turns at other intersections, or yet others, but we don't mind cruising down these roads lined with palm trees. From Azusa to Pasadena, the Road really runs in the southern foothills of the mountains. The traffic is moderately lively, but far from jamming. The jam is a short distance to the south on the freeway, so why should we drive there? We can travel just as fast on this road.

In East Pasadena the Road runs between hedges that prevent us from seeing the yards of rich people. Then we drive south, and the people living by the road get poorer. Once again under the freeway, and there stands the Rialto Theater on the right side of the road, a memory of the heyday of the Old Road, its best days behind. Then hills, more hills, and advertising signs in Spanish. Bridges and railroad yards, barred store windows. I would not like to live here, but this is not yet the Dream City. This is just Los Angeles.

City of Angels?

Los Angeles deserves a book of its own—and many have been written. Also songs and movies. It is where everything comes together. A new beginning and the end of the continent and of Route 66. It's the combination of the American dream and the American nightmare. One in all, and all in one. *E pluribus unum* . . .

"L.A. Is My Lady," sang Frank Sinatra, but Los Angeles is a generic name for a geographic area in Southern California. It is an expression referring to a large region between the Pacific Ocean and the San Gabriel Mountains. It is geography, but it is not a geographical concept. It is more of a cultural concept—or a cultural mess. Los Angeles is really eighty towns in 465 square miles. It reaches from Santa Clarita to San Clemente and from San Bernardino to the sea. It is Long Beach, Santa Ana, Fullerton, Inglewood, Glendale, and Burbank. And yet it is only Los Angeles in the middle of them all. It is a desert split by freeways. The small rivers here and there have been channeled into canals and sucked dry to irrigate the citrus gardens. It should have no prerequisites for life, but it lives nevertheless—maybe more powerfully than any other city in the United States. Its area is the ultimate destination of Route 66 and the goal of all hopes.

Some say that LA is no longer in the United States, or maybe it has never really even been part of it. Some say that LA today is what the rest of the United States is tomorrow. In David Lynch's film *Mulholland Falls*, the name referring to the hills northwest of the city, Nick Nolte plays a rough representative of law enforcement. "This is not America, this is LA." he tells a man he is going to kill, when the poor victim weeps that things like that are not done in America. The film also refers to the other end of Route 66 when Nolte says that Mulholland Falls was for the man he just killed a way to return to Chicago, as "there is no organized crime in LA."

Small groups of Indians lived here and there in the area, when Spaniards first sailed up the California coast. Most of the indigenous population lived on the fertile lands in the north or in the California Valley. In 1771, Spaniards built a mission dedicated to Archangel Gabriel in the desert, and the mountains north of it also got their name from the angel. San Gabriel became a link in the Spanish chain of missionary stations, each a day's trip from the previous one, although the trips then were made on foot, your own or a donkey's.

A couple of years earlier, Gaspar de Portolá had named the area Nuestra Señora La Reina de Los Angeles de Porciúncula after an Assisi chapel in Porciúncula, Italy, the home of the Franciscan Brotherhood. Thus, the name of Portolá honored not only the Virgin Mary but also the Franciscans. Later the words "our lady (Nuestra Señora)" and the reference to Porciúncula disappeared, and what was left was merely "Queen of Angels" (Reina de Los Angeles). Finally, even "Queen" changed into "village," and only the "village of Angels," El Pueblo de Los Angeles, remained.

The pueblo still stands, maybe not quite in the original site but north of the present Los Angeles city center. Originally, Route 66 ended here or began from here. It had several optional routes to the very heart of LA. According to some people the Road ended when it met the wall of Los Angeles City Hall. The road arrangements have since changed the face of downtown to the extent that it is difficult to say today where the Historic 66 runs, or should run, or whether it runs at all. There have not been road signs for a long time. Maybe the Old Road now lies under a railroad yard or the freeways in Santa Ana and Hollywood. Wherever the 66 runs or ran, we still have to stop at Los Angeles. Pueblo is its old town, and a few old houses still stand on their original sites. Olvera Street imitates a market street of a Mexican village. At the end of the street is a monument to the town's founding fathers.

The city hall is a stone's throw away. In the other direction you can throw even a larger stone and hit the railroad station, named Union Station here as well. It is not a very important station now, as today everybody either flies to Los Angeles or drives here, but it still is an important station. Union Station has lately become a stop on Los Angeles's new subway, the Metrolink.

The railroad was once an important factor in growing the area into the second largest metropolis in the United States. Only some five thousand wealthy Mexican rancheros and Anglo immigrants lived in the town in 1850. When the railroad arrived in 1880, it started the growth that still continues. At the turn of the century, the city already had 115,000 inhabitants. After World War II, the space and airplane industries served to increase the population. Today, eight million people live in the Los Angeles-Long Beach area.

These people are diverse, and they come from all corners. In this way, Los Angeles is similar to Chicago and most other big cities in North America. Los Angeles is the world's second or third largest Spanish-speaking city after Mexico City and perhaps Madrid in Spain. Some of the Spanish speakers are illegal immigrants. Especially since World War II, black people have been moving to the area from the South and the northern Midwest. Indians have come to the city in search of jobs from their reservations in Arizona, New Mexico, and South Dakota. Los Angeles has a Chinese district and a Japanese district and a Korean district larger than either of the others. In fact, LA has the largest concentration of Koreans outside Korea itself.

Suburban areas where families lived in detached houses with swimming pools and two cars in the garage became the symbol of the city after World War II. The houses were surrounded by orange gardens and the mountains towered in the background. Above it all shone the perpetual golden sun of California. All was just as in the neighborhood of the great space film *E.T.*

But the sun does not always shine down on all of us, at least not in a mental or psychic sense. The Los Angeles area is famous for its violence. With the old-time gangsters in mind, people have sometimes referred to LA as the West Coast Chicago. Has Route 66 brought the gangsters here from Chicago? Many drug gangs operate in the towns and districts of this area. Some of this face of LA is depicted in the 1988 film *Colors*, starring Robert Duvall, and directed by the old Easy Rider Dennis Hopper.

Los Angeles has not been able to avoid racial conflict, either. In August 1965, the Watts riot in the black district on the western edge of the city center resulted in thirty-six casualties, a number of destroyed buildings and broken hearts. On March 3, 1991, a bystander videotaped an incident in which white policemen battered Rodney King, a black man they had pulled over. A year later the court released the policemen, thereby provoking a wave of rioting. The episode was the largest civil unrest in United States history, accounting for some six hundred fires and fifty-five dead. Within the next ten years, 85 percent of the destroyed buildings had been rebuilt.

How about O. J. Simpson, the black football player who was suspected of murdering his white wife and her "boyfriend"? The police apprehended Simpson after a dramatic chase, much of which was televised. The trial turned into a massive media event. The defense managed to turn the charges into racism, and Simpson walked. One year later, however, a civilian court ordered Simpson to pay millions of dollars to the families of the victims.

Political violence is also familiar in LA. Presidential candidate Robert F. Kennedy was assassinated at the Ambassador Hotel in June 1968. Even the forces of nature sometimes give the area a hard time. The strength of the earthquake of 1975 was 6.6 on the open Richter scale.

But, as stated above, Los Angeles is not only the relatively small area of Los Angeles itself but also the other seventy-nine towns connected to it. The Okies of the 1930s did not take Route 66 to get to Pueblo of Los Angeles but to find work in Orange County orange groves. Actors and writers in search of their fortune were not driving on 66 to reach the Los Angeles Pueblo,  but to make a name for themselves at the film studios of Hollywood or Burbank. The families of the 1950s and 1960s did not endure the hardships of the long trip down Route 66 to get to Los Angeles but to visit Disneyland.

Disneyland is in Anaheim, some twenty-five miles southeast of Los Angeles City Hall. It is the home of Donald Duck and Mickey Mouse, the dream of every American child. Well, the dream of their parents, anyway. After more than fifty years, Disneyland still represents "pure American family entertainment." There are greater machines and wilder rides at most other amusement parks, but this classic attracts visitors in plenty. Perhaps too many, as you have to queue up even on a regular day and to the most popular places maybe even for a couple of hours. You need to buy the three-day ticket, therefore, if you want to see all of Disneyland.

You can see plenty of other places in Los Angeles for three days, too.

Even other amusement parks like Knott's Berry Farm at La Palma—or is it actually Buena Park?—some seven miles west of Disneyland. Knott's amusement park centers on the theme of the Wild West. The berry farm really exists, and you can buy Knott's berries and jams on the spot. The wildest roller-coaster rides are at Six Flags Magic Mountain in Valencia north of Hollywood.

For museum lovers, even thirty days would not be enough. The Museum of Contemporary Art has spilled over into the Temporary Contemporary, both inside Los Angeles proper on its western edge. That part of town is also a good place to look for a sense of the Old West and of travel before the 66 from the museum of the Wells Fargo stagecoach company, nowadays a modern banking and transport company. The Gene Autry museum in Glendale in the north gives you a taste of the life and great songs of this great western singer. A museum of women of the West has now been added to the original Autry complex. The county of Los Angeles, of course, has its own museum of art and museum of natural history. Naturally, there also has to be a museum of California science and industry. African Americans have their own museum. The naval museum lies in West Carson. The wax museum of the motion picture world is at Buena Park.

For sports fanatics, the region is full of memories and dreams. The Olympic Games were held here not once but twice. Los Angeles has football, baseball, and basketball: Raiders and Rams, Dodgers and Angels, Lakers and Clippers. Or *had*. The Angels have become the Anaheim Angels. The Rams have moved eastward but are still on Route 66 in St. Louis. They, too, played in Anaheim during their last years in the area before becoming "the white flight Rams."

The area even has hockey under the California sun. Plenty of Europeans, too, Finns included. Teemu Selanne and Jari Kurri have both played for the Anaheim Mighty Ducks, who finally won their first Stanley Cup in 2007. Before joining the Ducks, Kurri used to play as Wayne Gretzky's pair for the Los Angeles Kings. Now a third Finn, Saku Koivu, has joined the Ducks and left Montréal Canadiens behind with their cooler weather.

Education is easy to come by in the area, despite everything. The area has enough high schools of varying sizes, kinds and levels to suit any taste. Campuses of the University of California and California State University are in Los Angeles, Fullerton, and Irvine; the Catholic

Loyola Marymount University lies near Los Angeles International Airport; and the California State Polytechnic is in Pomona, not to mention smaller places of learning.

Dream Town Road

After the Pueblo of Los Angeles you are definitely on the right road, you spot a long-awaited Historic Route 66 sign showing you the way. The street, now named Cesar E. Chavez Avenue after the champion of farm workers' rights, runs west-northwest. Chavez was born in 1927 near Yuma, Arizona, by the Mexican border. During the Great Depression of the 1930s, the family moved to California among the many migrant workers picking fruits and vegetables as did the Joads in *The Grapes of Wrath*. Chavez served in the US Navy at the very end of World War II and in the 1950s began to get a reputation as a labor organizer or trouble maker, depending on your point of view. In 1965 Chavez and the National Farm Workers Association (NFWA) led a huge strike of California grape pickers. It irritated many but won the support of Robert Kennedy. Throughout his life, as any leader and maybe labor leaders particularly, Chavez was a controversial figure. Since his death in 1993, even his former enemies have begun to appreciate his dedication.

After Cesar E. Chavez Avenue, Route 66 changes into Sunset Boulevard, and soon you will have to decide what you want to believe. Did Route 66 run along Sunset Boulevard all the way, did it run along Hollywood Boulevard for a time, or is it the same street? Did Route 66 turn west onto Santa Monica Boulevard? Actually, who cares? In the dream town anyone can dream up the road for themselves. In Hollywood Route 66 is also the road of dreams.

No matter where Route 66 runs in anybody's imagination, we catch a glimpse of the famous sign reading "Hollywood" on a hillside to our right. The sign was erected originally in 1923 to advertise the lots in the area, and it read "Hollywoodland," but the tag "land" has been removed. Today, the sign is the symbol of the movie town.

Hollywood Boulevard is the town's tourist center. The sidewalk has the names of various movie stars, musicians, and directors, embedded inside stars. The famous Grauman's (Mann's) Chinese Theater along Hollywood Boulevard has a front yard with the foot and hand prints of many celebrities of the silver screen from Marilyn Monroe to Donald

Duck. The tradition began when an actress who came to see the building of the theater in 1927 fell by accident and landed on her knees on the wet cement.

Also on Hollywood Boulevard stands the oldest of the grand Hollywood hotels, the Roosevelt from 1927, still worth visiting, still worth spending a night or two. It is characterized by a wonderful entrance hall decorated in the Spanish Southwest style, a swimming pool hidden in the back yard among the palm trees, a hearty breakfast, and smiling faces. Charlie Chaplin cast in bronze will greet you when you enter.

Some haunting memories may also find you here. Hollywood is one of the most haunted places on earth because of the many tragedies that have happened there. Montgomery Clift stayed at the Roosevelt Hotel when he was filming *From Here to Eternity*. Some people still hear him play trumpet in room 928. Marilyn Monroe also stayed at the Roosevelt. The mirror that once hung in her room is now in the lobby. If you believe in ghosts, you may see her image in the mirror. According to the Travel Channel, Hollywood is ninth among the creepiest destinations in the world.

On East Hollywood Boulevard lies Musso & Frank Grill, the oldest eatery in Hollywood. It was established in 1919 and has a legendary reputation as a place where Faulkner and Hemingway drank during their screenwriting days and where Orson Welles used to go for big meals with his friends and followers. Some say the food is still good, but I cannot say. I once went there with my wife and my mother, having made a reservation, and pretty well dressed, even formally by Hollywood standards. The arrogant looking waiter did bring us our aperitifs but ignored my attempts to order.

At the corner of Hollywood Boulevard and Highland Avenue, the Hollywood and Highland Center has offered plenty of restaurants since 2001. Trastevere Ristorante Italiano is perhaps a little pricey, but it does offer excellent Italian cuisine. If you want California eclectic cuisine, try Twist next door. Also at the Highland Center are a bowling alley, some seventy-five shops, and a hotel.

Universal Studios, perhaps the most popular Hollywood tourist attraction, lies only a few miles to the northwest. A theme park built around the motion picture, Universal Studios includes a working film studio as well as tours, rides, shops, and restaurants. Although movies are still filmed there, most of the studios are located over the hill in Burbank. It's true though that nowadays they shoot the landscapes almost everywhere, and even originally they did much of it in Arizona and New Mexico, where the sunshine is as guaranteed as it is in Hollywood. Now television has joined the movies. Even *All in the Family* was filmed in Hollywood, although the Bunkers lived in New York.

Innumerable movies are set in Los Angeles: *Chinatown, Pretty Woman, Die Hard,* and *Naked Gun,* to name just a few; and even a movie called *Live and Let Die in L.A.,* whose theme song is Jerry Leiber's "L.A., L.A." In *The Species* the beast of a woman cloned from an extraterrestrial DNA chain finally meets her maker in the sewers of Los Angeles. The wild run in *Speed* takes place in a Santa Monica bus. And some of the street scenes in *Sketch Artist* from 1992 may even be right on the Old Route.

The film that really connects LA and 66 is *Repo Man* from 1984. While we read the credits at the beginning about the actors, cameramen, dolly grips, and such, the background is a map of the southwestern United States. It starts to move from around Los Alamos in New Mexico south to meet and follow Route 66 across the western edge of New Mexico, across Arizona, and to the eastern edge of the Mojave Desert. The shield of the double-6 is clearly visible. After the opening scene on 66, the rest of the film takes place in Los Angeles.

City of Angels by Brad Silberling takes place, of course, in Los Angeles. Nicholas Cage plays the angel who falls in love with the human Meg Ryan. Dennis Franz plays another "lovefallen angel." Some scenes of Los Angeles are seen, but the library, so central to the film, is in San Francisco. Originally, everything happened under the skies of Berlin, as this film is a Hollywood version, with more action and drama, of Wim Wenders's more European *Wings of Desire.* That partially black and white movie is filled with plenty of philosophy of life, Berlin, and being German. The angel (Bruno Granz) falls in love with a girl from a circus (Solveig Dommartin, at the time, wife to the director). In the European version the angel and the girl don't marry, and the girl doesn't die. Peter Falk plays the role of the previously fallen angel playing the role of himself playing the role of Columbo, the TV detective. The original German name is *Sky above Berlin (Himmel über Berlin).*

But Wim Wenders has also directed a movie of his own on Los Angeles, the American-French production of *The End of Violence* in 1997.

Like many Europeans, Wenders has a love-hate relationship with the United States. He depicts Los Angeles with both a smile and a grimace. The photography is as important, if not even more important, than the story. The Griffith Park Observatory has a major role as a locale, the same way as it had in the 1955 classic of *Rebel without a Cause* by Nicholas Ray, one of James Dean's three films.

My Family reminds us that Los Angeles was Mexican in the past and still is. At the beginning, this story is way too romantic, even pathetic, in representing the fifty years of a Chicano family on the east side of LA. It gets better by the end, however. It is a showcase for many Latino film stars, including Jimmy Smits, Edward James Olmos, and Jennifer Lopez. Great scenes of the city skyline are shown, and also many of its bridges, including the one on Route 66 or Cesar E. Chavez Avenue.

The first Route 66 movie is probably John Ford's film version of *The Grapes of Wrath* by John Steinbeck. The shield shaped sign of US 66 flashes so often on the silver screen during the movie that you could even call the movie a Route 66 advertisement. Several other movies, filmed in Hollywood or elsewhere, take place on the Road. *Thelma and Louise* from the year 1991 tells the story of two women who leave their homes to have fun, until the fun trip turns into a tragic journey west, yet a magnificent journey during which the two women get emancipated. Susan Sharandon and Geena Davis play their roles beautifully. There is no mention of the name or the number of the road, but towards the end of the movie the landscapes are clearly those of the Old Road in Arizona and New Mexico. It even feels that some of the scenes were filmed in California in the same place as *Bagdad Café*. Maybe they were.

The women's escapade ends when the police have them surrounded, and they choose honorable death rather than defeat, surrender, and a possible life sentence. Many American movies end like that with the hero or heroes choosing death. Thelma and Louise drive their Thunderbird off the rim of the Grand Canyon. *Butch Cassidy and the Sundance Kid* charge out from the small shack knowing full well that the police will mow them down. In another Western, *The Desperate Trail,* the hero saves a woman by driving her out the back door and charging out the front himself, shooting at the sheriff and the deputies to draw their fire, and allowing the woman to escape.

Why is all this? Do Americans have an instinct for self-annihilation, manifesting itself in movie endings? Does the US Declaration of Independence not guarantee everyone a right to "the pursuit of happiness?" If that pursuit does not succeed, is death the best alternative? Americans cannot lose, the cup is too bitter to drain, and therefore dying or self-destruction is more honorable. Maybe this is why the Vietnam defeat was so hard to bear. In a general sense, maybe death by hanging is better than the life of a slave, or a life of shame; an idea known also to Finns through one of their ancient heroes. And how different is it from the Japanese "hara-kiri?" Thank goodness Americans do it only in movies.

The mother of all road movies, Dennis Hopper's *Easy Rider*, also ends in tragic death. Two young men sell drugs and use the money to leave Los Angeles for New Orleans, traveling on Route 66 from west to east, the "wrong direction." One of the bikers is Peter Fonda, whose father Henry Fonda took the same road from east to west as Tom Joad in *The Grapes of Wrath*. Is it just a coincidence that the crossing of the Colorado River is such an important scene in both movies?

Many other movies take place "on the road," and people even talk about a distinct genre called the "road movie." In one example of the genre, Paul Mazursky's *Harry and Tonto*, an old man and a cat start their trip from New York, but their longest stretch is from Chicago to Los Angeles, and that can only mean Route 66. It's true that in this case the heroes travel through Las Vegas in Nevada.

Dean Martin and Jerry Lewis also travel through Las Vegas en route from Chicago to Hollywood in the 1956-movie *Hollywood or Bust*. Mostly they travel on 66 or near it. Around the middle of the movie there is a long scene of singing, during which the heroes drive their convertible across the Mississippi, across the Missouri, through Oklahoma, through Texas full of oil towers, and through New Mexico and Santa Fe, and peep into Arizona on the edge of the Grand Canyon before finally crossing the present Hoover Dam (still known as Boulder Dam at the time), from Arizona to Nevada, and then to Las Vegas. This part of the movie could almost work as a Route 66 music video. There are no road signs, but the magical Double-Six badge sign flashes finally past as the heroes turn from the main road into Hollywood.

The southwestern United States is also the scene of Sam Peckinpah's *The Getaway* from 1972 and its later version, directed by Roger Donaldson in 1994. The first film version of this Jim Thompson novel starred

Steve McQueen and Ali McGraw as the bank-robbing couple, the second starred Alec Baldwin and Kim Basinger. The latter pair drive Old 66 from Arizona to New Mexico and confuse the geography completely when they wait for a train to El Paso at the Flagstaff railroad station.

Television has also tried to make the Road its own. A total of 104 episodes of the series *Route 66* were filmed from 1960 to 1964. The series told the story of two friends in a Chevrolet Corvette on US-66. Bobby Troup was offended when his song was not chosen as the theme music; instead, Nelson Riddle composed a new title melody. The TV series described the moving, dynamics, and courage of the United States, and the adventurous nature of its people. The audience liked the idea, and the series was popular. Things were still going well for the United States in the early 1960s, before the Vietnam War. The series succeeded abroad as well, and even Finnish TV showed it. Route 66 became even more familiar.

Or did it really? The thing is, hardly any of the episodes were filmed on the Road. They did film in Chicago and Arizona, but also on the Northwest Coast and in Florida and New York. The location even in Arizona was more often Phoenix than Flagstaff. In principle, however, Tod Stiles and Buz Murdock traveled on Route 66 and had many adventures and misadventures there. Tod was the more liberal of the two. He came from a good family and had even studied at a university. Buz was a more abrupt character, a street kid whose stepfather had died of a drug overdose, leaving Buz an inheritance, with which Buz bought his first Corvette.

During the filming, the model of the car changed to a new one every year. At the end of the first production season the buddies wrecked their car completely in a crash. They saved the life of a rich man, however, who rewarded them with a new car. This explained the next season's new Corvette. But the car kept changing with every production season, and without further explanations. Chevrolet wanted to present their latest model each year through the TV series and did not want the boys driving around in an older model.

Martin Milner played Tod Stiles and George Maharis played Buz Murdock. Glen Corbett replaced Maharis and Buz as Linc Case for the last season. Other famous actors in the series include Robert Redford, Alan Alda, Robert Duvall, Rod Steiger, Gene Hackman, Lee Marvin and Jean Stapleton. Recently, Martin Milner has almost started a second career as a spokesman for Historic Route 66. You can see him often at Route 66 festivals and auto shows.

Nobody knows why they stopped filming the TV series. Another attempt at the story took place in fall 1993 with the launching of a new Route 66 TV series. It was really a remake of the original series: two guys and a cherry red corvette (the original show was black and white, so you really could not tell the color of the car). Despite plenty of handsome pre-publicity, the series flopped immediately in the United States. Some TV stations stopped broadcasting it after only a couple of episodes. After four episodes, it was cancelled. It had some success in Europe, however, and I understand that it was very popular in Germany and Norway.

The revitalizing of the Old Road has, of course, brought to light a whole number of TV movies and videos relating to Route 66. The 1998 film *Route 66* by Steve Austin, and starring, among others, Alana Austin, Pamela Hasselhoff, and Diane Ladd, is an example. More typical of the new genre is *Route 66: America's Main Street*. It's written and directed for TV in the year of 2000. The host is Peter Fonda, the old Easy Rider, Captain America.

Beaches and Piers

Los Angeles has something that all other major cities in North America lack: a hundred miles of beach and, at least by Nordic standards, water warm enough to swim in throughout the year. Well, if not to swim, at least to dip in. Starting from the south, the beaches are Newport Beach, Huntington Beach, Seal Beach, Long Beach, Cabrillo Beach (named after the Portuguese-Spanish sailor Juan Rodríguez Cabrillo, who sailed these shores in 1542), Royal Palms Beach, Redondo Beach (that is, round beach), Hermosa Beach (that is beautiful beach), and a few more. Other LA beaches are Manhattan Beach, Dockweiler Beach, Venice Beach, and Santa Monica Beach, where Route 66 finally ends. Every beach has a nature of its own. Early in 2002 the Travel Channel listed the ten top beaches of Southern California, judging Will Rogers State Beach number six as this is where many TV series, including *Son of the Beach*, have been filmed. Number one on the list was Coronado City Beach down in San Diego. Beaches are part of Los Angeles's charm, and all of California's for that matter. In Southern California life is beach.

At times even the Pacific Ocean is far from peaceful or "beachful," but most often it behaves gently and has soft swells in the San Pedro Canal. It raises waves just enough for surfing. Just enough waves to make the children lose their balance, laughing. Just enough rushing to lull the homeless to sleep under a palm tree, in the shade.

The most affluent living area in the United States is here, on a cape between San Pedro Bay and Santa Monica Bay. Rolling Hills Estates is a beautiful and independent small town inside its own walls. Only the dwellers, their guests, and their servants will get inside those walls. The rows of cars in and out of the gates are long. In this area of freeways the road is closed here. The 66 has no business there.

Route 66 reaches the beach some twenty miles farther north. You can already smell the ocean after Hollywood. Santa Monica Boulevard continues to West Hollywood, Beverly Hills, and West Los Angeles. At times the Road is lined with houses and at times by nothing but hedges. We pass the large Los Angeles area Mormon Temple on the left. When it was finished in 1956, the 250-foot tower made the church the second tallest building in the Los Angeles area.

Beverly Hills is also a place where rich people live. Most houses are hidden behind well-groomed hedges. If you want to leave the 66, you can visit Rodeo Drive to see if you can detect any movie stars or other trivial celebrities. It is a great place to lose the rest of your money, your own and the money you borrowed; that is, if you have any left at this final lap of the journey.

Santa Monica and the sea are very near. Venice Beach, immediately south of Santa Monica, is the beach belonging to "characters." Abbott Kinney dug a number of canals in the beach and planned to recreate the Mediterranean Venice in Southern California, but the water in the canals got dirty, and the area did not tempt the rich. Instead, it tempted some pretty strange characters. The beach is still full of them. There's one, juggling with a chainsaw. A fire-eater badmouths the audience who will not pay enough to see his show. A man with no hands or feet bangs drums with his stumps with a hat to collect money in front of him. Roller skaters, rollerbladers, and skateboarders cruise the asphalt path lining the beach in an unbroken chain. On the Travel Channel's list Venice Beach was number four, as the people peopling it are such a variety, and it is about two miles of constant entertainment with only one rule—there are no rules.

The path continues north and becomes tidier. Santa Monica Beach is a more peaceful area. On the Travel Channel's list it was number seven. At the turn of the century, the trip from Los Angeles to Santa Monica Beach was long and difficult along poor roads. The red streetcar made the trip far easier, but the 66 was the first really good connection. Now Interstate 10 shortens the drive here to half an hour.

Right on top of the embankment an Asian woman steps out from a Thai restaurant and starts to sweep the pavement in front. She wears a T-shirt declaring that Finland's national hockey team won the world championship in 1995. I explain to the woman in Finnish that her shirt is correct. The woman looks at me curiously and continues sweeping. I tell her in English that her shirt tells the truth. She still does not understand and is about to give us a lesson with her broomstick. Finally, I get my message through. She tells us that her daughter or niece sent her the T-shirt from Finland. We talk for only a moment, and she goes back into the restaurant. We are so taken by surprise at the incident that we forget to snap a photo. Too late now. She has locked the restaurant door behind her. Finland's national hockey team won the world championship again in 2011.

Santa Monica is a town in its own right, although the beach is closer to Los Angeles proper than any of the others. Therefore, the beach is frequently overcrowded. In the middle of the beach the Santa Monica Pier sticks out into the ocean, a colorful memory from the past comes alive again. You must have seen it in many ads, photos, and movies. In *Forrest Gump*, Tom Hanks runs into it, passing also some other Route 66 places, like Monument Valley, on his way.

You can eat and drink on the Santa Monica pier at hotdog stands, a hamburger bar, and even a couple of classier restaurants. An amusement park extends out over the sea. You can fish from the pier, of course, and that pier is where Route 66 ends.

But in fact, it doesn't. Most people claim it, but actually Route 66 hits the embankment a couple of blocks further north. You can see the Santa Monica Pier from the end of the Road.

Ocean Avenue runs on top of the steep bank. By the foot of the bank is the Pacific Coast Highway. You must cross it before reaching the ocean. Route 66, that is Santa Monica Boulevard, descends gracefully down to Ocean Avenue. Like a memory from times gone by, an old movie theater and an old diner stand beside the Road just before it meets its destiny. Some people claim that 66 originally ran its final yards along Olympic Boulevard, three blocks south of here.

Between Ocean Avenue and the embankment lies Palisades Park, a park of palm trees and pathways. Route 66 does not continue through it. In the park, however, at the end of the boulevard is a monument of the Road and its famous traveler. A small plaque on the ground is dedicated to Will Rogers, the globetrotter who traveled Highway 66, Main Street of America, into the hearts of his fellow Americans. The plaque was laid here in 1952, when the southernmost section of the Road was officially named Will Rogers Highway.

Ten yards from Palisades Park and the Will Rogers plaque is a safety fence. Below, the waves bury themselves in Santa Monica Beach, looking for peace. This is the end of the road, the end of land, the end of everything. The end of the West. Open seas ahead. Across them, other worlds. Here is only the sunset and the eternal longing for faraway places.

This is where Route 66 ends. Destiny fulfilled. Journey completed.

For the Road—
And Before

In addition to the interviews and discussions on the Road, and in addition to the field-work I have done along and in the vicinity of Route 66, I have also leaned heavily on the help of other travelers, researchers, storytellers, musicians, and artists while writing this book. The writings, songs, and films they have produced have been extra food for me while making this trip in writing. I have listed below some the most important sources I have used. I recommend those for everyone as additional nourishment for the Road.

To read: (but, please, don't read them while you're driving)

Abbey, Edward. *Desert Solitaire: A Season in the Wilderness.* 1968. Reprint, New York: Ballantine Books, 1991.
> Not a Route 66 book, but many travelers of the Old Road will probably like the peace and harmony of the desert surrounding most of 66 in the Southwest.

Bergheim, Laura. "Reminisce Down Route 66." In *Rand McNally 1992 Road Atlas*. Chicago: Rand McNally, 1992.
> Nice little essay attached to the Rand McNally Road Atlas of that year.

Cather, Willa. *Death Comes for the Archbishop.* 1927. Reprint, New York: Vintage Books, 1971.
> Masterpiece novel that is located in Santa Fe and elsewhere in New Mexico.

The Chronicle of the Movies: A Year-by-Year History from the Jazz Singer to Today. New York: Crescent Books, 1991.
> Gives interesting facts, and maybe a bit of fiction, too, of the history of the motion pictures.

Cline, Platt. *They Came to the Mountain: The Story of Flagstaff's Beginning.* Flagstaff: Northland Press, 1976.
> Tells the story of the early years of this unofficial capital city of Route 66.

Crump, Spencer. *Route 66: America's First Main Street*, 3rd ed. Corona del Mar, CA: Zeta Publishers, 1995.

> Not a great literary achievement that has beautiful colored pictures and a wonderful layout like the fanciest Route 66 books but, nevertheless, certainly worthy of reading. Gives a good personal account of the Old Road and contains stuff you cannot find in the fancy 66 books.

Crunden, Robert M. *A Brief History of American Culture*. Helsinki: Finnish Historical Society, 1990.

> Not a Route 66 book, but a superb and short introduction to what the United States is all about by a former University of Texas professor of American Studies. If you disagree with Crunden's interpretation, that's your problem.

Foard, Sheila Wood. *Harvey Girl*. Lubbock, TX: Texas Tech University Press, 2006.

> Great fiction based on interviews with former Harvey Girls. It could have been just like this—maybe it actually was.

Freeth, Nick. *Traveling Route 66: 2,250 Miles of Motoring History from Chicago to LA*. Norman, OK: Salamander Books Limited / University of Oklahoma Press, 2001.

> A standard presentation of the Old Road. Nice to look at and read but the language does not flow, nor is there any personal involvement by the writer.

Freeth, Nick. *Route 66: 2,297Miles from Chicago to LA*. St. Paul, MN: MBI Publishing Company, 2001.

> With more than five hundred photos and with beautiful layout, this book is one of the best Route 66 books to watch. Unfortunately, the text does not match the photos. The book is a pretty straightforward presentation by a London-born University of Cambridge graduate and a former music reporter for BBC, which makes one wonder even more about the poor style of his language.

Fugate, Francis L. and Roberta B. *Roadside History of Oklahoma*. Missoula, MT: Mountain Press Publishing Company, 1991.

> A good standard history of the roads in a central Route 66 state.

Gómez, Arthur R. *Quest for the Golden Circle: The Four Corners and the Metropolitan West, 1945-1970*. Albuquerque: University of New Mexico Press, 1994

> Very interesting look at the economy of the natural sights around Route 66 in the southwest. American Studies at its best.

Historic Route 66 Mainstreet of America. Mesa, AZ: Smith-Southwestern / Terrell, n.d.

> Thirty pages of old postcards by one of the largest Route 66 postcard makers and scenic photography by D. Jeanene Tiner. A beautiful and most enjoyable little booklet

Horgan, Paul. *Great River: The Rio Grande in North American History*. 1954. Reprint, Hanover, NY: Wesleyan University Press, 1996.

> Tells the story of this great American river with nice pictures. Classic.

Inside Guide: United States on the Road. Singapore: Discovery Channel/APA, 2001.
A guide to a choice of travel routes in the United States.

Jacka, Lois Essary and Jerry. *David Johns on the Trail of Beauty.* Scottsdale, AZ: Snail-space, 1991.
Beautiful history of the Navajo artist with great examples of his art.

Janelle, Donald G., ed. *Geographical Snapshots of North America.* New York: Guilford Press, 1992.
Covers almost all of North America. Not only for geographers.

Jensen, Jamie. *Road Trip: Cross-Country Adventures on America's Two-Lane Highways.* Moon Travel Handbooks. Chico, CA: Moon Publications, 1999.
Interesting reading.

Kelly, Susan Croce and Quinta Scott. *Route 66: The Highway and Its People.* Norman: University of Oklahoma Press, 1988.
One of the important books right at the time of the second coming of Route 66. Easy to read with great stories and great style. Superb black and white photos.

Kerouac, Jack. *On the Road.* 1955. Reprint, New York: Penguin Books, 2002.
One of the great American classics.

Lamb, David. "Romancing the Road." *National Geographic* 192, no. 3 (1997).
A little piece of Route 66 in a major magazine.

Liebs, Chester H. *Main Street to Miracle Mile: American Roadside Architecture.* 1985. Reprint, Baltimore: Johns Hopkins University Press, 1995.
Increases your understanding of not only American architecture but also American roads and America itself.

Our National Parks: America's Spectacular Wilderness Heritage. Pleasantville, NY: Reader's Digest, 1985.
One of the many beautiful books about the great national parks of America.

Past Imperfect: History According to the Movies. Society of American Historians. New York: Henry Holt, 1995.
If you learned most of your history from the movies as many of us have, this book will teach you not to trust the moviemakers.

Peters, Arthur King. *Seven Trails West.* New York: Abbeville Press, 1996.
How people traveled west and what routes they followed before Highway 66. A fresh look at American history.

Poling-Kempes, Lesley. *The Harvey Girls: Women Who Opened the West.* New York: Paragon House, 1991.
Important story of the important women in the history of the American West and Route 66.

Rittenhouse, Jack D. *A Guide Book to Highway 66*. 1946. Reprint, Albuquerque: University of New Mexico Press, 1989.

A Route 66 classic. The very first and still very useful guide book to travelers on Route 66.

Robson, Ellen, and Dianne Halicki. *Haunted Highway: The Spirits of Route 66*. Phoenix: Golden West Publishers, 2000.

Route 66 in the twilight zone. Spooky and fun.

Root, Waverly, and Richard de Rochemont. *Eating in America: A History*. 1976. Reprint, Hopewell, NJ: Ecco Press, 1996.

Tells the history of American food, much of it related to Route 66.

Sautelet, Patrick, Serge Labrune, Jean-Luc Moreau, and Philippe Fauconnier. *Route 66*. Besancon/Paris, France: Editions d'Art J.-P. Barthelemy / M6 TURBO, 1992.

A beautiful French look of the Old Road.

Schneider, Jill. *Route 66 across New Mexico: A Wanderer's Guide*. Albuquerque: University of New Mexico Press, 1991.

A detailed guide with easy maps and interesting photography by D. Nakii.

Scott, Quinta. *Along Route 66*. Norman: University of Oklahoma Press, 2000.

Another beautiful book by a writer who has practically started a new career with the comeback of Route 66.

Snyder, Tom. *Route 66 Traveler's Guide and Roadside Companion*. 2nd ed. New York: St. Martin's Griffin, 1995.

The essential guidebook for present-day Route 66 travelers. Well written and easy to follow. Without Snyder, you would get lost, but if you get lost with Snyder, that's probably a great adventure.

Stanton, Bette. *"Where God Put the West": Movie Making in the Desert, A Moab-Monument Valley Movie History*. Moab, Utah: Four Corners Publications, 1994.

Located north of Route 66, Monument Valley, nevertheless, is an important feature within Route 66 destinations. Nice story with nice black-and-white photos. But was it really God who put the West in Monument Valley, or was it perhaps John Ford?

Steinbeck, John. *The Grapes of Wrath*. 1939. Reprint, London: Arrow Books, 1998.

The great Route 66 classic. Most likely we would not be even talking about Route 66 had this book not been published. A most touching story of the travels of an Okie family to find their fortune in the West.

Teague, Tom. *Searching for 66*. With Bob Waldmire and Lon Haldeman. 2nd ed. Springfield, Illinois: Samizdat Books, 1996.

A product of the Route 66 comeback, but one of the very best.

Trimble, Marshall. *Roadside History of Arizona*. 1986. Reprint, Missoula, Montana: Mountain Press, 1994.

Tells what has happened along the roads in Arizona, another important Route 66 state.

Wallis, Michael. *Route 66: The Mother Road*. New York: St. Martin's, 1990.
> The book that really started the Route 66 boom. Beautifully written and good photographs. Especially nice vignettes about people of Route 66, including Bobby Troup and Martin Milner.

Williamson, J. W. *Hillbillyland: What the Movies Did to the Mountains & What the Mountains Did to the Movies*. Chapel Hill, NC: University of North Carolina Press, 1995.
> We need something like this about the roads as well.

Witzel, Michael Karl. *Route 66 Remembered*. Osceola, WI: Motorbooks, 1996.
> One of the best books in the field. Written with a good flow, nice pictures, old and new, and a beautiful layout. Proceeds thematically rather than state by state. At the end includes several reminiscences by people who have traveled on the Road to the West.

Witzel, Michael Karl, and Tim Steil. *Americana: Roadside Memories*. With additional photography by Jim Luning. Ann Arbor, MI: Lowe & B. Hound, 2003.
> This is three books in one; the first one is simply titled *Route 66*, the second *Gas Station Memories*, and the third *Drive-in Deluxe*. It is 285 pages filled with interesting photographs and little stories. Well written, too. The second book introduces several gas stations around the United States, and talks about pumps and signs and gas station attendants. The third book introduces many things related to the drive-in.
>
> *Route 66* is a pretty standard state-by-state treatment that interviews some of the perhaps less well-known people of the Road. It has interesting photos that have interesting subtitles, but in (too) many cases there is no reference to their substance in the actual text, and the reader is left to wonder. Overall, it looks as if this whole book were a spinoff of Witzel's previous book riding on the Route 66 boom; an easy way to make money on the same topic with not much extra work. Nevertheless, it's worth a look.

To listen: (this you can do while driving)

American FM. Nectar, 1994, compact disc.
> A good collection of pieces that Americans supposedly listened to while driving their cars a few decades ago.

Autry, Gene. *The Essential Gene Autry, 1933-1946*. Columbia Country Classics/Sony Music Entertainment, 1992, compact disc.
> An excellent collection of the great master of western songs.

Berry, Chuck. *Rock & Roll Music*. European Charly, 1993, compact disc.
> The basics of the grand old man of rock'n roll.

Blues 1. United Audio Entertainment, 1996, compact disc.
> Nice listening of American Oldies.

Burning Sky. *Blood of the Land*. Canyon Records, 1995, compact disc.
    Great music from a Native American point of view.

California Dreaming. Columbia/Sony Music, 1995, compact disc.
    Standard collection of California-related songs.

Coast to Coast, Route 66. Capitol Records, 1994, compact disc.
    Great musical journey across the United States by pieces from the Capitol
    archives.

Cole, Nat King. *Golden Memories*. Euros Oy, n.d., compact disc.
    A good collection of great songs, including the essential "Get Your Kicks."

Eero ja Jussi & the Boys. *Singlet 1964-68*. Castle Finland Oy Ltd, 1987, vinyl record.
    A collection of melodic rock from my home country by the people who
    made several versions of "Route 66."

Freeway: 20 Classic Driving Tracks. Polygram TV, 1996, compact disc.
    Music for the open road.

Get Your Kicks on Route 66: 100 Songs for the Road. Intermusic S.A./Movieplay S.A.,
    1993, compact disc.
    Plenty of music for the open road. With this collection, you can practically
    drive through all of Illinois.

The Golden Eagle String Band. *The Canallers's Songbook*. American Canal and Trans-
    portation Center, 1990, compact disc. Originally recorded 1984.
    Great songs from the times of the Erie Canal.

Guthrie, Woodie. *Library of Congress Recordings*. Woody Guthrie Publications/
    Rounder Records Corp., 1992, compact disc. Originally recorded 1988.
    A great piece of American history. Guthrie sings and talks—nostalgia at its
    best.

Mailroad. *Left Chicago*. Mailroad-Music, 1997, compact disc.
    Mr. Route 66 of Finland and his group play melodic rock.

Route 66: A Special Compilation Tribute to Route 66. California Historic Route 66
    Association, n.d., compact disc.
    These songs are all about the Old Road.

The Songs of Route 66: Music from the All-American Highway. David Sanger/Lazy
    S.O.B. Recordings, 1995, compact disc.
    More music for the open road.

Southern California with Fond Memories. City Songs, 1994, compact disc.
    Another interesting collection of California songs.

Street Dreams. Clay Dog Records, 1994, compact disc.
    Street music is seldom heard on records, and perhaps some of the feeling is
    lost, but this is a very interesting and ambitious collection of music played
    on the streets of the Windy City.

The Weavers. *Greatest Hits*. Vanguard Records, 1986, compact disc.

>A classic collection of one of the classic groups of American folk music. Some of the songs will still bring tears to your eyes.

To watch: (but, once again, don't watch these, or any other movies or videos while driving; just watch the road and the traffic)

Bagdad Café, also known as *Out of Rosenheim*. Directed by Percy Adlon. Munich: Pelemele Film Gmbh, 1987.

>A German look at the American Southwest. One of the best movies ever. Demonstrates cultural differences between Europe and America but also analyzes American society deeply. A sad and happy film set right on the Old Road.

Cars. Directed by John Lasseter. Pixar Animation Studios and Walt Disney Pictures, 2006.

>A great animated feature film for lovers of cars and Route 66. All "actors" are cars or machines with voices of celebrities including Jay Leno, Michael Schumacker, Paul Newman, and Jim Carrey. A rookie racecar Lightning McQueen gets detoured on Route 66 to Radiator Springs, where he regains his spirit as does the sleepy town. Everyone will like this film. The more you know about Route 66, and the more you know about cars, the more you can enjoy this good old fashioned motion picture.

Charlie's Angels: Full Throttle. Directed by McG (Joseph McGinty Nichol). Columbia Pictures, 2003.

>Totally unnecessary additional movie based on the TV series. Shows several famous landmarks of Hollywood, including the Roosevelt Hotel, Walk of Fame, and the Musso & Frank Restaurant.

Duel. Directed by Steven Spielberg. Universal TV, 1971.

>An early Spielberg and a good road movie. Dennis Weaver plays a salesman who is bullied by a truck driver. Great scenes of the Southwest. Shows a Southern Pacific train with some Burlington Northern cars.

Easy Rider. Directed by Dennis Hopper. Columbia Pictures, 1969

>The mother of all modern road movies. Probably the second best film on my list. Great performances by Peter Fonda, Dennis Hopper, Jack Nicholson, and others. Great southwestern scenery, wonderful music, but not just fun and laughter. Shows also a dark side of 1960s America.

Forrest Gump. Directed by Robert Zemeckis. Paramount Pictures, 1994.

>A great American Studies film, that takes the viewer to most events and music of the United States after World War II. Tom Hanks plays the main character, who also runs on Route 66 to the Santa Monica pier.

The Grapes of Wrath. Directed by John Ford. Twentieth Century Fox, 1940.

>The mother of all films about the Mother Road. Practically an advertise-

ment for Route 66. Probably the best film on my list. Great performances by Henry Fonda, Jane Darwell, and others. Screenplay by Nunnally Johnson, who changed the original, and stunningly moving, ending of Steinbeck's novel to better suit film audiences.

Harry and Tonto. Directed by Paul Mazursky. Twentieth Century Fox, 1974.
> Art Carney plays the role of a retired teacher, who travels with his cat Tonto across the United States to find a world they have never seen and perhaps also to find themselves (if you can say that of a cat). Beautiful and nostalgic road scenes.

Hollywood or Bust. Directed by Frank Tashlin. Paramount Pictures, 1956.
> One of the many Jerry Lewis-Dean Martin comedies, and their last movie together. In this film the guys travel across the continent through Route 66 country.

My Best Friend's Wedding. Directed by P. J. Hogan. Predawn Productions, 1997.
> A romance/comedy with some Chicago scenes. At one point the main characters Julianne Potter (Julia Roberts) and Michael O'Neal (Dermot Mulroney) take a cruise on the Chicago River and go under both bridges of Route 66 (Adams and Jackson).

The Negotiator. Directed by F. Gary Gray. Regency Enterprises, 1988.
> Story of police corruption (once again) and a hostage situation in Chicago. Street and El scenes. Starring Samuel L. Jackson and Kevin Spacey, who says that he once negotiated a man out of blowing up the Sears Tower.

On the Road. Directed by Walter Salles. IFC Films/Sundance Selects & Lionsgate & MK2, 2012.
> A long waited film based on Jack Kerouac's book.

Repo Man. Directed by Alex Cox. Edge City, 1984.
> Starts off on Route 66 east of Los Angeles. Later turns into a strange film of UFOs and aliens.

Road to Perdition. Directed by Sam Mendes. DreamWorks SKG and Twentieth Century Fox, 2002.
> Gangsters in Chicago and the surrounding Illinois in the early 1930s. Plenty of dead bodies, fewer scenes of Chicago. The Chicago River, however, is crossed on a Route 66 bridge. Good scenes of Illinois prairies. Gives us a great example of a classic diner at Englewood.

Route 66, television series. Aired from October 7, 1960 to March 13, 1964. Lancer-Edling Productions and Screen Gems Television, 1960-1964.
> Mostly written by Stirling Silliphant. Originally paid little attention, if any, to the actual Route 66 but, nevertheless, has later become part of the 66 nostalgia.

Thelma & Louise. Directed by Ridley Scott. Metro-Goldwyn-Mayer/United Artists, 1991.

One of the greatest road movies ever. Susan Sarandon and Geena Davis want only to break away from their dull lives for a day or two, but unintended acts force them to run farther than they anticipated. Absolutely great scenes of the American Southwest, some possibly on Route 66.

Wonder Boys. Directed by Curtis Hanson. Paramount Pictures, 2000.
This is one of the many movies that has nothing to do with Route 66, but which, nevertheless, has an interesting reference to the Old Road. The story is about an English professor (Michael Douglas) trying to finish his long overdue manuscript for a book. In one scene his young student James Leer (Tobey Maguire) is watching TV and surfing from channel to channel. One channel shows (a rerun of) the TV series on Route 66. You can see the Corvette on a bridge and listen for a few seconds to Nelson Riddle's music in the background.

ZZ Top. *Greatest Hits: The Video Collection*. Warner Music Vision, 1992, video cassette.
ZZ Top of Austin, catches some of the mood—and even landscapes—of the Old Road in their video *Gimme All Your Lovin'*. In the video, a red car decorated with a lightning figure (ZZ) whizzes down a two-lane road in the Southwestern desert. Characters include a shy boy and some beautiful girls, an old gas station, and, of course, the bearded guys from the band.

And never forget to take with you the latest *Rand McNally Road Atlas*. Without it, I would have been lost several times while on the Road and while writing this book. It is your best key to America.

If you want to be in touch while en route, use a cell phone with a hands-free device. My phone is, of course, Nokia E66.

The Remembrance

The most American of all the American places is Chicago,
Center of the Old West
and from there the Road leads you even further west
to the center of the New West,
the populous of Los Angeles;
from Windy City to Tinsel Town

The Road, too, is American,
part of the American dream and optimism
it switches around
and avoids New England, the East Coast, and the Deep South,
the more European parts of the United States.
And like most of its predecessors, it too
is a part of the Western legend,
a part of the great migrations,
the greatest of them all in human history.

The Western way—and I sigh—
The flat boats pulled by mules on the Erie Canal,
The wagons leaving their trail on the short grass to Oregon,
The pioneer path of the Santa Fe Trail,
and then, the iron horse, Union Pacific, Central Pacific, and others,
Then another engine and the rubber wheels,
on the asphalt and the concrete,
until the airplane
and people left the earth.
No tracks any more on the ground
by this new route to West.

As there first was the travel,
then the Road,
and now, but memories and nostalgia.

The short grass on Oregon Trail has grown longer.
The path to Santa Fe covered with sand.
Forgotten the dream of gold on the Bozeman Trail,
dried and filled the canal,
broken the asphalt of the Old Road.

Under the full moon
only the wind carries the silent song of a lonely jackalope
and in the shadows
whispers the spirit of Bobby Troup:
"Get your kicks . . . on route . . . 66."

. . . for me, and other wanderers whose souls are held captive by the open road, Route 66 never really died, no matter what the maps may say.

David Lamb, *Romancing the Road*

Index

Page numbers in *italic* indicate illustrations

About the Author

McDonnell Douglass Chair of American Studies at the University of Helsinki, Markku Henriksson has lectured on Route 66 in Estonia, Sweden, and Canada, as well as Finland and the United States.